Learning To Live In The Violent Society

by
Professor Eric Moonman

authorHOUSE™

1663 LIBERTY DRIVE, SUITE 200
BLOOMINGTON, INDIANA 47403
(800) 839-8640
WWW.AUTHORHOUSE.COM

First published by AuthorHouse 12/20/05

ISBN: 1-4208-7724-0 (sc)
ISBN: 1-4208-7725-9 (dj)

Library of Congress Control Number: 2005908548

Printed in the United States of America
Bloomington, Indiana

This book is printed on acid-free paper.

FOREWORD

RT. HON. LORD WEATHERILL DL

A key issue confronting the British public today is the manner and futility of extremists who kill and maim. The London bombings follow similar activity in New York and in cities and towns throughout the world.

Professor Moonman's message is not merely a commentary on the British scene but his views and advice have universal reference, confirmed by his case studies of terrorism world-wide.

What he has achieved in this book is to identify many levels of violence; how it intrudes into our working and domestic lives, into sport and on our streets. Racism and violence are a cruel feature of our society — long after Nazi Germany was defeated sixty years ago.

The late Lord Scarman, in a foreword to a previous book by Eric Moonman, The Violent Society, described the author's thesis, this way: "The subject is complex, but I cannot do better than to invite you to read from cover to cover this challenging, exciting and sobering work."

I feel precisely the same about Eric Moonman's new work.

In summing up, the various manifestations of violence are constantly changing and often confusing to the lay public. The author shows a deep insight into the many issues involved and this enables him to provide the reader with a framework of the subject which is clear, fair minded and always absorbing.

Despite evidence of the many serious and troubling issues involved, for instance, he does not shirk from expressing the failure of European countries to cooperate in confronting terrorism, Eric Moonman ends on an optimistic note.

It is his belief that the public can be reassured as to the future. He is challenging and the message is unlikely to be lost on those countries whose citizens have had their lives and families torn apart through the acts of the terrorist.

I believe the book is a timely insight into the challenges facing our country today and I warmly commend the important contribution he has made.

Bernard Weatherill

TABLE OF CONTENTS

Everyday in Britain and the United States there is street violence.
No section of the community or class is free from the turmoil
which arbitrary violence brings. Evidence of incidents may
be found in both the rural area as well as the inner city.

What is the nature of violence? Where does it spring from? What are the
modern manifestations? Is it endemic to people and societies? What are
the implications of planned violence? What is the political dimension?

Information about violence has inevitably been drawn from the criminal
statistics and this is briefly indicated. But there is also a significant body
of evidence about violence visible outside the criminal justice system.

Football, contrary to popular opinion, has not invented violence or
racism. Indeed soccer has in recent years played an important role
in providing black youngsters with a means to visible success and
that very visibility is a crucial positive factor. On the other hand,
football has provided a worrying level of spectator violence.

What is important is that these notions serve to underline two
fundamental truths: first, that for large numbers of people the football
ground is the only stage on which they can expect to play out their
frustrations and aspirations; secondly, and in consequence, an
increasing level of violence is to be found at all levels of the game.

Mention of violence and sport usually turns on football, but there
are other experiences of crowd behaviour in sports, which are
both positive and negative. How has cricket and rugby escaped
the spotlight of attention? How far is spectator violence a British
phenomenon and to what extent is it affecting other countries?

Chapter 5: International Violence and Terrorism

Terrorism has been a permanent fixture in human history. In contrast with its antecedents, modern-day terrorism is often institutionalised, technologically advanced, and global in its consequences.

The proliferation of weapons of mass destruction raises the stakes. Thus we have the potential for "super terrorism" - biological, chemical, nuclear, information abuse and cyber-terrorism.

Hence, there exists the need to educate policy makers and the public in general, on the nature and intensity of the threat of terrorism in the Twenty First Century.

Chapter 6: Telling the Public

The need for a consistent message to the public.

Chapter 7: A Roll-Call of What We Should be Aiming to Do

What remedies are available in the short and long term? Can governments and city authorities make a significant difference in controlling violence?

INTRODUCTION

There has been a rush on the literature of counter terrorism but sadly, the writers have chipped away at the subject with such a narrow outlook that with few exceptions, the total picture eludes them. And if they describe the total scene with all the manifestations of violence, it is hardly surprising if students of the subject or the public are in ignorance of the how and why of violence.

Of course, it is ambitious to try and bring all the strands of violence, crime and terrorism together for study and review but it is possible with one proviso. The author of such a thesis has to have a wide command and experience of the various sectors of public reporting and government responsibility as well as a good research approach. Eric Moonman fits that role perfectly because he has something to offer, a down-to-earth understanding of what the public wants to know. He is a former MP and communications expert.

Counter terrorism is now so complicated an issue because there are many attempts, by government and various agencies to create a fog around the issues. Here Professor Moonman sweeps through the density of the subject and enlightens us. The book is admirably titled-and therefore despite the gloom surrounding terrorism, he offers hope and enlightenment.

He starts by exploring street violence. No section of the community or class is free from the turmoil which arbitrary violence brings. Evidence of incidents may be found in both the rural area as well as the inner city. To this he moves on to the nature of violence. Where does it spring from? What are the modern manifestations? Is it endemic to people and societies? What are the implications of planned violence? What is the political dimension?

The scale of violence is then presented through much research and study. Information about violence in Western societies has inevitably been drawn from the criminal statistics and this is briefly indicated. Eric Moonman argues there is also a significant body of evidence about violence visible outside the criminal justice system. It is interesting that he chooses examples from the health and social services.

Sport is not ignored. The author is well placed to examine football and other games. Mention of violence and sport usually turns on football, but there are other experiences of crowd behaviour in sports, which are both positive and negative. How far is spectator violence a modern phenomenon and to what extent is it affecting other countries?

International violence and terrorism is a central part of the book. Terrorism has been a permanent fixture in human history. In contrast with its antecedents, modern-day terrorism is technologically advanced and global in its consequences. The proliferation of weapons of mass destruction raises the stakes. Thus we have the potential for "super terrorism" – biological, chemical, nuclear, information abuse and cyber-terrorism. There exists the need to educate policymakers and the public in general, on the nature and intensity of the threat of terrorism in the Twenty-First Century.

After all, if we contribute to a better understanding of the past record of both conventional and unconventional attacks perhaps the international community would be able to provide "good practices" strategies to minimise potential risks. As the philosopher, George Santayana already taught us, "those who cannot learn from history are doomed to repeat it." The July 7 and July 21, 205 terrorist attacks in London reinforce Santayana's wise warning.

To sum up, Professor Moonman asks the crucial question, Can we live in this violent society?" What remedies are available in the short and long term? Can governments and city authorities make a significant difference in controlling violence? I would state, in my judgement, that Eric Moonman honestly and fairly lays it all out. The concluding chapter will enlighten and provide helpful support to those who believe, as I do, that it is vital we learn to live in a violent society.

Professor Yonah Alexander
Co-Director of the Inter University
Centre for Terrorism Studies
Washington, D.C.

OTHER BOOKS BY ERIC MOONMAN

The manager and the organisation

Communications in an Expanding Organisation

Reluctant Partnership (a critique of Government Industrial Relations)

Industrial Innovation and British Computers

The Alternative Government

The Violent Society

PREAMBLE

What is nature of violence? Where does it spring from?

The question is frequently raised by all manner of groups and of all ages: how does violence start - is it a natural part of our self and our being? There is a great deal of evidence that takes into account influences on children and there are even some studies which fashion the problem to the nature of our genes.

What are modern manifestations?

We will try and answer some of these questions, but in the main we will focus on the immediate results of violence and the critical areas to be examined, identify and possibly control.

Is violence endemic to people and societies? Is it inevitable in the battle for rights, property and recognition? Is it limited to the way we live, as Margaret Mead and many more recent anthropologists have observed of the aggression in society. There are also societies where the life is peaceful and harmonious.

What are the implications of planned violence?

This type of violence is premeditated and highly organised to achieve the aims of the power groups in societies covering large-scale wars, internal strife as well as violent, horrendous acts of terrorism, such as New York, September 11, 2001, and in Bali over a year later.

At a lesser level on the scale we have the riots which, out of control, create havoc to the police and essential services, such as the attacks on the City of London and in Whitehall (2000).

Violence on the soccer field is a growing source of interest. The Observer (1 June, 2000) leader put it bluntly that society is to blame; football thugs are made; not born.

"Typically, bullying and aggression stem from the weak, rather than the strong. The drunk violent, bare-chested English football fan, tattooed

with the cross of St George, is the product of a winner-takes-all society in which he has little chance, but which gives him the chance to ventilate his frustration by identifying foreigners as the enemy".

Strong stuff, but borne out by the facts both internationally and what we know of the street clashes in Britain.

What is the political dimension of violence?

Terrorism is a tool to engage in a cheap war within a country or beyond its boundaries to destabilise the political system. Terrorist groups can transfer their skills and weaponry to other like-minded operators and in a number of instances they share the same "banker".

Assassinations, hijackings and riots have all been shown on television before an audience of millions. The issues become obscured by the sheer drama of the events being played out; familiarity breeds contempt, or at the very least, indifference. Hijackings are still sufficiently rare and attract huge ratings; overturned cars, stone throwing and burning cars have become so familiar as to be boring. It is an appalling comment on contemporary society that these matters, which should revolt the consciousness, have become models for the criminal, the terrorist and the desperate, judged in terms of their entertainment value for the general public by the information providers.

There is a media related linkage between terrorism, small-scale war waged by bands of undisciplined recruits on civilian targets and regular wars waged between nation states fought with sophisticated and devastating weapons. Vietnam was the first war to be televised, but it was not until the 1982 war in Lebanon that modern technology brought a war into our living rooms as it was happening. There is no question that this new dimension to warfare heightens international tension and stimulates the political debate surrounding any conflict. Some would argue that this is "a good thing," but we should not blind ourselves to the dangers arising from the greater involvement of huge numbers of people misled by biased reporting through mass communications in international conflict. Violence is a necessary part of survival, from the level of the local neighbourhood to the world arena. Neither should we ignore the enormous responsibility the whole phenomenon places on the media. Television cannot yet decide who wins a war, but it can already decide who we think is winning.

On the other hand, let us consider the iniquities of the exclusion of the mass communications element. Look at the Soviet involvement in Afghanistan, Mugaby's Zimbabwe, or the bloody and protracted conflict in Iraq. Limited media access has not reduced the bloodshed or the injustice, but it can assist in a state of amnesia among the wider public.

To the public then, conditioning in terrorism is taking place whether by individual interests, groups or superpowers. In the United Kingdom for example, a family on the mainland will know of the tension and terror experienced directly if they have family or friends living in Northern Ireland.

Along with the conditioning comes direct personal experience. Whether it is a mugging in one's neighbourhood; a burglary of an old age pensioner with precious little to take; a hit-and-run driver who wrecks a family by killing a father or child; or the soccer hooligan who terrorises the streets both before and after the game, it is all seen and felt personally. No longer is it a detached film on TV. It is here and now with terrible consequences for families, in which the destroyers have no respect for age, children, or circumstances.

We will seek to examine the connection between these different levels of violence, warfare and terrorism, and whether measures taken to curb or even eradicate the phenomenon in the domestic context will have any effect at the other, international end of the scale. Does one feed the other?

If violence is an inevitable, even necessary part of human existence can ways be found of channelling it into constructive as opposed to destructive activity? The basic question with which we are concerned is the difference between aggression and violence, life-giving energy and death dealing force. We will move from the specific to the general, from the pragmatic to the philosophical, an inevitable process if this book is to throw any light on the nature of contemporary violence.

CHAPTER 1

The scale of violence inevitably increases, as terrorism becomes the means of destroying communities, regions, even countries. However, violent actions in local and domestic settings - against the person, the vulnerable and aged have similar objectives, perhaps not so explicit, but to destabilise the regular order of society and to create fear in the public mind.

1. THE WORKPLACE

Within the workplace in Great Britain there has been a growing number of incidents, which have caused the Trades Union Congress to express considerable concern about the need for more effective monitoring.

In particular, nurses, security and care workers are most vulnerable to attack or abuse from the public at work, whilst young women are almost twice as likely as young men to be attacked or verbally abused, as Violent Times, a TUC report revealed as far back as 1999.

The report reveals that one in three nurses have been violently attacked or abused at work, closely followed by security workers (one in four) and employees in care homes (one in five).

The report also shows that younger women are more likely to be assaulted in the workplace, 11% of women aged 25-34 had suffered a physical attack compared to 6% of men in the same age group.

Several industries note dramatic increases in assaults on their staff - 70% of teachers believe that violence in schools is rising, attacks on employment service staff have increased 12-fold since 1987, and assaults on railway workers have more than tripled in recent years.

Although Violent Times looks at workers in a wide variety of employment settings, the report identifies several factors common to all work sectors. In many cases, a lack of training leaves staff vulnerable when it comes to dealing with aggressive people, managers are often unsympathetic when staff are attacked and adequate support is only rarely provided.

2. DISTRICTS

Whilst violence in the workplace may seem a new phenomenon, the dangers arising from the hostility in a particular district is not. London has emerged as an increasing threatening area. Donal Shanahan, a senior consultant surgeon from London's Homerton Hospital, says somewhat provocatively *"Soweto is statistically rather safer than East London"* (Times, 30 April, 2002).

The figures to which he is referring are indeed disquieting: Homerton, in Hackney treats 55 knife or gunshot wounds each month; the Chris Hani Baragwanath Hospital sited in South Africa's most notorious township, sees six times as many cases - despite serving a population ten times larger.

Is one of the poorest parts of London really more violent than a notorious township in one of the world's most crime-ridden nations? Possibly not, yet there is disquiet amongst the British police and authorities that guns are readily on the streets in a way never contemplated or planned for even ten years ago.

District violence, however is not a new phenomenon, as we are reminded by Martin Scorsese's remarkable "Gangs of New York" (released early 2003). The film begins in 1846 with a hard fought battle in the centre of New York slums. The contestants are a gang of Irish immigrants (known as the Dead Rabbits) and a band of Xenophobic Protestants (the Natives). The resentment of those first in the country to those who arrive later produces the gang warfare. This warfare, be it over space, district, streets, can be traced in other countries and at many periods since 1846.

The film, cleverly executed, tells the story of the anger arising from and perceived "advantage" new immigrants seem to hold. It highlights prejudice, economic exploitation (in establishing the big city and the nation) and pure tribal revenge.

On a personal note, as an MP for a New Town in Essex in the 1970s, I encountered a noisy campaign directed against the most recent arrivals in the town, *"Keep Basildon for the Basildonians - out with Bethnal Green".* Yet we are talking of a distance of around twenty miles and to add to the irony of the protest most of the Basildonians came from Bethnal Green and East London - or their parents did.

Writing in the Times (7 Jan, 2002). Christine Wheeler was the victim of a violent assault only a few steps from her "safe" house address, while Julian Lee's wife Nicole, was battered as her bag was stolen. Both incidents revealed a complete disregard for their victims plus an additional tussle with the police administration and the hospital.

Wheeler writes *"November 8:15pm. They came out of the darkness into the yellow pool of streetlight. Six of them circling me like a pack of hyenas, smirking, hissing, and daring me "Go on, Run". And thus I became one of those statistics showing that, since September 11 when many police have been pulled off their beats and deployed on anti-terrorist duties, violent street crime in London has more than doubled. Every impersonal number is a story of a life turned upside down and it comforts me not one jot to know that I and many others have suffered from the worthy cause of keeping the free world safe from Osama bin Laden.*

Was this build-up a tentative testing of uncharted territory where word had it that low life could now roam unhindered looking for rich pickings? But we are wide open. The local police station is under constant threat of closure and functioning only part-time".

The second case highlights street warfare in which crimes appears to be dismissed too easily.

Scene: North London, Nicole is walking along the street in the late afternoon at around 5:30 pm speaking on her mobile when suddenly it is dragged from her. Her husband takes up the story.

"She doesn't know what the intruder wants and out of instinct she hangs onto her bag and screams, only to pay for it when he flings her violently across a metal gate with such force that her wrist is broken in three places and her face and eye are badly bruised and gashed. Twenty-five minutes later, the police turn up. They begin questioning Nicole, barely conscious and laying on the pavement in her blood, surrounded by onlookers. They record the incident as a robbery. No account is taken of her injuries".

A series in the Daily Express (2 June, 2003) described a wanton most frightening attack on an 87 year old, who was brutalised when a mugger ripped away her Zimmer frame in broad daylight. Violet Bentley, who cannot be without the frame, was crashing to the pavement when the thug snatched her shopping bag packed with groceries she had bought for her tea. The extremely disturbing feeling in the case is the wider issue of causing millions of elderly people into prisoners in their own home. A view confirmed by the Charity Age Concern, which reports that vast numbers of old people remain indoors, because they fear abuse or attack. Age Concern polled 8000 older people, revealing that 37 per cent of the over 50s and 47 per cent of the over 75s are now too afraid to go out at night.

There is little that can be said to the victim in such cases, other than immediate expression of sympathy. The media however, demand "more action". An increase in police on the beat is the most common suggestion by politicians and the media. The government has responded by directing a significant budget in making the police more available and determined.

The fact remains that two thirds of people in England and Wales feel unsafe walking alone in their neighbourhood at night, according to a Home Office Study published December 30th, 2004 (The Citizenship Survey, based on interviews with 14,057 people aged over 16).

In the two years 2002-4, growing numbers of householders no longer feel safe when out after dark and fewer people say that they definitely enjoy living in their neighbourhood. The Citizenship Survey also found a higher proportion of people who believed that Britain was more racist than it was five years previously and that racial prejudice would increase. The findings were a setback for the Home Office which, despite falls in overall crime has been unable to alter the public's perception that offending is getting worse.

The public will continue to tolerate the injuries and threats to their peace of mind, but they will expect the politicians to "do something" about law and order. It is a major item on all the political party agendas and it is unlikely to drop out of their agendas for the foreseeable future.

Yet for all the politicians' concerns, law and order is constantly being challenged by organised groups in running or controlling shoplifting, or provoking attacks against the vulnerable in our society.

3. THE MOB

The original violence of attacks on the streets is now refined with the use of technology and in particular, the mobile phone.

It does seem somewhat ironic that anarchist leaders in recent street demonstrations, including those in London on May Day, used a variety of "capitalist" symbols like the mobile phone to co-ordinate their plans.

Previously the organisers made it easy for the police by posting their intentions on the Internet. Now, to avoid being trapped by the police they have taken to sending text messages, not only of their intentions to act, but also revealing how many police are on a particular street and cross roads and how they are being deployed.

One security source said that some of the groups under surveillance were believed to have been using simple grid references from a map of Central London so that they needed only to text a couple of digits.

"They use what is called the "information tree". Everyone in the group knows the code to use and the first person sends a text to one other. The recipient sends the message to two others and they each do the same, so it gets around fast. It then takes only a couple of people at the front of the march to head off in a particular direction and the rest follow on". The implication of this organised approach to demonstrations will be referred to later.

4. CHILDREN AND CRIME

The killing of a four-year old boy in Nagasaki horrified the whole of Japan in 2003. As a result of the examination of closed-circuit footage, it emerged that the killer was a child.

Richard Lloyd Parry (Times, 10 July, 2003) reflected this was similar to the agony felt in Liverpool after the murder of James Bulger, 2, who was killed by two 10-year-old boys in February 1993. Now 7000 miles away, the same awful story is acted out in Japan. Eight days after the death of Shun Tanemoto, police in Nagasaki said that they had solved the murder. The four-year old boy died when his naked body was thrown off the top of a multi-storey car park. A full confession from a 12-year-old boy followed. The similarities with the Bulger case are eerie. First there is a physical horror. Then comes a painful incredulity that such a thing could happen in a country that prides itself on being one of the safest. And finally comes anger that, for such a young killer, there is little that society can exact in the way of punishment. Some positive things occurred in Liverpool in the years following the Bulger case. It brought home to the police, the public and the social services of the need for much closer coordination; the closed-circuit cameras were no longer regarded as a threat to an individual's rights, but a support and possibly a deterrent to those likely to plan crimes.

In Japan there was an attempt to explain such actions as part of the malaise in society. It was argued that two generations ago, Japanese children grew up in large extended families. Today, families are smaller, many mothers go to work and more and more children grow up alone and isolated.

Japan's mania for gadgetry may have an influence, encouraging young people to spend time alone with video games or to communicate via their mobile phones rather than meeting in person.

In Britain, the gang culture is growing and attracts many young people often with serious consequences. Status and street credibility are the aim for the thousands of boys in Britain's cities who have joined gangs styled on the Chinese Triads.

Although police have known of their emergence for several years, it was not until a Triad-style gang was held responsible for the death of the London headmaster Philip Lawrence, that the public became aware of their existence.

Nathan Brown, who killed Carl Richard with a machete, fits the police blueprint for a gang member. The emergence of the schoolboy gangs is rooted in the activities of a real Triad gang known as 14K, which began recruiting youngsters in the early 1990s. Youth of all races and backgrounds were drawn in, mainly in London to help them to extort money from restaurant owners.

Groups of youth would go into restaurant premises and cause trouble for the owners, but police, who did not then realise they were part of a larger criminal organisation, would often not take a tough line with them.

A response given by some commentators and educators is that such behaviour is due to broken homes and TV influence. But the issues involved are somewhat more complex.

A report by the Joseph Rowntree Foundation in 2002 (Youth at Risk) dealt with a study of 14,000 children, which highlights a picture of a large minority of young teenagers drinking heavily, sniffing glue, smoking cannabis and slipping into a broad range of juvenile crime. Half those questioned said they had broken the law at some stage. The most frequent offences involved shoplifting, vandalism, and burglary. Children as young as twelve admitted to binge drinking.

The authorities were particularly troubled by the high incidence of binge drinking, an issue which seldom reaches the headlines. A quarter of school children in Year 9 - those aged 13 and 14 - admitted that in the previous month that had consumed five or more alcoholic drinks in one session. Drinks including beer, wine and spirits. 43 per cent of boys and girls in Year 10 - those aged 14 and 15 - had been binge drinking, rising to 59 per cent of boys and 54 per cent of girls in Year 11 - those aged 15 and 16.

It is inevitable that some children are moved to copy their elders or peers, and this was confirmed in the research. There is no doubt that alcohol abuse is an expensive item to the nation and the NHS in particular, certainly no less than £3 billion a year.

A survey for the department of Health in 1999 on these issues showed that 40 percent of men and 20 percent of women regularly imbibe more than the recommended limits. The medical community admits that tutoring the public about what constitutes a healthy consumption is not easy. There is not even concrete consensus among medics about safe limits - while the Royal College of Physicians and the British Medical Association play it safe with weekly figures of 14 and 21 units.

When people intake more than the weekly limits, they are putting themselves on a drinking spectrum that runs from alcohol abuse to alcoholism. As well as pounding their liver and heart, they are at greater peril from stomach ulcers, brain damage and depression. When abuse tips over into dependence, the price may be a lost job, a broken marriage, social isolation, financial penury and violence.

5. TELEVISION AS AN INFLUENCE

This subject is constantly discussed with little general agreement. The initial case for opposing restraint in the media was made nearly 20 years ago by the talented playwright Hanif Kureishi (Times, 28 Dec, 1985) and few have expressed the particular arguments quite so well.

"Since there is already adequate provision to prevent ordinary people being shocked by unusual or unlikely sex or violence, it is increasingly apparent that this renewed call for censorship is a fig leaf concealing the desire to suppress work which is morally or politically challenging. The extent to which the authoritarian suppression of dissent - be the dissenters trade unions, artists or the BBC - is becoming more general in our society now is already worrying enough. But this fresh attack is deeply dangerous. As it is through the imaginative arts that we tell the truth to ourselves, writers and directors who seek to explore the serious and difficult issues of sex and violence are essential to any society that considers itself tolerant, sceptical, pluralist and self-aware. This is not only a question of the freedom of the artists, but one about the importance a society attaches to criticism".

Mr Kureishi was answering correspondence on the showing of violence in television serials. But whilst he stressed the 'rights' of artists and writers to express themselves freely he offers not guidance to help an audience to understand, to relate or even to refute what he sees. Besides, it is one thing for writers to intellectualise on the Royal Court stage for a minority few hundred each evening, but it is a very different thing when the message is transmitted on TV to millions of young people, indiscriminately, able to see in their own living room a series of violent acts. Television has the power to create models and remains a pernicious and persistent factor in many lives.

How far do the violent images on a TV and movie screen influence behaviour? The latest examples of images into real life concerns the film "2 Fast 2 Furious," which glorified high speeds and danger. Within a few days of the premier of "2 Fast 2 Furious," a young family cruising down an avenue in Miami were hit by a car hurtling along at about 100mph. But it was all too late. The family car was clipped and the BMW zigzagged across the highway. The result: the accident seriously injured the three adults and two children (in the family car). Sadly this is another example of a deadly illegal sport-drag racing highlighted in the film.

Apparently, in the first week of the film's distribution. US police were dealing with at least one racing-related crash every day. Hours before the film's opening, one Los Angeles street racer killed a 15-year old bystander, and another hit an electricity pole, knocking out the power to 1,300 homes in North Hollywood. Fearing an even greater number of crashes now that 2 Fast 2 Furious was in cinemas, Los Angeles police were given emergency powers to seize all cars used in suspected races.

But what of violent crime? Is it increasing because television teaches young people that aggression and dishonesty are normal? This is the crucial question which those who disagree have to address - how television influences and touches the young mind by demonstrating that normality is very tough, demanding and without too many scruples.

Sir Edward Crew, head of West Midlands police reported a 17 per cent rise in street robberies over the previous year and said that violent crime would continue to rise in England and Wales (Times, 28 June, 2002). This is due to the way such behaviour was portrayed in peak-time dramas which are meant to reflect real life.

Viewers' groups welcomed the chief constable's warning. The broadcasting watchdog shared many of his concerns but said it would not condone a sanitised schedule.

Support for Sir Edward's view came from the Broadcasting Standards Commission. They reported that complaints about violence during soap operas shown when children were likely to be watching were a great concern. Norman McLean the BSC deputy director said *"Audiences expect realistic portrayals in soaps but we have warned the BBC about scenes of violence in EastEnders"*.

Hollyoaks Channel 4's teenage soap opera has dealt with 'taboo' issues such as male rape, but generally in late night specials. The BSC believes Hollyoaks "treats issues important to teenagers in a responsible manner". Nevertheless, letter columnists in the press dispute this assertion.

Programmes depicting car chases and crime re-enactments have attracted an enormous amount of complaints. Mr McLean said, *"If programmes portray criminal acts in an easy to imitate manner they are censured"*. A possible answer would be to give parents some guidance with programme categories similar to the cinema, reflecting certificates around the 15-year mark.

This is not an automatic option as Daniel Rosenthal pointed out in the Times (28 Feb, 2002).

"Twice in the past two months I have emerged from an intensely violent Hollywood war movie asking myself one question: "How could this be awarded a 15 certificate?" I'm 31 and have never considered myself squeamish about cinematic gore, but I was numbed by the footage of battlefield surgery, severed limbs and charred flesh in Black Hawk Down and the Mel Gibson vehicle We Were Soldiers".

A major investigation into the effects of TV violence on children as complaints about disturbing scenes in top soaps hit unprecedented levels. The Broadcasting Standards Commission (BSC) announced 17 July, 2003, that it was commissioning a study into the impact of violent images on nine to 13 year-olds. The BSC said it was acting after its annual review showed that more viewers than ever before are complaining about the amount of violence and foul language.

The watchdog said it has received a massive rise in complaints about the soaps and warned television executives to clean up their act. It singled out EastEnders and Coronation Street for their use of *"protracted scenes of violence in domestic settings"* before the 9pm watershed.

BSC director Paul Bolt said, *"Broadcasters of soaps ought to have regard to the fact there is a very substantial part of the audience who are children."* He said families often watched soaps together *"so broadcasters have to look at the way soaps affect particular viewers"*.

Complaints about violence and offensive violence now make up 30 per cent of total complaints, the BSC's review revealed. Previously, they accounted for 19 per cent. The largest number of complaints for a single programme in 2002-2003 was over violence in the drama Spooks. There were 154 complaints about a scene in which a woman was tortured in boiling fat.

The BSC received a total of 6,900 complaints last year. The BSC also criticised offensive language in the BBC sitcom My Family and an advert for Pot Noodle, which described the product as "the slags of all snacks". It does seems strange given the evidence referred to earlier as the evidence from the BSC that such an enquiry has not taken place prior to this view.

On cause for some relief in Britain is that guns are not so readily available as they are in the United States but the scene is changing very rapidly. To commit a certain level of violence you only need the wherewithal and the criminal element know where to buy the gun. Indeed in an excursion made in a London borough one evening in December 2004, I was offered everything from out of bond cigarettes, drugs and in one case a small gun. *"You just have to ask,"* I was told.

With so few brand new guns in circulation a "clean" weapon usually means a newly reactivated one. A 2002 Home Office study found that at least 30 percent of guns used in London shootings had been reactivated. With certain models, particularly machine guns, the process is relatively simple and needs only a few tools. The National Criminal Intelligence Service also warned that Brocock ME38 Magnum air pistols can be converted to fire .22 ammunition with relative ease. The guns, which can be bought brand new, without any kind of licence for £120 have been linked to a handful of murders including that of taxi driver Mohammed Basharat, who was shot dead with a converted Brocock in Bradford in October 2001. Another was used in the attempted murder of two police officers in South London. Several other cases have alarmed the Association of Chief Police Officers, which has called for a change in the law to ban Brococks so that they can no longer be illegally converted.

During the mid-Nineties, it was widely reported that dozens of petty criminals set themselves up as underworld armourers, each holding a selection of guns and hiring them out to anyone who needed them. It meant that villains didn't have to risk having a gun on them all the time, but could get access to one within minutes.

The guns are the essential equipment to demonstrate a gang's strength and to resolve disagreement. Hence the increasing number of gangland war is over territory.

This results in the haphazard shootings of people of different nationality, the new people on the block who also want a share of the 'take'. There is also the haphazard school shootings. In the German school shooting (26 April, 2002) a youth Robert Steinhauser, had been expelled earlier in the year after constant conflict with the teaching staff and was barred from taking the school leaving exams. He took his revenge as former colleagues sat the tests. Using a pump action gun, the youth ran amok, chasing teaching staff and secretaries through the corridors. Some were killed while hiding in the lavatories. Others were shot dead while in the staff room or the school secretary's office. Although he killed two girls this appears to have been a mistake: he was gunning for adults.

The United States has seen many such shoot-outs. The authorities have had some success in thwarting the shootings and this is due in main to the procedures insisted upon including high security admission, barrier checks for weapons and a defined educational programme set up by the Secret Service after the Columbine massacre in 1999.

Pre-emptive arrests have also prevented a string of attacks of pupils in Fort Collins, Colorado, San Jose, California, Hoyt, Kansas, Elmira, New York and New Bedford Massachusetts. In New Bedford, for example, a girl told a teacher that she had overheard a boy talking about bombing the school and shooting pupils as they fled. The teacher told a "school resource officer" who had just been appointed in line with the Secret Service's recommendations.

A two year study, conducted by the Secret Service in co-operation with the Department of Education, of 41 children involved in the 37 school shootings in America since 1974, found that in about three quarters of the cases the perpetrators told someone of their plans in advance.

Secret Service Agents have been meeting school officials around the country and have issued a "threat assessment manual" to help them identify potential killers.

6. ANGER ON THE ROAD

Road rage and violent reactions between drivers is increasing in Britain as it has in the United States. At first hand, in several states, I witnessed spontaneous and speedy retribution of "justice" for those drivers who were pursued and threatened or attacked.

The US National Highway Traffic Safety Administration (NHTSA) considers that about 28,000 deaths on America's roads each year, or two thirds of the total are wholly or partly the result of bad temper.

Ricardo Martinez, the head of the NHTSA told a congressional committee on 17 July, 2002, that cases of "violent aggressive driving" were growing by 7% a year. Other causes of death on the roads however were falling. In particular, the share of fatal crashes involving drunk drivers had dropped from 57% in 1982 to 41% currently.

But why rage? Firstly congestion on the roads, since 1987 the number of miles of roads in the United States has increased by only 1%, but the number of vehicle miles driven has gone up by 35%. The numbers of cars has increased by 27% and most journeys are taking longer than drivers think they should. Second, traffic policing has been reduced.

It is also a reflection of US society where order and justice can be dispensed by the individual if you feel you have been used or intimidated.

In Britain, an increased number of cars on the roads, poor back-up facilities for parking etc, could well see incidents of road rage rise.

7. DEMONSTRATIONS

One may support the good intentions of a peaceful demonstration, but not the rowdy and violent single-issue hazards witnessed in a number of cities around the world.

There are threats and counter threats even before the demonstration takes place.

The Observer 25 Feb, 2000, revealed that extremist groups opposed to blood sports were planning to wreak havoc on the property of members of the Countryside Alliance when they left their homes and began their march through the capital on 25 March, 2000. Because of the publicity the mood was set, encouraging both demonstrators and counter-demonstrators to strike a determined new belligerent attitude.

There are various plots by the counter-demonstrators to infiltrate the march and there are many misleading pieces of information to divert all hostile elements to another scene. As one marcher proclaimed to me: *"it's all the fun of the chase"*.

Sadly damage and injuries occur and at the end of the day there are few winners and little alteration to the "policy" the demonstrators wanted. Certainly this is true of all the globalisation demos. After the noise and the damage, life goes on as normal, whether in Switzerland, Canada or Italy. But considerable damage is done to the fabric of law and order and physical injury to the police and those running the public services. The wider public is becoming increasingly aware that such riots are far from spontaneous, but they are highly planned, marshalled and directed, often by the extreme left.

The inevitable consequence in that a critical public within the individual countries will react more harshly than hitherto or will demand much tougher methods of control by the police. The consequence will not be pretty.

8. ANIMAL RIGHTS ACTIVISM

Terrorism is about disorder. We will discuss causes, weapons and suffering of innocent victims. But the campaign for animal rights – although well meaning - has adopted methods used by determined violent groups. Their campaigns use or threaten the use of violence. Target selection is symbolic. Those hit are arbitrary, although there is a higher risk of being maimed or killed if one happens to be working in a laboratory (no matter how valuable the research might be in saving human life), or guarding a location which the campaigners believe to be connected with the abuse of animals. Peter Singer's "Animal Liberation" for instance, describes how animals have "equal rights" parallel to those of humans. Several lobbies of Parliament have taken place, but now the campaigns have an increasingly serious mission.

The central body is the Animal Liberation Front (ALF), which began, in the early 1970s. Its purpose is to carry out direct action against animal abuse, rescuing animals and causing financial loss to animal abusers, usually through the damage and destruction of property. Their short-term aim is to rescue as many animals as possible and directly disrupt the practice of research where animals are used. Their long-term aim is to end all animal suffering by forcing companies out of business.

ALF do not view property damage as violence. The ALF uses a variety of methods, including arson, the releasing of animals and the super gluing of locks. They are determined to destroy in a manner expressed by William Paton in Man and Mouse (1993) Oxford University Press. More than £250,000 worth of damage has been attributed to the ALF in its first twelve months of activity. Other less violent groups, followed on, including the Animal Liberation Leagues which aim to investigate claims of research being conducted on animals.

The Animal Rights militants stepped up their campaign with letter bombs, contamination threats and car bombs. This escalation in tactics gave rise to the more militant group, the Animal Rights Militia (ARM).

Six minor bomb attacks on scientists' homes in 1986 shocked the nation. Tim Daley, a prominent ALF leader was quoted as saying *"in a war you have to take up arms and people will get killed, and I can support that kind of action by petrol bombing and bombs under cars and probably at a later stage, the shooting of vivisectors on their doorsteps."* (David T Hardy's "American's New Extremists" 1990).

The ALF claims that it carries out 15 to 20 actions every night and that the level of incidents have increased. It is difficult to see why the campaign has become so destructive, but as anarchists and other left-wingers gravitate to the cause the campaign has become a rallying cause for other factions "against the system". Fortunately, the law has been pro-active and in its reaction, has confronted the worst excesses of the animal rights campaign. Some 350 prosecutions have been made, most of them successful and some involving long sentences.

As with other areas of terrorism, there is the direct confrontation with the public, which inevitably lead to people being maimed if not killed, as well and the subsequent spreading of fear. Sending of hypodermic needles through the post and planting car bombs signals a similar threat and arouses a similar degree of fear.

The London-based Aegis Defence Services in a report published December 2004 warned of the dangers of animal rights activists. Aegis which employs hundreds of specialists in region such as the Far East and the Middle East says that animal rights "terrorists" in the United Kingdom could do as much damage to the economy as a single spectacular terrorist attack.

At stake is an annual investment of up to £16 billion in the pharmaceutical and biotechnology industries. These extremists will become a growing threat over the next two years.

As the UK government and industry fail to act effectively against animal rights extremists, says the report, so the activists will maintain their momentum in establishing offshoots in a number of European Countries, especially Italy, the Netherlands, Sweden and Russia.

A particularly sinister aspect of recent events occurred in September 2004 when a training camp in the Kent countryside was deployed for hundreds of animal liberation front activists who were taught how to kill as extremists break the law. (The Times, Dec 10, 04)

9. VIOLENCE AND RACISM

It worth drawing attention to the racist element which wishes to break up the formal lines of good citizenship and law and order.

a) The racists confront the public in a number of ways: (Evening Standard, 10 Sept, 1997.)

"A policeman's son was critically ill in Great Ormond Street Hospital today after having his skull fractured in a playground racial attack. Daniel Moore 12 underwent emergency surgery early today to remove a blood clot from his shattered skull after being beaten senseless with a broken house brick by a gang of Asian youths in Hounslow"

b) "Lies and distortion" (from the Oldhamer publication in reaction to the BNP in election leaflets): (April 2002).

Asians get jobs because of their colour. (BNP allegation).

Oldhamer replies: It is false. Unemployment among Asians is higher in every age group than among whites. Even the council employs a lower percentage of Asians than their proportion of the town's population.

All Muslims are fundamentalists (BNP allegation).

Reply: It is false. Every religion has extremists. They might make a lot of noise and get lots of publicity, but they are in the minority. Most Muslims, like Christians, just want to live their lives in peace.

Mosques have been paid for by council money (BNP allegation).

Reply: It is false. The mosque in Coppice and the planned mosque in Chadderton were funded by local Muslim people.

c) Additional material produced by Oldhamer at the 2002 election.

In some detail it ran a feature on the extreme right-wing group Combat 18. Olhamer advocates:

To ship all non-whites back to Africa, Asia, Arabia, alive or in body bags, the choice is theirs; to execute all queers, to execute all white race mixers. To weed out all Jews in the government, the media, the arts, the professions. To execute all Jews who have actively helped to damage the white race and to put into camps the rest until we find a final solution for the eternal Jew. To form a white commonwealth containing Europe, America, Canada, South Africa, Australia etc.

Whilst legislation, is on the increase, both nationally and in Europe, to search out and identify racism, the ability to 'deliver' and deal with racism through the various national courts within the countries of the European Union is less impressive.

Within Europe, there is a defined structure, through the European Commission against Racism and Intolerance (ECRI). This is a mechanism, which was established by the first Summit of Heads of State and Government of the Council of Europe member States. The decision to establish ECRI is contained in the Vienna Declaration adopted by the first Summit in 1993. The second Summit, held in Strasbourg, October 1997, decided to strengthen ECRI's action. Now, ECRI is taking their responsibilities further.

In 2004, it is clear that ECRI's task is to combat racism, xenophobia, anti-Semitism and intolerance at the level of greater Europe and from the perspective of the protection of human rights. It aims to confront discrimination and prejudice faced by persons or groups of persons, on grounds of race, colour, language, religion, nationality or ethnic origin. ECRI's members are appointed by their governments on the basis of their knowledge in the field of combating intolerance, and they are nominated in their personal capacity and act as independent members.

The programme of activities comprises three aspects: the country-by-country approach, work on general themes and relations with civil society. ECRI's strategy for constantly enhancing its activities is to take a step-by-step approach, building on the work it has already accomplished by evaluating, consolidating and extending its action. There has been criticism that perhaps this way of dealing with complaints does not deal effectively or quickly enough. However, the widespread propagation of theories which claim that cultural differences are insurmountable is a dangerous tendency, which is likely to increase feelings of racism and intolerance in the public consciousness. In this context, an insidious form of racism has resurfaced, which tends to define cultures not only as set in stone, but also to classify them, as though there were cultures which are in some way "superior", or "inferior".

There has also been a sharp rise in prejudice against Muslim communities, observable in many countries after the attacks of 11 September, 2001 in both society at large and in some public authorities. This climate of hostility has led to acts of violence, harassment and discrimination against persons who are or who are believed to be Muslim, and to a further increase in the generally negative attitude and stereotypes towards Muslims and their communities.

At the same time ECRI has also reported "a rise in the spread of anti-Semitic ideas. Acts of violence and intimidation against the members and institutions of the Jewish communities and the dissemination of anti-Semitic material are increasing in a number of European countries."

Related to ECRI is the European Union Monitoring Centre (EUMC), which has established one project concerned racism and diversity in the mass media, which has created much interest. The media often receives complaints made about their treatment of issues concerning the black community in Britain. The report provides a guide with a most comprehensive overview of media research with regard to racism and examples of good practice on anti-racism and cultural diversity in all the EU Member States. The aim of the report is to provide reliable data about, and to chart the main characteristics of reporting on ethnic minorities and migrants.

It highlights a number of different initiatives to promote cultural, ethnic and religious diversity taken by mass media organisations, such as developing codes of conduct, recruiting broadcasters from the migrant and minority communities and training multi-ethnic personnel.

An instrument to measure racist attitudes is a necessary requirement for any research group to function, and this has been set up by the EUMC in close co-operation with Prof. Wilhelm Heitmeyer from the Interdisciplinary Institute for Conflict and Violence Research at the University of Bielefeld in Germany.

The EUMC desperately needs the support of governments, NGO's and the wider civic society. Unless it is able to achieve this, the pursuit of action again race discrimination will pass to countries who may not prioritise the action required.

Meanwhile in Britain, the extreme right-wing fascists have not made any significant headway in Parliament although they have been successful in local elections in Burnley, Oldham and Halifax. This has not stopped the determination of organizations like the British National Party (BNP), to make racism and the deportation of immigrants their core policy.

The BNP will often use a 'safe' national issue to disguise their racist ideology – and a gullible public in some areas will buy the proposition. An example of this was during those elections, when a local newspaper - the Southport Champion - ran a long interview with the BNP candidate, and when I pointed out to the Editor that such publicity was contrary to NUJ guidelines, he replied that he was surprised the candidate agreed to his instruction so he had to go ahead, and anyway he considered it a scoop!

Steve Silver of Searchlight confirmed to me (2004) that there is a naive, gullible, local newspaper attitude. He says that the press were merely turning the BNP press releases into major articles all too easily. However, Silver told me however, he is heartened to see the trade union and labour movement supporting so much of the anti-fascist work that is being carried out at the moment. It seems likely that the best people to get the anti-racist message across to the white working-class are the organised groups, like the professional bodies and the trade unions.

The racist confrontation continues in Britain. Whilst their political penetration is not reflected in our Parliament as it is in other European assemblies, notably in France and Austria, it would be foolish to ignore the determination of the racist party's membership and the infrastructure of their leadership.

Whilst this campaigning is almost totally against the black community, it would take little change of policy to sway it towards Jews and gays. Searchlight's fight over many years is a constant reminder of not letting up.

Credit must also be given to the changing attitude in the police force, prompted by the Stephen Lawrence case.

In combating racism and the consequences of its insidious effects, we need the formal authority to act through legislation as well as the willingness of police and the authorities to provide adequate resources.

Ireland presents a complex picture. For the tourist, the country is known as the land of a "thousand welcomes", but as black or coloured people enter the job market or pursue a property purchase many see little of their "welcome". A case in point was well described by Paul Harris (Observer, 19 Aug, 2001):

"Jean-Pierre Eyanga is a lucky man. He fled death squads in his native Congo and was granted asylum in Ireland two years ago. He is free to find work. To the thousands of refugees rejected each year he is a rare success.

But Eyanga has discovered booming Ireland – the so-called Celtic Tiger – has no place for him. He holds a veterinary degree and a master's in food science, but each day he trawls the streets of Dublin looking unsuccessfully for work. His briefcase contains more than 40 rejection letters.

For him there is one simple conclusion. A black or brown skin is unwelcome, even in an economy operating at almost full employment. "I have lived in France and Belgium but I never experienced what I've had here. I have been called nigger and monkey on many occasions," he said.

Yet the immigrants are still coming to Ireland and black faces are to be seen on the streets of Dublin, although not on the West Coast. Many are living in a tense situation and working with some fear. Harris further reported, *"Petre Tanase knows all about racism in Dublin. In the back of his restaurant the Romanian former asylum-seeker keeps a bag of broken cups and a jagged concrete block – all thrown at him in the restaurant he founded and runs".*

One Irish government spokesman, the then Minister of Justice was determined to send the asylum seekers home with an economic bounty – in this case to Nigeria. With such ignorance it is not surprising that social unrest, even violence seems not too far away.

OTHER MANIFESTATIONS OF RACISM

There is a further cause of likely racism in Britain today due to the possible involvement of British Muslims in any world conflict involving their fellow religionists. This occurred when Muslim volunteers went out to Afghanistan and took up the Al-Qaeda cause. One has to admit that this is not an ongoing issue to disturb the two million Muslims in Britain, but for every one who is influenced and possibly brain washed by the visiting mullahs, it will undoubtedly exacerbate tension to race relations, and therefore it will be exploited by the extreme right-wing movements.

Imran Khan, a 30-year old DJ wrote a most revealing account in T2 (8 March, 2002) in which he described how Muslims who previously were only interested in clubs and girls have become fundamentalists. As a result of the travelling teachers in the mosques, the whole pattern of the faith of the young has changed. They have put aside drugs and clubs, says Khan. Yet there are ambiguities as Khan asks *"But if Islam is this clean beautiful religion and all my friends want to do is to live a simple life, why are young men who grew up like me taking up arms and fighting in far-off lands?"*

Khan says, *"The answer lies in the politicisation of Islam and some of the newer more militant followers. For them, Islam is being dismantled by the forces of the West, which has nothing but capitalist self-interest at heart".*

Omar Sheikh, the former British public school boy accused of murdering the American journalist Daniel Pearl, was just in his twenties when he kidnapped three British tourists and held them at gunpoint in his fight for the Muslims in Kashmir. The methods of the visiting Muslim "teachers" are to brainwash. They aim to destabilise British society and it gives the enemies of a multi racial society the opportunity to work their venom on the "strangers".

The likelihood of achieving racial harmony and stability is not encouraging. How far strategies can be deployed to meet the challenges will be examined in this book. Our aim is threefold:

First, to examine the past in order to assess the various trends and malfunctions, which create disorder and violence.

Second, to relate this historical perspective to the contemporary scene: is there a greater degree of violence today, and if so, what form does it take?

Third, what can be done to reassure a growing, anxious public as they observe brutalities within their neighbourhoods, affecting their families and friends, as many of our social institutions appear to be breaking down?

Further, the public wants answers to the questions of international terrorism and why it appears to go unchecked and apparently uncontrolled. The people, on behalf of the next generation, want answers now. What sort of future is it going to be?

CHAPTER 2

Information about violence has inevitably been drawn from the criminal statistics. Over the last decade the picture in Britain – as in many parts of Europe – is disturbing. Yet there is little serious debate and inevitably all who speak merely reflect the latest press release from the Home Office or the various police forces. Thus the very nature of the argument is defensive with predictable comments from the Government spokespersons and the opposition. Equally predictably is the press reaction to 'galloping crime'.

The Health Statistics Quarterly continues to reveal a troubling contemporary picture of Britain. The number of people shot dead in England and Wales for instance, has increased by two thirds during the past 20 years but shootings account for only about 60 of the 700 murders a year. The death rate from homicide among young men has risen 50 per cent over the same period.

The number of people killed with a knife has risen from an average 175 to 211 a year over the last 20 years - an increase of more that 20 per cent - according to the Office of National Statistics. The statistical breakdown reveals that stabbing is more common in Scotland, where the death rate from knife wounds per million of the population is double that in England and Wales. Scotland comes across as the 'stabbing centre'.

1. CRIME STATISTICS

The general picture in Britain is gloomy. There have been quarterly figures showing an improvement but the inevitable trend is high on the increase of violence. However charitable one might be of the difficulties facing the Home Secretary, street muggings and robberies seem to be getting out of control. Crimes involving firearms, increased by 35 per cent in 2002.

Vicious drug wars, mobile phone thieves and a dramatic increase in young offenders are blamed for the epidemic which is blighting urban Britain, at a time when many crimes are falling.

It is curious that officials insist the true picture is less bleak, because police forces were now being forced to record more offences. Yet, although police recorded 5.5 million crimes it is believed that another seven million victims did not bother to report a range of crimes including vandalism and other minor assaults.

"Some crimes have reached epidemic levels," said Norman Brennan, chief executive of the Victims of Crime Trust. (Daily Express, December 2002).

Dave Rodgers, vice chairman of the Metropolitan Police Federation, added, *"Many of the problems stem from contempt for society in general among young people. Robbery is in vogue because it offers easy pickings with very little chance of being caught."*

The figures show that 83 per cent of robberies were in a handful of key areas – London, the West Midlands, Merseyside, Greater Manchester, West Yorkshire, South Yorkshire and Northumbria.

They also show how the number of young people committing and subjected to robbery has spiralled – one in every 10 men in the 16-24 age bracket was a victim of violent crime last year, while in London the number of robbery suspects aged under 15 has risen fivefold in the past 10 years.

In short, Britain's record is dire. England and Wales top the Western world's crime league, according to The UN Interregional Crime and Justice Research Institute study 2002 and 2003. The UN research reveals that people in England and Wales experience more crime per head than people in the 17 other developed countries analysed in the study. Researchers found that nearly 55 crimes are committed per 100 people in England and Wales compared with an average of 35 per 100 in other industrialised countries.

The UN study analysed Home Office crime statistics for England and Wales and also carried out telephone interviews with victims of crime in the 17 countries surveyed, including the US. Britain has the worst record for "very serious" offences, recording 18 such crimes for every 100 inhabitants, followed by Australia with 16.

"Contact crime", which is defined as robbery, sexual assault and assault with force, was second highest in England and Wales – 3.6 per cent of those surveyed. This compares with 1.9 per cent in the US.

2. PUBLIC PERCEPTION

The public perception of crime and confronting it is even more serious a social issue than the crime figures suggest.

One particular local community is more scared of crime than people from almost anywhere else in Great Britain. The annual British Crime Survey shows people in the Merseyside region have among the "highest levels of worry" about violent crime and disorder, even though a smaller proportion than in comparable areas were actual victims. The Merseyside Police Authority has revealed a 5.7 per cent increase in the overall number of reported crimes in the survey, which has long been established as the most reliable reflection of crime in the UK. In Merseyside, 24 per cent of those questioned said they had a high level of worry about violent crime. 27 per cent said they had a high level of worry about disorder on the streets. The percentages for every other county apart from Greater Manchester and South Yorkshire were lower, averaging under 20, where fear of crime was concerned. Yet only 7 per cent of Merseysiders have actually experienced "personal crime", the survey reveals.

In contrast, 10 per cent of people in Greater Manchester have experienced "personal crime," as have 9 per cent in Lancashire and 8 per cent in Cheshire.

Confronted with these statistics the Merseyside assistant chief constable said, "The fear of crime bears no resemblance to the risk of actually becoming a victim. We want people to have an informed view of the reality of crime."

Statistics clearly demonstrate that the people most terrified of crime are pensioners. But those most at risk are people aged 18-25. It has been pointed out by police officers previously that it is those members of society who are, in fact, least likely to feel challenged, who are attacked every day.

Are our present difficulties on the street quite so unique? Evidence shows that there is a long history of fears on the streets (see Geoffrey Pearson, The Violent Society 1985).

Interest in violence is one thing but the many characteristics of the damage and destructiveness it brings is another. The authorities are attempting to codify the many incidents, which occur daily in all parts of the country and share the information, to some extent also with police and governments abroad. But violence is not a new phenomenon, although many current incidents have shocked the public, provoking intense reaction.

Reasons offered by the media and the public include the lack of parental authority, the absence of restraint, the wildness of extremes, the confusion of newfound liberties, and the wholesale drift away from churches.

These views are similar to those reported many years ago, by a Christian youth worker, James Butterworth, as written in 1932 Clubland (Epworth).

"Again and again in the mid-1800s onwards there are many examples of violence on the streets and with a corresponding declaration by writers and politicians bemoaning the fate of society and/or the government. There was a style of dress, a 'clubbing together' and a youth culture, which expressed itself dramatically and often, violently".

Geoffrey Pearson put it this way: Bell-bottom trousers cut tight at the knee and with a tasteful buttoned vent in the leg; colourful neck scarves and a distinctive style of cap; boots said in some quarters to be toe-plated with iron and calculated to 'kill easily'; ornamental leather belts with designs worked in metal pins; and a characteristic 'donkey fringe' hair cut: these were the elements of the London Hooligan style. (The Violent Society, E Moonman 1987).

In other cities, youths with the same clothes (and the same street-fighting habits) were known and feared by different names. In Manchester there were the 'Scuttlers', where the name and style went back at least until the late 1880s, who were followed by a new generation calling themselves 'Ikes' or 'Ikey Lads'. In Birmingham the gangs were known as 'Peaky Blinders' or as 'Sloggers'."

In Liverpool and London violent gang loyalties were thus reflected in a vigorous code of loyalties and commitment to each other and to the group acceptance of right and wrong. Similar gangs were to be found in Australia and Canada.

However, in parliamentary debates, there were politicians who discounted this talk of violence and they said the gangs were press manufactured - again an echo of some of the expressions today by those who attempt to play down the destructiveness of the violent society. Charles Booth's remarkable Survey of Life and Labour of the People in London (1903) declared that hooliganism has been exaggerated. However in so many parts of his survey, incident after incident is recorded which hardly suggests that all was quiet and calm in London.

Fear marks many potential gang members. One-tenth of urban teenagers are joining inner-city vigilante gangs out of fear for their own safety, according to study by a government-backed think tank, the Foreign Policy Centre 2002. The report, the first into ethnic tensions among young people after 11 September, 2001 paints a startling picture of city centres at breaking point.

Researchers found that nine out of 10 Asian school children believed carrying a weapon for self-defence was "acceptable" because they had been attacked, bullied or insulted.

A sixth of all teenagers surveyed have been driven to depression and suicidal thoughts because they feel vulnerable and let down by police and schools. Young people said they broke the law only because they felt at risk.

Contemporary violence has, in many ways, become far more organised. In France, a weekend brawl between rival gangs over young people and their "affections," had little of the romance and musical adventure of West Side Story. In February 2001, following some excessively violent incidents, it was necessary for CRS riot police to pursue the hooded sweaters of the gang called 'The Barbarians'. Up to that time, gang fights were private and out of sight, today violence has been brought out into the public arena.

In Chanteloup and Mantes-la-Jolie many of the immigrants are from North Africa. In the grading system of French racism they figure at the top. In France today it is Arabs rather than blacks that supporters of Jean-Marie Le Pen and Bruno Megret reserve their hatred for.

French people don't visit the council blocks where many of the gangs live, ironically not too far away, is one of the wealthiest areas of France: the council blocks are tucked away from sight of the expensive blocks not far from Versailles and St. German-en-Laye to the west of Paris. The gang battle is about power and ethnic pride. There are more than 70 ethnic groups and with high unemployment the tension seems inevitable.

Alongside the ethnic conflict is the religious divide and here Northern Ireland has been a fertile training ground both within its boundaries as well as exporting its menace and terrorists to other parts of the world. Another additional dimension to the support of terrorists from Northern Ireland was the help offered in the past by two outside groups, the neo-nazis and also the Palestinian extremists.

Not only is there close communication and support between the various groups, as with terrorists across national boundaries, but even a fiercely loyal gang of right-wing skinheads will merge with other groups when the time and opportunity for violence is deemed to be worthwhile.

The progress of the former skinheads who were disrupting concerts in the 1980s still continues in venues in Britain and Europe.

Young Irish loyalists, who formed the core of the now defunct National Front branch in Belfast, are now the cadre of Johnny Adair's C Company of the Ulster Freedom Fighters – the assassination arm of the Ulster Defence

Association. These men were at the centre of the Ulster loyalist feud, and claimed three lives, have been ferociously loyal to each other over the last two decades. The Nazi roots of the group are profound, and while the British and Irish press may portray these feuds as squalid turf wars over drugs there is a deep hatred of all Catholics and nationalists, hence the attraction of the Nazi philosophy.

The image and reality of the intense prejudice was brought home – through our television screens – of the horror experienced by children as they walked to Holy Cross School in the Ardoyne. We saw a group of Catholic parents and girls stoned and abused on their 300-metre walk to Holy Cross through a Protestant area. On the worst days the girls were in tears as their parents tried to cheer them up with songs and cover their ears against the worst of the abuse as they made the simple procession into school.

"They called us Fenian bastards and spat at us, but sometimes it was more personal so you know it's you they mean," one mother said.

Four sets of parents have been warned that they will be killed if they take their children to school through the loyalist area again. The threats come from the Red Hand Defenders – regarded by the police as a cover name for dissident members of the Ulster Defence Association (UDA).

These examples in Ireland highlight the force of outside influences and the determination to destroy even if it means innocent people will suffer. To abuse children going to school is shown to be determined, predictable and violent.

A poisonous atmosphere is created in which people, who in other circumstances would like to get on with their neighbours, are drawn into violence. (Violent Times, see earlier)

3. AT WORK

Methods of obtaining information of violent acts at work have improved, particularly in the public sector, so that there is an intelligent basis to examine the various incidents and trends of violence.

The TUC continues to pursue initiatives on the hazards at work. It followed when Jenny Morrison, a social worker, was fatally stabbed by a patient. A UNISON survey of meat hygiene inspectors revealed that many are subjected to physical and abuse when they visit abattoirs to enforce the laws aimed a preventing "mad cow" disease. And an airline steward was attacked with a broken bottle, which left her scarred for life. These are just a few examples of recent violent incidents at work. But there has been a steady drip of cases in the news, from Dunblane to the series of attacks on casualty nurses.

These cases are not rare. Violence at work is a serious problem for all people whose work brings them into contact with members of the public. As well as the immediate physical effects, it can lead to stress and depression, and it can undermine the effectiveness of the workplace.

Younger women are the most likely to be attacked, with 11 per cent of women between the ages of 25 and 34 reporting a physical attack compared to 6 per cent of men in the same age group. 24 per cent of women and 17 per cent of men of this age had been threatened with attack.

Other findings of this report are:

- Nurses are most at risk, with one in three attacked; second most at risk are those working in the security industry (one in four), followed by care workers (21 per cent) and education and welfare employees (14 per cent);

- The vast majority of security guards – often employed to protect other workers – get no training in dealing with aggressive members of the public;

- 70 per cent of teachers believe that violence in schools is increasing;

- Assaults on employment service staff have increased 12-fold since 1987;

- Assaults on railway workers have more than tripled between 1995 and 1998;

The number of violent incidents in the retail sector has risen by 44 per cent.

The TUC recommended improved training and awareness seminars, but much more needs to be done. The law on violence at work seems to be adequate, yet TUC's main concern is that employers seem to have adopted the attitude that violence is unpredictable and therefore cannot be prevented.

Unions were urged to take a lead in workplaces on violence, not only expressing the fears and concerns of working people, but also pressing employers to accept that it is their legal responsibility to prevent violence in exactly the same way, as they would address any other threat to health and safety.

Employers may work with the unions to:

- Assess the risks of violence to their staff;

- Take steps to prevent or minimise such violence or protect employees from it.

- Ensure that, when violent attacks do occur, they are recorded and the victims receive appropriate assistance.

A TUC officer - following the publication of the report - stated, *"These are not just isolated newspaper headlines. We are under attack."*

Being honest about the problem should help. Introducing an effective reporting system may clearly demonstrate that the problem is getting worse. It will make staff more aware of the problem, show up the potential danger points and help avert a more serious incident.

As the TUC report has shown, within the public sector there has been much abuse of staff. The health service has seen various levels of violence, particularly in the A and E departments. The Department of Health released figures in 2002 and 2003 to show that alcohol is behind one in six admissions to hospital casualty departments, rising to eight in ten at weekends and during holidays. The problems posed by alcohol were starkly illustrated at one London hospital where patients have been caught in their pyjamas and dressing gowns attempting to buy alcohol at a nearby 24-hour shop. Another London hospital, which is working with police to solve these problems, also found a patient leaning on his drip, drinking outside a nearby shop.

It is estimated that there are 65,000 violent incidents against NHS staff each year, with almost two-thirds of cases involving nurses.

As part of a campaign aimed at reducing the number of incidents against NHS staff by 30 per cent, the Government has issued guidelines on dealing with persistently violent patients. (21 Dec, 2002, Dept of Health).

They advise that such patients should be removed from NHS hospitals and denied treatment for up to a year. But these guidelines do not apply to people with mental health problems, and those requiring emergency treatment. The Government has also endorsed a football-style yellow and red card system, piloted at Barts and the London NHS Trust, to warn abusive patients that treatment might be withheld.

In my own experience as Chairman of two large London Health Authorities I visited A & E deliberately in the late evening to support the staff in their confrontations. Inevitably, I found the families of patients - often ethnic - often deeply aggressive.

Liberal-minded folk would challenge that we should not turn the hospital admission and ward visits into a security operation, but the hazards of violence to staff are too great to ignore. A leading New York hospital, when admitting a patient, insists that the family do not enter the building, and they have security to ensure this is done. Subsequent visits by relatives are monitored and supervised closely. It is not inconceivable that we may turn to such a system here.

4. DOMESTIC VIOLENCE

What is the appropriate response to domestic violence? This complex question, still without clearly defined answers, is the subject of intense controversy and debate.

What is domestic violence? Domestic violence is violence between heterosexual adults who are living together or who have previously cohabited. The term is broadly defined and it is acknowledged that definitions are largely dependent on descriptions by the police, assailants, and victims.

In an important appraisal of the subject, Smith and Straus. ('Understanding Partner Violence' 1995) concludes.

Partner violence has many causes. This is one of the reasons why there is no single solution, but at times there may be found at different levels: i.e., community-wide, through the legal system, within the violent partner relationship, and at the level of the individual batterer or victim, a community level solution – shelters for battered women.

It is claimed by some researchers that only about 2 per cent of incidents of domestic violence are reported to the police. This would account for the lack of reliable evidence on why it occurs and the kind of people that are involved.

Now the government intends to act as a result of much lobbying on behalf of many community workers and wives who have been the victims. A government initiative will be to record the names of wife-beaters on a national register. Men convicted of beating their wives will be named in the "domestic violence register" under government plans to help police to track the men's movement and warn new partners about their past. Modelled on the sex offenders register, the register would contain the names of anyone sentenced to six months or more in prison for assaulting their partner. Those on the list would be forced to inform local police when they move home. The register would be made available to all the relevant agencies including the NHS, social services and some benefits agencies.

Plans for the register have been backed by police chiefs and senior prosecutors. Details of how the register would operate are contained in a document drawn up by the Association of Chief Police Officers (ACPO) and the Crown Prosecution Service.

Action is essential as domestic violence has one of the higher recidivism rates of any crime so it becomes all the more important for a clearly defined action plan when an offender moves into a new neighbourhood.

5. TELEVISION AND ROLE MODELS

We have considered this earlier and, of course, there is a considerable amount of varied advice as to the likely causes and influence. But I mention just one research proposal undertaken by Professor Jeffrey Johnson of Columbia University and published in Science (March, 2004).

Professor Johnson's team tracked more than 700 children and took into account the "chicken and egg" question: Does watching television cause aggression or do people prone to aggression watch more television?

Professor Johnson concludes that responsible parents of adolescents should not let their children watch more than one hour of television a day. Even youths with no history of aggressive behaviour were much more likely to commit aggressive acts if they were watching more than that per day. There was also the issue of what they were watching and whether parents were sufficiently determined to prevent children watching over the late evening watershed. In many cases, there was no discipline.

The link between watching television and behaving violently remained intact after the researchers had taken into account other factors such as childhood neglect, or family income, or psychiatric disorder during adolescence. But the study confirmed earlier enquiries that teenagers are affected to a considerable extent if their watching goes beyond one hour per day and can provoke violent tendencies. A similar research project is now likely to take place under similar conditions in the United Kingdom.

SPOT THE DIFFERENCE

CHAPTER 3
VIOLENCE IN SOCCER

1. THE BRITISH SCENE

Violence and sport seem an unlikely combination but the two are much closer than at appears at first sight. Thus it is increasingly talked about, scrutinised and researched. Perhaps the competitiveness and the determination to 'win' contribute to this. Ironically England has often been charged with a lack of a winning attitude. "To win at all costs" is, it is said, is part of the Australian make-up, whereas the English lack that will. English players should toughen up and the results will follow! Perhaps we have the measure of this advice in view of the success of the Rugby team in 2003 and the winning of the Ashes in cricket, 2005

Spectator violence on and around the grounds has continued for years, while Football Club Chairmen and Politicians have argued, *"it is not our problem, it is society's."* A former Minister of Sport, Neil Macfarlane, said, *"the problem with spectator sport at, and associated with football matches is indeed a serious one but the origins of the problem do not lie within football."* (Centre for Contemporary Studies Conference Updated, 2003).

Irrespective as to whose responsibility it is, soccer violence damages the image of the professional game and can have repercussions on the non-professional game. More insidiously, and more significantly for the future of the game, it may well also deter parents and schools from encouraging children to take the game seriously. It certainly discourages family attendance at professional soccer matches.

Within the game violent play is identified and the rules ensure it is dealt with. Players respect the rules, to a greater or lesser extent and with some serious exceptions.

Spectators, who have no such rules, are merely constrained by the stewards in the ground and the police outside.

To look more deeply into the sport/violence equation demands that we examine social behaviour generally. The organisations within football have to understand the social process at work. A question which requires an answer is not "why hooliganism or violence?" but "why in football?" For example at the England World Cup game in Rome 1997 (before H.M. Government took a tough line with hooliganism). It was reported that up to 700 known football supporters would be present. The British police identified (6 Oct, 1997) between 60 and 70 "Category C" fans who are the worst offenders likely to instigate crowd trouble. (6 Oct, 1997.) At least another 600 "Category B" supporters, who would get involved if trouble presented itself, were also travelling. Even though 95% of these hooligans had convictions for football-related violence, police were powerless to stop them travelling unless they already had court-imposed restriction orders.

Detective Inspector Peter Chapman, head of the National Criminal Intelligence Service football unit, said his Italian counterpart would be monitoring the troublemakers as they touched down on Italian soil on more than 50 flights from all over the UK. Chapman went on to say "not to worry...the Italian Police are probably the best in Europe." (Evening Standard, 1 Oct, 1997). In the event, it was a disaster. In an editorial, The Times (14 Oct, 1997) reported that *"the Italian policing of Saturday's World Cup qualifying match in Rome was a model of how not to proceed"*. The indiscriminate baton charges in the stadium injured English supporters who played no part in the violence; worse, casualties would have resulted had there been a stampede by panicking spectators. Italy has much to learn about British police techniques of isolating troublemakers and taking them out of the stands at the first sign of trouble. If containment failed, so did proven methods of prevention. Gate checks were offensively intrusive in searching bodies but culpably lax in checking tickets and seat assignments. Groups of English fans were not properly isolated, and some were admitted who should not have been.

Many English fans abroad behave far worse than they do at home. The Football Association's ticket schemes have not stopped fans travelling without tickets on the assumption – often correct – that they will be allowed into stadium for fear of riots if they are excluded. However inexcusable the police brutality in Rome, the background to it is the apprehension that still attends the arrival of English supporters.

It was a bad day all round. The Italians overreached at the match, but left gaps unsupervised in the city. Before the game, drunken, aggressive English supporters raised the tension when they vandalised Roman cafés, cars and shops, littering parts of the city with broken glass and forcing shopkeepers to ring down their shutters. It did not take many to induce a climate of fear.

2. DIMENSIONS OF VIOLENCE

The police have tried to marginalize the timing of matches and the corresponding travel movements of supporters. The fourth round of the FA Cup (January 2002) witnessed a clash of interest, during which the BBC and the Metropolitan Police found themselves at loggerheads over the scheduling of Liverpool's visit to Highbury. The BBC had hoped to air the fixture during prime time, but the authorities deemed a 7pm kick-off too high a security risk, given that forces would already be stretched to cover the half dozen other London ties to be played that weekend. They were reluctant to agree particularly because of the problems that were caused a week before, when a crowd invasion was staged at the match between Cardiff City and Aston Villa.[1]

Soccer violence can, and often does, carry racist overtones.

Oldham is a city burdened with racial disharmony, and so it is not surprising that in April 2001, Stoke City supporters travelled up on an away game with the intention of causing trouble, after hearing reports that Asian[2] youths had set up 'no-go zones' for whites in the area. Trouble is believed to have started following the chanting of racist slogans. It escalated outside the Boundary Park ground into an exchange with a group of Asians, in which petrol bombs were thrown at Police.[3] Although the skirmish may have been arbitrary in its sudden outburst, the raison d'être behind it most certainly was not, as on this occasion a particular grouping was discriminately targeted for abuse.

A good case illustration of racism in football violence is when trouble flared in Highbury after Arsenal's penalties defeat in the UEFA Cup final (2000) against Turkish club Galatasaray when trouble flared in Highbury.

As frustrated fans spilled out of pubs in Highbury and Finsbury Park, up to 400 hooligans threw missiles, smashed shop windows and intimidated residents in Blackstock Road. Kosovan refugees living above a 24-hour grocery told of their terror as a gang of raging yobs burst into their flat. The intruders were armed with a knife and bottles and forced them to escape through the first and second floor windows (Islington Gazette, 25 May, 2000).

Edmia Cocia, 19, said, *"we heard them smashing the shop windows downstairs and when we looked out of our window they started shouting abuse at us. "They kicked through the front door and about 15 of them ran into our flat, they smashed up all of our things – television, table and chairs – and said they were going to kill us. We escaped through the windows, it was very frightening."*

Three police officers were injured in the violence. Six arrests were made for a series of offences ranging from affray to being drunk and disorderly. One Arsenal fan was injured falling from a window in Blackstock Road.

Instead of celebrating a great sporting triumph, Islington's Turkish community were left to count the cost of the damage caused to their shops by drunken hooligans.[4]

The Turkish fans were by no means the victims on other occasions during this tournament. En route to lifting the trophy Galatasaray beat Leeds United in the Semi-finals, a Turkish man, Ali Umit Demir, stabbed and killed two Leeds supporters. He was later sentenced to 15 years imprisonment for the crime. Buses carrying Leeds fans were bombarded with bricks and stones as they were taken to the ground less than half an hour before kick-off.[5]

The game was patrolled by 10,000 armed officers. Many covered the ground with dogs or sat in armed personnel carriers.

Football violence can sometimes be a very deliberate and precise action. Sections of clubs illicitly form themselves into gangs, or 'firms', and just as their respective clubs compete on the football pitch, these gangs take to the terraces, streets and pubs in and around the ground to go head to head with one another.

One of the most fearsome firms in England is the Chelsea FC Headhunters gang, and was led by Andy Frain, alias Nightmare. According to the Evening Standard and a BBC1 TV programme MacIntyre Undercover, he is believed to be a ringleader behind an alarming rise in organised football violence (10 Nov, 1999).

The report in the Evening Standard stated that for him, the sport is a sideshow to a type of alternative entertainment, where the goal is battering rival firms with missiles, knives and iron bars. It would be comforting to dismiss Frain and others like him as mindless, but it would also be a mistake.

In a chilling TV exposé[6] Frain is seen laughing as he uses his mobile to rally 150 cohorts for an away-day riot. The language is military as he gives reference to troops, snipers and advance guards. The organisation is Machiavellian, as the gang take three separate coaches through three different routes in order to spread the risk of capture.

Perhaps the most scandalous instance was Frain's attempt to orchestrate violence between the Headhunters and Leicester City's firm, in which he sought to arrange a 'head to head' with his opposite number as a 'starter' to the match. They knew each other by name and were evidently used to playing a 'brutal poker' with the number of men they'd line up against each other. It looks as if two boxing promoters were arranging a title fight.[7]

These examples are by no means isolated in their occurrence. Football's anti-hooligan squad warned me that especially the late 1990's heralded a marked increase in the cases of disorder around British football grounds.

The National Criminal Intelligence Service (NCIS) published a report in 1998, which concluded that it is but a matter of time before someone is killed unless the dramatic rise in soccer-related violence is tackled. Brian Drew, NCIS's head of specialist intelligence strategy said, *"In the Premier League and First Division the opportunity no longer exists for hooligans to engage in the behaviour we saw in the 1970s. But this level of violence ...has not been seen for a long, long time. The signs now so early in the season are not encouraging."*[8] The vast majority of incidents are happening in streets and pubs in the locality of grounds. There is a growing tendency for trouble to break out on trains and other modes of public transport long before or after matches.[9]

A dossier published by the NCIS contains information on several incidents of criminal chaos caused by football thugs, many of which spilt over into the public domain. It includes for example details of a mêlée involving 200 supporters from Manchester United and Coventry City that broke out on a train in September 2000; a Leeds United and Bradford City game which led to 59 arrests; an attack on a pub used by Arsenal supporters after a derby match with Tottenham Hotspur; and robberies and fighting on a train carrying Sheffield United, Chesterfield and Nottingham Forest fans.

In all 22 incidents were detailed, all occurring within a few weeks of each other.[10]

This type of 'spill-over' violence hurts the local community, as it is left to pick up the pieces after such incidents, while the perpetrators may walk away with little more than a slap on the wrist.

Violence does show its unruly face *within* the football ground too. In many cases the spill over of hooliganism occurs from having at first been nurtured inside the stadium. When Derby County played Nottingham Forest in April 1999 there were no problems until the hosts scored in the 85th minute. The majority of Forest supporters left their seats and gathered in the concourse under the stand: It was later found that seats and facilities had been damaged. The Forest group of 200 then proceeded slowly toward the East Car Park. As they reached the stewards line on the southeast corner, they surged toward the departing Derby supporters with an omnipotent roar. Police were forced to use batons to prevent serious disorder. The Forest supporters were eventually corralled and numerous arrests from both parties followed.[11]

No area of the Beautiful Game is safe from aggression, as such episodes occur throughout all levels of the sport. Cambridge United's encounter with Peterborough (4 April, 1999) saw a number of fights and confrontations take place away from the ground, both before and after the match. Seventeen arrests were made throughout the day.[12]

Chelsea and Sunderland are top of the league of football thugs arrested whilst Wycombe Wanderers are the best behaved supporters. In the 1999/2000 season Sunderland, had 223 fans arrested, mainly due to a result of extensive policing operations. On one occasion 53 Wearside fans were arrested on a coach before they even reached the game with Derby County, after Officers learned that they were planning attacks on rival supporters. This was also the case with Chelsea, where 168 arrests included a group of 100 thugs stopped by police from attending a game against Tottenham Hotspur. They were arrested after authorities found weapons including a meat cleaver and bottle of ammonia which they planned to use on a rival Tottenham gang.[13]

Why does so much violence take place on football grounds? These are places where people of a particular interest congregate and whose attention is focused upon a particular activity. One may reasonably infer that the actions of the same football players have some degree of influence over their audience, creating copycat behaviour. It can however, have a positive influence. For example, when a player altruistically kicks the ball out of touch in the event of another falling injured, the crowd often respond positively, cheering to express their support for the act of kindness. A player behaving aggressively will influence the conduct of his audience to a like manner. Hence where badly behaved supporters off the pitch are often referred to as hooligans, so badly behaved players are equally to be considered as 'yobs'.

The yob culture in the professional game has been discussed at the highest level in government. Football's bad boys have been branded as 'yobs' by senior ministers and members of H.M opposition. Tessa Jowell, the Secretary of State for Culture, Media and Sport, claimed that players like Chelsea's John Terry and Liverpool's Jamie Carragher were wrecking the national game's reputation (Evening Standard, 4 Feb, 2002). Midway through the 2001/2002 season, the sport was rocked by a series of violent incidents. In their respective incidents, Carragher escaped police charges when he threw a coin into the crowd at Highbury, and John Terry, Jody

Morris and Wimbledon's Des Byrne, were charged with assaulting a nightclub bouncer.[14]

These episodes occurred alongside the fiercely controversial backdrop of the Lee Bowyer and Jonathan Woodgate court case, where the Leeds United duo were at the centre of an alleged racist attack on a young Asian student. Woodgate was later charged with affray.

The problem doesn't stop there, for the question of football violence within the professional game also extends to management. One of Britain's best known football Chairmen outside the Premier League had forged links with a group of hooligans who have provoked mayhem across the country. Sam Hammam, owner of Cardiff City FC, has bought champagne for his club's Soul Crew thugs, travelled with them and forged friendships with men who have serious criminal records. He refused to help police identify Cardiff hooligans and claimed that a riot at the club's Ninian Park ground did not involve violence. The Cardiff Soul Crew has acquired a reputation as Britain's most feared soccer gang by attacking rival fans, confronting police and causing chaos at games in England and Wales. Police dread visits by the club because of the likelihood of disorder. At the Welsh Cup Final against archrivals Swansea City in May 2002, Cardiff fans threw stones and bottles at police outside the stadium. A total of 112 Cardiff followers were banned from matches (more than any other British club). A NCIS spokesman said, *"Banning orders are the most accurate barometer of football hooliganism because they have been issued by a court against those the court has already decided pose a threat to the game."* Police have criticised Hammam's links with the wayward fans, saying that he has encouraged misbehaviour and damaged the club's image.[15]

The trade unions have been used to protect an alleged football hooligan. A major unofficial walkout crippled the postal system in February 2002. The stoppage came as a result of the dismissal of two clerks, brothers Tom and Mick Doherty, who were sacked in May 2000 after being caught on camera apparently fighting at the UEFA Cup final between Arsenal and Turkish Club Galatasaray in Copenhagen.

Photographs in the national press showed Mick Doherty throwing a punch at a man who appeared to be a Turkish supporter during a wider clash between rival fans.[16]

Again, we would imagine that the problem needs to be tackled holistically, as it affects society at large.

However, as the perpetrators of the crime do not conform to society's norms and carry little regard for law and order, tackling soccer violence has not and will not be a straightforward task. The thugs do not care if they are derided as scum, if they are despised and detested; they thrive on hate, their attitude is incomprehensible to sane, intelligent people, and there is little point trying to rationalise with them.

They do not look like average fans and claim that they avoid fighting with 'shirts' (supporters who wear replica kit). They gather in gangs and seek out other gangs, using football grounds as a meeting point in which to stage their unruly expressions of violence. Many of the individuals involved also harbour links to other major disturbances, such as the race riots in Oldham.[17]

The pictures would be even more worrying, were it not for the efforts of the authorities and the police. The demands and claims on the police force by hooligans were most vividly described in a fly on the wall documentary in Sheffield. The hooliganism creates a considerable financial cost to the police force management. (Dispatches, Channel 4, 10 Aug, 2003).

Having looked at the somewhat morbid reality of football hooliganism in England, we have to note that on the positive side there are programmes in place, set up by football clubs, which aim to tackle the issue in a proactive manner.

Millwall for example did try to stamp out the problem by banning away-supporters from attending certain fixtures that are deemed to be of high-risk.

Agreements with Wolves, Burnley, Nottingham Forest, Stoke Portsmouth and Leicester meant no visiting fans were allowed in when Millwall played them in Division One (Evening Standard, 11 June, 2002). The club announced a series of measures, which also included the club selling its tickets only to members and season ticket holders and building a walkway between its ground and South Bermondsey train station for away fans. The moves followed violence at The Den when hooligans went on the rampage after Millwall lost their play-off semi-final.[18]

The police have continually demanded that the Government make it compulsory for anyone convicted of football violence to be barred from travelling abroad as a supporter. Home Secretary Jack Straw had earlier run into criticism from supporters' associations after investigating moves to prevent hooligans from travelling to the World Cup matches, and by forcing them to report to police stations during matches. He urged judges and magistrates to make greater use of their existing powers when dealing with people convicted of football-related violence.

As the police identify the leaders and their tactics, the villains take to new ways and equipment to pursue their ends. In a clash in 2002 between Cardiff and Millwall it emerged that many of the thugs involved used an Internet web site to help organise their activities. The site, run by self-confessed hooligan Paul Dodd included a bulletin board where visitors could post messages. It contained a number of references to the Cardiff-Millwall clash, including details of where the violence would start and even a running commentary on the fighting. This has confirmed fears concerning organised gangs of soccer hooligans turning to new technology to avoid police crackdowns.[19]

Hooliganism has adapted to anti-violent measures, exploiting technology to further its interest.

The authorities' efforts to counter the brutality of football-related violence have recently shown encouraging signs. A NCIS report (February 2002) stipulated that the number of thugs banned from watching football domestically and internationally increased from 100 before Euro 2000 to just over 900 two years on.

The value of the orders were seen when 59 suspected troublemakers were prevented from travelling to Amsterdam for England's friendly against Holland. Of those stopped at airports and ports, 17 had already received banning orders which prevented them going to any ground in England or Wales and travelling abroad to watch England or English clubs on designated match days.

Those banned now total 1000, but nearly 10% of those bans come from one club; Cardiff City. Consistent with earlier discussion, the Welsh club has the largest army of thugs subject to banning orders, standing at 99. They are just ahead of Stoke City with 87 and Leeds United with 64. Millwall, according to the report, are London's worst club with 17, two more than Chelsea.[20]

The gangs of thugs have not only a rivalry with other club gangs, they also dispense justice if any member became wayward. They share a common lifestyle and even their own songs, all with the purpose of intimidation.

The Observer published a report by a journalist who was forced to remain anonymous (9 Dec, 2001). He described a game at Millwall, when the Manchester City team and supporters were greeted with: *"Fuck off you northern monkey! Oo, oo, oo, oo, oo"*, *"Fuck off you stunted coon! Oo, oo, oo, oo, oo"*, they screamed at Wright Phillips.

"Fuck off you Paki!" was the welcome for Ali Benarbia the first time he touched the ball.

"Fuck off you fat Jew," was the inevitable insult hurled regularly at Eyal Berkovic.

"No one likes us, no one likes us, no one likes us, we don't care, we are Millwall, Super Millwall..."

This is the flavour of the tension and violence around the stadium.[21]

With pitch invasions likely to become more common, attention has again been focused on rail fencing. It is worth noting that crowds on the Continent are still behind wire. In this country, fans were given the freedom to watch games without being caged and hopefully we don't have to return to fencing. Fencing is intimidating and humiliating, nevertheless everyone in the game has a duty to protect the players and genuine supporters.[22]

3. THE INTERNATIONAL SCENE

It was a quiet town in Italy. People were perhaps taking a siesta. Suddenly, the arrival of a football game created a whole new environment. Tim Parks, an ardent Verona fan, says:

"Everybody was hopeful and chattering, everybody marching to the stadium, entering the realm of compulsion. How exciting I thought, and then a bottle exploded on the pavement beside me. Then came the blast of a siren. That meant the Verona buses were arriving. In seconds the innocuous crowd around me had been replaced by a 100 or so hard-core romanisti with scarves tied around their faces and caps pulled down over their eyes. The police had sounded their sirens, but they hadn't radioed ahead to warn their colleagues to have the big gates into the protected sector opened." (Times Magazine, 9 March, 2002).[23]

It is a great myth that only Britain provides the football thugs. Not true. Yes we do have the thugs, - far too many - and we certainly have contributed to the hooliganism at many soccer tournaments. But thugs are to be found in all the countries. Who would deny that the evidence of the last 10 years with violence and damage initiated by, among others, Turkish, German, Dutch and Italian groups.[24]

The Dutch thugs even have designer combat gear. The firm Hooligan Streetwear launched a new range designed to give troublemakers at major soccer events their own 'uniform'. The company's sales pitch for mail order mayhem on the web was branded 'repulsive' by leading English fans' groups and condemned by the Football Association. Holland, the tournament's joint hosts, has one of Europe's worst reputations for soccer violence – and their thugs soon snapped up hard-core hooligan accessories. The T-shirts, baseball caps, sweaters and coats that carry a distinctive devil emblem were produced specially for the tournament.

Serie A was one of the finest leagues in the world. But within the last few years, scandal and intimidation has seeped into several clubs and the governing boards.

Malaise has engulfed the Italian game. There have been ambushes, stabbings and beatings as violence has spilled from the stadiums into cities with *ultras* (the hard-core fans) turning Serie A, B, C into battlefields. There have been attacks on players by their own supporters. Incidents have included besieged dressing rooms, assaults on players' relatives and a firebomb attack on a team bus. There has been widespread evidence of corruption, from match fixing and bribery, to positive dope tests and dodgy passports. Finally a disbelieving and disgusted international audience has witnessed an apparently endemic malicious racism among both fans and players that is all but tolerated in Italy itself.[25]

Scorn and potential violence is commonplace and apparently affecting all groups in society. A coordinator of Football against Racism in Europe, Michael Fanizadeh, was shocked to see women and children hurling abuse. Those fans that do not join in sometimes grimace, sometimes smirk, but mostly look as if they don't hear anything. Maybe they don't. *"Maybe the taunting is so routine they no longer notice,"* an Observer enquiry commented.[26]

There is a strong political tone to many of these acts of disorder. During a 1997 trip to Poland, the Italian National squad refused to accompany federation officials on a visit to Auschwitz. A journalist who wrote the story was threatened. Meanwhile Gianluigi Buffon, the Italian national goalkeeper, has worn a T-shirt sporting the fascist slogan, *'Death to those who surrender'*. Buffon, who plays for Parma in Serie A, also raised a few eyebrows last year when he picked '88' as his shirt number for the new season. The decision upset Italy's Jewish community, which pointed out that the figure is sometimes used as a neo-Nazi symbol, it is the 8th letter of the alphabet, so '88' equates with 'HH' or 'Heil Hitler'.[27]

However, in another case, some Italian players showed solidarity with their black colleagues. Treviso footballers smeared their faces with black shoe polish. The Treviso players made the gesture of support for striker Schengun Omolade during a 2-2 draw against Genoa in Italy's Serie B, the equivalent of England's Division 1. In a previous game, fans displayed a banner declaring 'we don't want a black player on our team' and walked out of the stadium when Omolade came on as a substitute. Omolade, 18, who scored against Genoa, dedicated the goal to his teammates. Treviso goalkeeper Marco Fortin said, "We sent out a message that has nothing to do with soccer but is perhaps much more important."[28] (Metro 5 June, 2001)

Across Europe at present, there is no standard procedure to deal with hooliganism. Under Danish law the names of deportees could be passed to British police and UK laws brought in to crack down on hooliganism, including a ten-year ban on travelling to overseas games.

Attempts are made for Britain's NCIS to coordinate campaigns against the football hooligan, including warnings by Chief Superintendent Eddy Curtis who advised colleagues in 15 European countries, *"We should let local police commanders and central law enforcement officials know the nature of the worst element of our supporters, which is a very small minority, without making them feel that they have to treat everyone with an English accent as a potential hooligan."*

Sometimes it is an uphill battle says NCIS spokesmen. Only when a serious incident occurs do police authorities take notice, as was the case with the murder of two Leeds fans in Turkey, when Kevin Speight and Christopher Loftus were stabbed to death. The murders soured relations between supporters of British and Turkish clubs and led to further violence. A legal marathon dragged for two years.

The Istanbul Court reduced sentences on each of seven defendants, and 13 were acquitted owning to lack of evidence, after the prosecution concluded that the crime had been committed "under provocation" by Leeds fans. Ali Umit Demir, found guilty of murdering both men, was first sentenced to 48 years, but then reduced to 15 years. Further appeals were immediately raised. Leeds were not blameless, they provoked the fight by disturbing passers-by, breaking cars and shop windows, burning Turkish banknotes and rubbing the national flag against their genitals.[29]

Ticketing and crowd movement requires supervision and control. Prior to the England vs. Germany World Cup qualifier, ticket sales were not merely disorganised but they became a mystery.

Six weeks prior to the game (1 Sept, 2001) the FA had been given 6,000 tickets, but thousands more England fans planned to travel to Germany in the hope of getting into the Olympic Stadium, which holds 60,000 fans. Hundreds had already bought tickets for areas of the ground reserved for German fans, threatening plans for strict segregation of the crowd. Troublemakers amongst both teams' supporters were threatening to attack their rivals in a series of increasingly aggressive messages posted at Internet hooligan websites. Both sides pledged to assault the other. Hooligan 'firms' who follow different English clubs such as Chelsea and Leeds United were urging each other to set aside their often violent rivalries, and join together to fight their German counterparts.

The xenophobic elements among England's supporters saw the game as a chance to resume hostilities with Germans'. *"Many regard this as a World War Two rehearsal, with us invading them in their own stadium,"* said one English police officer involved in trying to prevent trouble. (Observer, 15 July, 2001).

Although the match had been sold out for months, scores of tickets for the home supporters' sections of the stadium were still on sale to England followers from several websites and travel agents not licensed by the FA. Dozens were being snapped up daily, with fans paying up to £150 to secure a seat in England's biggest game in years. Some England followers went to the Olympic Stadium's website, in defiance of a ban on non-Germans buying tickets from home areas.[30]

It looked grim, the chaos was evident for all to see, despite a blunt warning from NCIS as the German police would treat any violence with equal punishment and jail. Due to an extensive security campaign by both German and the British police forces the damage was much less than was expected but it was a close run thing.[31]

4. WORLD CUP 2006

What a\re the lessons for the world Cup 2006 as a result of our own experiences on the tournaments staged in Japan and Korea? What have we learnt for Europe? The experience in both countries was extremely valuable to assist in all sporting events over the next few years.

We learned that increased travelling distance and the location in Asia was a significant factor. The cost of between £4,000 and £7,000 was a deterrent even to those who wanted to plan acts of crime and vandalism.

We learned that crowd control and seating patterns are important. Without much fuss the Japanese and Koreans had a thorough review[32] of all the elements of likely disorder and their stewarding reflecting a higher ratio to each thousand spectators than was the case in any of the previously European Cup or international games.

We learned that the banning orders preventing travel for a large unruly number contributed most significantly. Several people did try to evade the ban, but the airline authorities were on to them. As a result of the British initiative other countries also attempted to freeze travel for those with known records of violence.[33]

We learned that the ultimate threat by the Japanese police to impose prison sentences should there be violence and disorder, got through to those on the fringe of the gangs and the 'troops' themselves. An effective PR job was done during the previous 15 months. Police in many forms of combat training against likely rioters were shown on TV and in the press. On radio, myself and others punched the message home that the Japanese are ready to shove rioters in 'jail and throw the key away.' It helped.[34]

More specifically, there was a high hit list of banned British fans. The banning order applied to those fans who had convictions for football-related offences, or who were strongly suspected by the police to be troublemakers. They were ordered to report to a police station and surrender their passports at least five days before the World Cup, which began on May 31st 2002. This practice will be taken up in other planned sporting events.

In addition, the police supplied their Japanese counterparts with the names of up to 200 suspected troublemakers who were barred from entering Japan. Senior Japanese officers who were shown British surveillance videos of football disturbances were so shocked that they issued a warning that they might resort to ordering their men to open fire on English hooligans.

However Japanese officers were issued with a new 'Spiderman' gun designed to trap hooligans. The device shoots a reinforced nylon net five yards and is capable of trapping two or three people at a time.

"It's a bit like casting a fishing net," the police said. *"Anyone caught will not be able to get out."*[35]

This tough approach helped the 9,000 British supporters who were genuine in wanting to enjoy the games without hassle.

In the case of the World Cup in France, Madam Spinosi, Security Director of the World Cup, had a small army of helpers including a pool of some 18,000 security stewards, one third of whom would be professional security staff and the rest volunteers.[36]

More than 5,000 CRS riot police, with truncheons, helmets and body-armour were also available. But Madam Spinosi acted too late and was overwhelmed.[37]

In relation to Euro 2000, Rob Hughes in the Sunday Times forecast the hassle that was to occur. He wrote (28 May, 2000), *"From the wringing of hands, the noises passing like a buck between the FA and Lancaster Gate and the members of all political parties in Westminster, we know that Euro 2000 is all but two weeks away".* The FA issued a statement...calling for emergency legislation *"to stop known hooligans heading for Euro 2000".*

The warning came too late. The Home Office responded predictably by telling the FA that parliament was in recess. "It would therefore be impossible to introduce new legislation". Moreover a Labour spokesman blamed Tory backbench MPs for wrecking a statute 12 months previously intended to impound passports of suspected hooligans.[38] All very interesting but totally irrelevant.

There was also much political quibbling about the civil liberties argument of not interfering with the rights of "Englishmen to travel," meanwhile the yobs travelled.

The Germans effectively earmarked 8000 potential criminals and prevented 2,700 of them travelling in the Low Countries.[39]

Nevertheless, with all this experience, 2002 World Cup was free from the hazards of the previous tournament. Banning orders, the cost of travelling to the Far East, and the desire amongst decent supporters to restore England's reputation, all combined to make the Word Cup a largely trouble-free event.

"Before we came into this world Cup", said Keith Cooper, FIFA's director of communications, *"everyone was all doom and gloom and talking about the possibility of rioting and hooliganism. The Japanese and Koreans were terrified. English supporters have looked at the Danes and the Swedes and seen that they can have a jolly good time, enjoy their games and not get into any trouble. England fans have decided to do the same, Hats off to them because they have been fantastic."*[40] (Daily Telegraph, June 22, 2002)

One curious episode of violence related to the World Cup, occurred not where the games were held, but thousands of miles away in Russia. Hundreds of football thugs, enraged at Russia's defeat by Japan, turned the centre of Moscow into a battlefield, looting shops, setting fire to cars and attacking passers-by. One man was stabbed to death in his car and more than 30 injured. The trouble began with fans throwing bottles at each other and then it turned into a major riot damaging many city landmarks. Hooligans broke away from viewers watching the game on a big screen even before the final whistle and laid a trail of destruction past the Parliament building and the Bolshoi Theatre towards the Lubyanka, headquarters of the Security Service.

The mob smashed the windows of the Duma, the Hall of Columns where the bodies of Soviet leaders used to lie in state before burial, wrecked luxury boutiques, overturned cars and ransacked kiosks.[41] This was no minor demonstration. Who was to blame?

Maybe it arose, in part, out of anger at the political malaise and economic hardship in Moscow. According to Giles Whittell and Alice Lagnado, correspondents in Moscow for The Times, the most chilling[42] fact to emerge was that the violence was inspired by British hooliganism. They reported: *"Violence or the threat of it is virtually routine at Russian football matches, especially in games involving Moscow's three richest clubs – Spartak, CSKA and Dynamo. Inside the stadium it takes the form of seats ripped off their mountings and fireworks aimed at the pitch. Outside, the spill over affect consists of ugly drunken brawling and uglier ties to racist and ultra nationalist hit squads fond of taking out their bitterness on market traders from Caucasus".*[43]

Most of the 60 who were arrested and many of the thousands who were not, belong to an unofficial fan club with British names, British slogans,

British looking paraphernalia and something close to reverence for that unlikely role model, the British yob.[44] The Moscow 'gangs' attend matches where the George Cross is sold, and consider Chelsea and Millwall to be their models.

The Russian thugs had watched the bullies in the World Cup of previous years and, in particular, the confrontation on the streets of Marseilles. Many millions saw the damage done by British gangs, so that following the Russian defeat by Japan they set out on a path of destruction.

In the same article of 11 June 2002, The Times reported a quote from one of the leaders of the hooligans. *"I watched it all on Sky. Now Russian hooligans know more about British hooligans then even the British hooligans themselves."*[45]

Nonetheless, World Cup 2002 was not all character assassinations and violence. The Japanese hosts seemed to abandon their reserve: Thousands of noisy Japanese football fans sang and danced in the narrow streets of Osaka in celebration of their team's first win in a World Cup finals match. In extraordinary scenes in a country known for its reserved culture, young men and women waved flags and relentlessly chanted "Nippon, Nippon" after the 1-0 win over Russia. Huge crowds gathered on the Dotonburi Bridge as scores of men leapt 30 feet into the river below, not in despair but joy!

The security budget of £13.5 million with a stern promise of 'zero tolerance' to hooligans was justified. It is likely that the hosts in 2006 will be tempted to cut back, but it would be a foolish, over-optimistic gesture.[46]

The floating prison was also a harsh reminder of the lengths the Japanese were prepared to go to. The Ministry of Justice acquired the ship, a transporter ferry, able to hold 630 people. The Minister said, *"It is very expensive but we think we will need it at least two or three times. English hooligans will be locked into cabins onboard, some may even be put in the hold, and taken to a detention centre in Ushiku, near Tokyo."* The Minister added, *"Once arrested, fans will be processed then deported"*.[47] In Japan, hooligans can be held for 27 days without charge.

Regarding the 2004 European Cup in Portugal, a sanguine attitude prevailed amongst the police and security forces until a year prior to the games. Once the government realised that their own prestige was at stake, work on roads and security fencing was speeded up. These measures owed much to the chief operating officer, Martin Kallen, acting in cooperation with other European police networks.

These lessons – and the need for action two to three years in advance have not been learned for the upcoming 2006 World Cup which suggests that, once again, the approach to tacking Hooliganism is merely to react to events. There are several areas to consider for the 2006 Games and beyond.

The first concerns communication, where it states that football disorder overseas cannot be divorced from its wider social context. Governments and club management used this as an excuse for passing responsibility. Football authorities should constantly review their links with supporter groups, to show that they recognise fans as stakeholders as well as customers. (This is something that is hardly ever acted upon.)

Secondly on the overseas conduct of English fans, Government, police, football authorities and supporters need to act in unison to tackle football disorder. (This is improving all the time but has still a long way to go.)

Thirdly, we should encourage police to adopt an intelligence-led, high profile, low friction strategy along the lines of the Dutch *"friendly but firm hospitality-oriented approach"*. Further research into impact and other public safety tactics on supporter behaviour is advised, as well as ensuring that stewards should be provided to travel with their supporters.

Finally, we require a pool of accredited club stewards capable of developing a rapport with English supporters. Supplementing their number with bi-lingual locally recruited stewards familiar with the host country's culture and legal system and equipped to liase with the local police would also be beneficial. Ground stewards should be given training on issues of cultural awareness and tackling racism. Clubs are acting slowly but at least they have started. While the Dutch 'friendly' approach to supporters is an option which has been tested with success, the hard-line Japanese approach offers more flexibility.

There are of course, some odd twists concerning football supporters – not all bad! For ten years one football supporter in Belgrade, Alexander Bozic, was a wild card, organising his supporting fans against other teams. He was the regular target of the Belgrade police. But it was he who was the inspiration and the key figure in the overthrow of the political system.[48] Bozic, the Red Star Belgrade football club supporter leader led the attack on the federal parliament. The supporters long been at the forefront of the Anti-Milosevic opposition and had clashed regularly with police forces. In May 2000, they beat the Special Forces into retreat during a battle in the centre of town, chanting the opposition hymn: *"Slobo serve Serbia and kill yourself."* (Deeply embarrassed the Milosevic regime prohibited the singing of the hymn at football matches.)

"We had no fear of the attacks on us. At some point you forget all fear." Mr Bozic said in an interview at the time. He marshalled the crowd and they advanced a second time when the unexpected happened. The police

stopped the beating and withdrew. *"I grabbed the shield of the policeman right in front of me and for a few seconds we were tearing it back and forth,"* Mr Bozic said. *"I looked him in the eye and suddenly he let go."* In a second everything had changed and the Serbian revolution was truly underway. A football 'hooligan' was in the front line and leading!

How do we get the right response to some of the questions raised in this chapter. We might start by urging support for two of the organisations set-up, quite informally, but dealing with an aspect of soccer violence, namely racism.

"Football Unites, Racism Divides", is a small agency based in Sheffield, which provides an administrative service working with the community and central to that is the use of football as a gateway with young people, enabling the youth worker or teacher to talk with them about racism, first in football and other sports, before moving on to the wider ramifications of racism in society itself. Thanks to a lottery grant from the Community Fund, the FURD Education youth worker started operations in January 2000 with a growing number of schools, colleges and youth groups together with other organisations and agencies working with young people, such as SHED drugs project, Roundabout Young Homeless project and Cherry Tree Residential Home.

The FURD Resources and Information Centre has proved invaluable in providing ideas and materials for use in anti-racist education for young people. Along with discussions with teachers or youth workers, the resources available enable the youth worker to devise individually tailored programmes of work. FURD has worked with the Institution of Citizenship to help develop curriculum materials to be used in citizenship studies.

In breaking down the barriers in soccer between black and white fans, there are a number of examples as to what *Football Unites* has achieved. Desbon Bushiri's story is not untypical:

"I arrived at my Shoreham Street flat, behind Sheffield United's Kop. I didn't know anybody in Sheffield. After a few days I started to look for somewhere to play football.

Eventually I found Mount Pleasant Park in Sharrow, where Luis Silva and Keith Ward (MV) were running the FURD Summer coaching scheme. Luis saw me playing with a ball, and liked what he saw.

Soon I met Kamran (MV) and Alan from FURD, who were starting a new Sunday league team, 'Sharrow United'. They signed me up for the team, as a Millennium Volunteer, and I scored two goals in our first game, which we won 3-1.

Next Luis recommended me to Sheffield United and I trained with the juniors, and played three times for the reserves, scoring on my debut against Bury.

After four months United decided they would not offer me a contract. I was very disappointed, but soon I met Tommy Spencer, who signed me to play for Matlock Town in the Unibond First Division.

I've met lots of different people at FURD, whereas in my own country, Burundi, I was often afraid of people I didn't know. FURD has given me a lot of help, and its nice to come to The Stables to meet everyone, and read books from the library.

I still hope to become a professional footballer."[49] (Fund Annual Report, Sheffield 2001 and other examples 2003.)

Another organisation which deals with racism directly is *Show Racism the Red Card*. Education is a key to the success of this operation as well. Within recent years, its main task was to promote videos, and magazines as widely as possible. In the course of one season for instance, they were able to organise 24 events throughout Europe to promote the dangers of racism in football. A total of 64 professional footballers, many managers and celebrities have attended these events supported by over 24,000 guests.

The work of this particular organisation extends from political lobbying to meetings with European associations. The lobbying includes meetings with government departments, including the Department of Education.

All in all there are genuine and determined efforts to respond to racism and violence. The organisations have small budgets but it does not prevent carefully prepared planning of events backed up by an educational service. However, there is still a long way to go if the organisations are to get the 100% backing of all players and managers.

In addition to the work of organisations aimed at eradicating racism from sport, individual clubs have given publicity to Holocaust Day. A typical example is Everton FC who devoted two pages of their Saturday programme (26 Jan, 2002) with a message from the local MP, Louise Ellman, on ways in which supporters could help to involve themselves in the community.

Government initiatives may also be seen through the European Monitoring Centre on Racism and Xenophobia in Vienna, where a number of research and action programmes, including sport and racism, are in operation. The central theme of their programming is to identify positive responses to violence and abuse in Europe and to then ensure they are made known to all, in sport, players, supporters and the media.

What may be further achieved to overcome violence and hooliganism in football? There is one healthy reaction affecting crowd behaviour:

"Kick It Out" is a national campaigning organisation whose role it is to eliminate racial abuse, harassment and violence within football and to make access to the sport fair and inclusive. The campaign is supported by all of the stakeholders in the game, including the governing bodies, statutory organisations, such as local authorities and supporters' groups.

To their credit, "Kick It Out" has defined the parameters for all the parties concerned, including supporters on the terraces. *"There is a clear distinction to be made between football hooliganism and racism in the game. Whilst both problems are rooted deep in local cultures and the political history of Britain, differing factors bring about these very distinct problems. Hooliganism is essentially a problem of violence, often pre-organised between groups of fans. Racism has found expression in the national sport as a result of the attitudes and views of supporters and the attitudes and practices of those involved in running the game".* (Kick it Out Annual Reports, 2003/4.) Violence in the sporting arena and in the public domain are one and the same, requiring care and control. Often the common language for a small, but worrying number of English supporters abroad is associated with racism. Kick It Out admits that the rise in hooliganism is likely to take place by fans around the stadium, rather than on the terraces itself.

By encouraging directly with the clubs on various activities, Kick It Out has made real progress in helping the majority of spectators to react when they see or hear examples of racism on the ground.

There is, however, always the risk of publicising concerns of crowds control at events or major events, because such publicity may act as a challenge to the would-be wrecker. But the amount of pre-publicity for the 2002 World Cup highlighted what the Japanese and the South Koreans would do to hooligans and such threats proved effective in preventing disturbance. (One report warned that *"you'd be locked up and the key will be thrown away!"*). Similarly, the Japanese authorities used their imagination in dealing with likely wreckers before their own game against Tunisia in Osaka, by protective policing methods which included wrapping traffic-light poles in barbed wire to prevent fans climbing them. The Portuguese European Cup (2004) benefited from this experience as will the 2006 World Cup.

Greater use should be made of CCTV on football grounds. At club level, Millwall did not hesitate to make available the footage of their cameras, with the result that the police charged a stockbroker following a riot between their supporters and those of the Birmingham fans.

The trouble was branded *"the most serious street violence ever seen in London"* by the Met's Deputy Commissioner, Ian Blair. Film footage showed bricks and pavement slabs being hurled at police ranks (May, 2002). Millwall are actively involved in confronting the soccer hooligan, yet they had setbacks with their supporters in 2004.

Banning orders have played their part in getting rid of disruptive English fans. This was used with great effect prior to the 2002 World Cup in Japan and South Korea, and Portugal 2004.

Several weeks prior to the games, John Denham, the Home Office Minister who visited Japan in advance said, *"There is no doubt that the spectre of English hooliganism has become quite large in the Japanese media."* He then acted with the banning orders, which were issued against 932 fans who had convictions for football-related offences, or who were strongly suspected by the police to be troublemakers. They were ordered to report to a police station and surrender their passports. Banning orders was issued under the Football (Disorder) Act, 2000. British police then supplied their Japanese counterparts with the names of up to 200 suspected troublemakers. Senior Japanese officers were also shown British police surveillance videos of football disturbances. They were so shocked that Japanese officers were issued with the new 'Spiderman' gun designed to trap hooligans by reinforced netting.

The law has had a lot to say and do against organised hooliganism. Stiffer sentences for offenders have, in the mind of several supporters' organisations, made a difference; for instance, a football hooligan aged 56 was jailed for five years for kicking a police horse and urging fellow Millwall fans to run riot. Raymond Everest, a former match steward at the first division club, was seen on closed-circuit television to be laughing after launching a karate-style kick on the horse during violence outside the club's New Den ground. Everest was convicted of rioting at Woolwich Crown Court and Judge Philip Statman told him, *"You are the oldest of all those arrested. You had shown no remorse from the start to the finish. You have brought shame on the club you purport to support".*

In June 2004, Matthew Carroll, a Judge's son was amongst 400 thugs who threw bricks, bottles and glasses at police and caused more than £250,000 of damage after England went out of the Euro 2004 competition. The court saw CCTV footage of Carroll – who had consumed 14 cans and bottles of lager as well as 4 shots of tequila – hurling bins at police and shop windows. In court, Carroll appeared alongside five others, all of whom pleaded guilty to violent disorder. They were all banned from football grounds for five years and banned from watching England games in pubs. In these and other recent cases, those convicted have been largely "middle class".

The future of football remains in jeopardy. The Football League has already warned that professional football is now so dependent on finance from television, that one in three clubs could go bankrupt. If this sounds unduly pessimistic, the general warning is appropriate. Clubs tottering on the brink now include not only the lower-league cases, but also big names in the Premier division. Whatever the circumstances for the clubs, they cannot afford to neglect the cost and scale of security.

It would be foolish to return to the days when the clubs made 'savings' on reducing police numbers. At a fixture between West Bromwich Albion and Bristol City in 1998/99, a serious outbreak of disorder did occur inside the stadium where no public police were on duty. The violence involved hundreds of supporters and lasted for 15 minutes before a semblance of order was restored. The police were summoned to deal with the incident.

The police have also argued for more cash to be available for security and to fight hooliganism. Bryan Drew, head of specialist intelligence at the National Criminal Intelligence Service, said, *"With the spread of pay-per-view TV and the television dictating when certain matches are played, there is a lot of money in football which police forces could make use of. We would like to see some of the huge sums being generated by football being earmarked for policing – not just in the grounds but also away from the stadiums where the problems continue to fester. There is a nasty, ugly and anti-social element in society that clings parasitically to football and just won't give up".* He added that in dealing with the problem, police were *"continually being stretched beyond their capabilities".*

As the grounds are structured to keep different sets of supporters apart, there is also the additional potential for violence that, when buying a ticket from touts, no such security applies, so that there could be serious trouble for the purchaser of an illegal ticket. Touting rings have, in the past, made tens of thousands of pounds from the sale of tickets to London Premiership football matches, but Scotland Yard has now succeeded in closing a loophole in ticket sales. Police fear that hooligans – already banned from the grounds – will use illegal agents to buy tickets in order to cause trouble inside stadiums. (The Evening Standard, 15 Jan 2002.) An undercover surveillance operation carried out by the Metropolitan Police Football Intelligence Unit, in liaison with National Criminal Intelligence Service officers, uncovered the illicit trade.

There is a limit to what the police can do. For instance, when there was a near-riot on a plane full of Celtic supporters returning from a game in Spain, no police support was present. Two flight attendants were assaulted. Eventually, the plane was diverted to Cardiff and the RAF provided a helicopter support on landing.

In the study of aggression and violence on the football ground, one cannot ignore the other element in the mixture, the players themselves. Do they incite the crowd? Can their behaviour influence the yobbos? Whether intentionally or not, the sight of players attacking one another can raise the blood of the crowd. This often follows a 'sending-off' or a referee losing game control. Such incidents highlight the affect on the crowd of bad behaviour on the field. This is illustrated in the following episodes:

a) **Jamie Carragher** (Liverpool, January 2002) threw a coin into the crowds. During the match at Highbury, Carragher was the subject of what the FA believed was a bad tackle by Dennis Bergkamp. As he was recovering from the challenge, he was struck by a coin thrown from the crowd, while other coins thrown by home supporters landed close to him. Carragher's reaction was deemed to have been prompted by physical as well as verbal provocation. Unlike the former Manchester United forward, Eric Cantana, who was involved in a similar incident and had a poor disciplinary report, Carragher immediately apologised for his actions - and was saved from a lengthy ban. Still Carragher's reaction was unwarranted; he was fined £40,000 by his club.

b) **Roy Keane** (Manchester United, August 2002). A dreadful, premeditated foul on Alf Inge Haaland provoked an enormous public reaction, visible for all to see because it was screened on Sky TV. Keane also draws attention to the incident in his own autobiography. (Keane, Penguin 2003). David Mellor, former Sports Minister and now an Evening Standard football columnist angrily writes: *"Here is a man being paid £60,000 a week and he still feels that he can behave like a pub brawler outside the Dog and Duck on a Friday night. He has got away with it twice: first when it happened and now by making money out of it through his book and its serialisation."* Keane has admitted that he allows vendettas to influence his game. One such vendetta with Alf Inge Haaland, now of Manchester City, had a three-year history, with Keane gloating over an injury to his adversary that ruled Haaland out of football for almost a year.

c) **Dennis Wise**. During a pre-side friendly with Leicester City, Wise broke the jaw of his team-mate, Callum Davidson. This was grounds for Leicester to terminate Wise's contract. Following his appeal, however, the weakness of the Football League revealed itself in an extraordinary judgement. *"After a six-hour hearing, the commission concluded that Wise did assault team-mate Callum Davidson. However, it was felt by the commission that this offence did not warrant the termination of Wise's playing contract"*. Leicester Chairman Martin Gough, expressed astonishment that, *"Football League regulations do*

*not permit the dismissal of a player who has committed a serious and
unprovoked assault on a fellow professional".* (The Daily Telegraph,
25 Aug 2002.)

Fortunately, such shameful incidents are offset by the behaviour of the
majority of players, who are likely to contribute generously to the local
community, activating good works and training in schools. Kevin Keegan
made a remarkable gesture in the late 1990's by assisting a school not in
his club area, but St. George's in Maida Vale. The school's reputation was
troubled. It was here that headmaster, Philip Lawrence, was murdered.
Indeed, the school had been closed following a breakdown in discipline.
Kevin Keegan's visit (along with one or two pop stars) helped enormously
in getting the "*business going again*" said the head. St George's reputation
as a good local school was restored.

These issues of player and club activities suggest more research needs
to be conducted into all the circumstances. However, research directed at
the football supporter needs to be simplified. It was clear from the derisive
comments of the fans in a recent research project that there would be no
"takers", and, sure enough, no questionnaires were returned. Hopefully
the good work of the Sir Norman Chester Centre, which prepared the
questionnaires, will continue to pursue their research, as much more needs
to be understood about all aspects of the game.

Additional information is also needed about sports generally. Crowd
violence may be described as a complex social phenomenon related to
three factors:

- The action in the sport event itself;

- The crowd dynamics and the situation in which the spectators
  watch the event;

- The historical, social, economic, and political contexts in which
  the event is planned and played.

Some interesting references have already been mentioned. For
instance, if spectators perceive players' action on the field as violent, they
are more likely to engage in violent acts during and after the games. This
point is important, because spectators' perceptions often are influenced
by the way in which events are promoted. If an event is hyped in terms
of a likely violent clash, spectators are more likely to engage in violent or
challenging acts with their rival fans. Does this make the promoters of the
event responsible? Yes to some extent, but the behaviour of the players and
supporters is key.

Spectator violence is likely to vary with one or more of the following factors:

- Crowd size and the standing or seating patterns among spectators;

- Composition or the crowd in terms of age, sex, social class, and racial/ethnic mix;

- Meaning and importance of the event for spectators;

- History of the relationship between the teams and between spectators;

- Crowd-control strategies used at the event (police, attack dogs, or other security measures);

- Alcohol consumption by the spectators.

An awareness of the historical, social, economic, and political issues that often underlie crowd violence is important. Restrictive law-and-order response to crowd violence may be temporarily effective, but they will not eliminate the underlying tensions and conflicts that often fuel violence (Sport and Society - Coakley, J.J, McGraw Hill, 2001). The wider issues of government policy also play their part, so that during a period of economic downturn with oppressive forms of inequality, and unemployment, such factors are often at the root of oppression.

Also needed are greater efforts to establish connections between the teams and the communities in which they are located. These connections can be used to defuse potentially dangerous feelings among groups of spectators, who may plan for a confrontation with their rivals. It does not mean that teams merely need better public relations. There must be actual connections between the teams and the facilities and the communities in which they exist. Players and coaches also need to be engaged in community service.

The goal of these guidelines must be to create generally accepted norms of non-violent behaviour and conflict resolution. The need for such guidelines has been made amply clear, not only in soccer, but in all sports.

In Literature and the Gods, Robert Calasso writes about the current yearning for community. (Vintage, 2001.) In an age of mechanisation and multiplicity of choice, they are looking for a sense of group identity, something that will enable them - to literally - hold hands with their own kind and sing along, submerging the identity of the individual in a shared enchanted group experience. To achieve that, they need a shared belief or cause. There has to be something to sing about. A cause also implies that there are those without a cause, or with a different cause, so one can sing against them. Hence the sports fan!

CHAPTER 4
THE WIDER WORLD OF SPORT

Mention of violence and sport often implies football, but other sports also reveal unruly crowd behaviour.

In Britain it is cricket and rugby. There have been serious attempts by cricket and rugby authorities to examine what triggers violence and to measure its impact on the games. One usually regards American spectators as less vocal and less likely to be involved in hooliganism, but the goings-on in the American football (akin to rugby) suggested otherwise. The Philadelphia Enquirer (19 Sept, 2002) quoted the Director of Security of the Eagles team on a serious brawl: *"Between the fights and the people trying to get out of the stadium and our guys puking, man, it looked like Dante's Inferno".*

The incident began with a players' brawl, which quickly spread to involve a large number of spectators. Bill Lyon of the Enquirer reports: *"In the closing minutes of the Eagles' 37-7 blow-out of the Redskins, fights began to break out at several sites inside the stadium, including skirmishes behind the Birds' bench. This, by the way, is hardly a unique experience at any stadium on any given Sunday in the NFL, with its hypocritical homage to violence."* In this case, events became increasingly dangerous. In an effort to quell one of the fights, a policeman used a pepper spray. The chemical wafted to the blowers being used to cool players on the visitors' bench., showering them with spray:

"The effect would have been fine...on a felon. Not so fine on a football player. Several of the Eagles began to choke, tear up and vomit. Their distress was shown on national TV. The scene was surreal. Play stopped on the field. Players, some shielding their eyes with towels, some still vomiting, wandered around, dazed. Confusion was everywhere. The referee, Bob

*McElwee, announced that "a foreign substance" had been found. It was
"too dangerous to continue play", he said".*

A. RUGBY

Rugby is not devoid of crowd violence, but on much lesser scale than
football. Widness Vikings (Aug, 2002) began a crackdown on violent
and threatening behaviour among supporters by issuing banning orders
preventing five fans from attending matches at Halton Stadium, and
passing on their details to other Tetley's Super League clubs.

A sports rage survey was commissioned in the summer of 2002 by
FHM Bionic magazine and 78 percent of those surveyed said they had been
involved in a heated argument on the pitch. 51 percent admitted being in
a physical fight during a game. Aggressive behaviour is not confined to
contact sports. The study found 35 per cent had been involved in a row
during a tennis match.

Also in rugby, racism seems to be the trigger for much violence, with
the result that a report on the nature and extent of racism in the Rugby
League and its violent consequence was considered a priority. Discussions
took place between the Rugby Football League (RFL) Leeds City Council
and the Commission for Racial Equality (CRE). Generally the situation in
rugby league is not as bad as in football, but racist abuse and occasional
incidents of banana throwing and monkey chants have all been recorded
at rugby league matches. Concern about racism at matches has also been
expressed in the letters pages of the rugby league press. Players have
spoken on television about their own experiences of racism.

In consequence, Leeds Metropolitan University was asked to survey
attitudes in a wide-ranging project, with the investigation having three
main components:

- the attitudes of the clubs

- the attitudes of (black and white) players

- the attitudes of spectators

The response from the supporters' survey was very good with a total of
2,364 questionnaires used in the analysis (67% response rate). The survey
of officials also received a high response rate for a postal survey (60%).

A large majority of all respondents knew that some clubs had been
taking part in campaigns to stop abusive chanting. Their awareness
came largely through PA announcements, programme notes, papers and
magazines. Most fans also thought that such action was a good idea.

While the referee was the most prominent target for abusive chanting, almost half the respondents reported hearing chanting against black players and 5 percent said that they were the most frequent targets. We are told that the majority of people do nothing if they hear racial chanting, but as many as 22 percent said that they complained either to stewards/police or directly to those chanting.

Like the fans the vast majority of officials reported hearing chanting against the referee, and a third said they had heard chanting against black players at their own club. Two thirds said that their own club had been involved in a campaign to combat abusive chanting and a similar proportion thought the campaigns had made things better. Half of the respondents agreed with the statement: *"if we have ethnic minority players in the side they get picked on at some clubs"*.

Two thirds of club officials reported that people from ethnic minorities were welcome at the club if they wanted to come, while less than a quarter said their club actively encouraged them. Yet for all these positive responses the interviews with Asian and black players showed a different picture.

The interviews revealed that all had suffered racial abuse of one kind or another, largely from spectators, which varied in intensity from club to club. Interviews with white players confirmed that racial abuse in the form of shouts at players from the crowd are seen as commonplace. They conceded that black players were more prone to abuse than other players simply because of the colour of their skin.

Again, there are two sets of impressions. Racial abuse from certain players was also said to occur on the pitch. While the black players said they had suffered racial abuse as a 'winding up' tactic, not all the white players said it happened. Black players also suggested they had to work harder than white players as they had to combat racial abuse and racial stereotyping. These stereotypes about the ability of black players were used by white players and to a lesser extent by black players.

The players felt action against those who shout racial abuse should be stricter, and that any development and encouragement of the game among ethnic minorities would be for the good of the game.

Still, overall the research team concluded that there is a small but significant problem in Rugby League accompanied by a lack of awareness on racial issues on the part of some. The loyalty of Rugby League fans and their pride in the game could be used to good effect in any action to combat racism in the game.

The threat of violence occurs not only because of racism but also because of supporters' anger with a referee's decisions. The events of 10 August 2002 caused a demand for tighter security. One minute into the second half a spectator evaded 400 security officials to launch himself at Mr McHugh, the referee, as a scrum was being set. Mr McHugh was hurled to the ground before several players intervened. The spectator, a Mr Van Zyl, said afterwards that he *"took matters into his own hands because the referee was biased!"* Unfortunately, the average Afrikaner rugby fan supported him, including several players who offered support without fees in a legal action.

Similar incidents are also intrusive. The following have been noted: In August 2002, two people streaked on the pitch on Sunday as a player was about to take a penalty (he missed). In May 2002, a teenager attacked George Gregan, the Australian captain during a Super 12 match. The Australian coach at the time urged litigation to stop these intrusions. Action is certainly needed but it is unlikely that the law would help. Nevertheless, Rugby Union has been lax and a policy in ground security is a priority.

Brawls by players outside the game are not always given prominence, but the jailing of two Leeds Rhinos players for what the judge called *"mindless, dangerous and drunken violence"* outside a Leeds club in 2002, made headlines. The Rugby Football League's response following the hearing that there was nothing they needed to do as the matter had been dealt with by the courts was a complete cop-out. In addition to breaking the law, which should have been addressed, there was a responsibility to their clubs and rugby football. The case was summed up by the Recorder who said to the players, *"Each of you has brought disgrace on the good name of Rugby League, on your clubs, but most of all on yourselves"*.

The sports authorities, whether in Rugby Football League or soccer, must show their determination to deal with hooliganism and violence on every level. The behaviour of the fans is only one part of the equation, another is the way players act on and off the field.

B. CRICKET.

The same level of security has not been felt necessary in cricket, but trouble does flare up in all the main centres. In the last couple of years, Melbourne was the scene of a hectic angry demonstration during a 3-nation tournament with New Zealand. Up to 10 people were arrested and more than 200 ejected after objects were thrown from the infamous Bay 13. Some missiles landed near New Zealand fielder Mark Richardson. What ignited the trouble was not immediately obvious, but the assumption was that drink was at the root of the loutish behaviour. This was the third time in recent years that Melbourne crowds had caused disturbances during one-day internationals.

Following this, there were a number of worrying physical incidents in the Nat. West Series. Fireworks were thrown at several grounds and in particular at Trent Bridge. It was a scary experience - fireworks, and firecrackers everywhere, whilst crowds were trying to get on to the pitch and the Australians walking off.

Shane Warne wrote in the Times (23 June, 2001) *"it is clear that in Australia the first time somebody comes on to the ground he is banned for 12 months and fined. A repeat offence gets a bigger fine and a five-year ban and if he does the same thing again the result is a life ban from any sporting venue in Australia".* Warne and others who play at international level say it doesn't matter whether the crowd who run on are malicious or not because when it involves about hundreds of people, with stewards trying to block them from the players and umpires, then anything can happen.

At the 2001 Nat. West final the MCC introduced a series of security measures some of which are now being routinely used: any spectators caught on closed-circuit television committing offences, during the final of the Nat. West Series at Lord's risks being prosecuted. Cameras and stewards were positioned on perimeter walls, to stop supporters illegally entering the ground for a match that was sold out. Spectators entering the ground are searched "robustly" at entrances for missiles and flags, which are confiscated (Times 23 June, 2001).

Pitch invasion is not a criminal offence in Britain as it is in Australia where individuals can be fined £2,000 and face bans from attending matches as Shane Warne has described.

Racism can also trigger violent behaviour as was seen earlier and has also been a matter for review and enquiry. The review by the ECB (England and Wales Cricket Board) produced an action plan to deal with racial equality in cricket. Their original report recognised that some positive work had been attempted.

Earlier, the ECB Inner City Community Cricket Project launched by the then Minister for Sport, Kate Hoey MP, illustrated the determination of all those associated with cricket, to ensure ethnic minorities have equality of opportunity.

The report, resulting from the commissioned Questionnaire Survey, served as a validation for much of the anecdotal knowledge and evidence on the matter of racism in cricket. The contribution of those consulted endorsed the view that racism existed. However, only 12% of the 1037 Questionnaire Survey respondents thought that racism was ingrained in English cricket. In response to the question, "Do you believe there is racism in English cricket?" 58 percent believed there was. White players, followed by spectators, were deemed to be the major perpetrators. Specifically there were several topics/issues which recurred in many of the interviews: ground/pitch/facility provision; exclusion from mainstream cricket; selection; lack of ethnic minority representation on committees at county/national level; poor levels of appreciation of culture and traditions between white and ethnic minorities; restriction of banners, flags, musical instruments at, and ticket sale policies for Test and One Day International Matches;

The cricket authorities were still somewhat cautious with the findings. They said, "We have established a fundamental principle that racism in cricket must be properly identified. Racism must be distinguished from other factors such as socio-economic inequalities". However, the 'Race-Card' is often used to cloud the issue and sometimes, as a result, perpetuates racism and/or hidden agendas that are counter-productive to ethnic minorities and cricket. The lack of ethnic minority representation on County/National committees must be rectified in relation to girls'/women's cricket and cricket for the disabled. The right of individuals to form clubs or groups to form leagues is recognised. However, a priority must be to encourage integration of ethnic minorities, both on an individual and club/team basis, within an inclusive structure.

As a result of the recommendations in their report being accepted, the ECB were encouraged to set up Action Plans, especially in those areas where there are significant ethnic minority populations. The working party reiterated the message that all involved in cricket must accept a responsibility to ensure every opportunity is afforded to all to pursue an involvement whether it is in playing, coaching, administration, etc. *"It is incumbent upon all clubs from the smallest to County clubs to state and operate an open membership policy and welcome players/members irrespective of ethnic origin".* At the same time, they asked all ECB affiliated clubs to implement a Code of Conduct for players, officials, members and supporters, prohibiting racially abusive comments and actions against fellow players, official, members and supporters.

The reports both in rugby and cricket and the action plans are an essential first step in outlawing racism.

There has been much interest in the specific issue of sports' anger. One FHM Bionic report (August 2001) referred to the fact that "men can't control their sports rage!" More than three-quarters of all men think *'society is more aggressive today than it was ten years ago'.* The report reveals aggression has spilled into sport. Of 3,000 men questioned nationwide for the Sports Rage Survey, commissioned by the FHM Bionic magazine, 78 per cent said they had been involved in a heated argument on the pitch. Fifty-one per cent admitted being involved in a fighting during the game.

Aggressive behaviour is not confined to contact sports. The study found 35 per cent of males had been involved in rows during a tennis match. The tantrums of US player Jeff Tarango have kept crowds more entertained than his tennis. In 1999, during a Kremlin Cup match in Moscow against Vincent Spadea, he broke his racket over his knee when he lost a point. Sixty-two per cent of the men questioned blamed the rise in male aggression on living in a more stressful society. Nine out of ten admitted to becoming more violent and competitive when they took part in any type of sport or visited a gym, with 93 per cent saying they wanted to win. Yet 86 per cent considered violence was unacceptable in sport.

There were marked differences in frustration and anger by the players between the sports. For example, on the subject of whether professional players made good role models, 87 per cent of golf respondents said yes, as did 85 per cent of tennis spectators and 70 per cent of cricket fans, but only 40 per cent of football enthusiasts.

Golf is a sport with a strong ethical foundation. For example, 90 per cent of golf fans thought their players showed respect for the officials, whereas only 24 per cent of football spectators thought the same of their sport.

When the Ryder cup was a success for the United States, there were acrimonious reactions when the United States players celebrated victory before the end of play, but examples of bad behaviour are few. It was slow play and anti-social behaviour that were rated as the most offensive characteristics – such as the time when Tiger Woods arrived for his Open practice session early in the morning and had left the course by 8am when spectators arrived to see him. This is clearly not in the same category as boxing, for instance, with Mike Tyson's ear biting and general hoodlum behaviour – both in the ring and outside.

There were several interesting dilemmas highlighted by the survey. For example, in tennis, standards of behaviour were judged to have improved over the years, largely because of John McEnroe's retirement, according to the anecdotal evidence - yet McEnroe topped a poll as the most popular tennis player.

The Sports' Rage Survey also reported on likely causes of crowd reaction when there is slow play, such as the match at Wimbledon between Jennifer Capriati and Serena Williams. The feigned injuries and toilet breaks were thought not to be in the spirit of the game. The players themselves might well argue that they were using psychological tactics.

In rugby, cricket, tennis and football, 84 per cent of spectators disagreed with the statement that it was "ok for professional sports persons to bend the rules". In short, most spectators want more from sports people than a win-at-all-costs outlook.

93 per cent of football spectators said players should throw the ball back to the opposition after it had been deliberately kicked into touch, to allow medical treatment for an injured player. Nearly two-thirds of tennis spectators thought that players should alert the umpire if they had benefit from a bad line call. And 82 per cent of cricket fans thought that batsmen should "walk" if they knew they had got an edge.

A majority of cricket spectators (54 per cent) thought that video/third umpires should be used to settle leg-before decisions and 63 per cent of football spectators thought that TVC replays should be used to help referees to make decisions about penalty kicks.

However revealing this particular survey, a further qualitative survey will be necessary before serious conclusions may be ready. Nevertheless, it is because of the unpredictable nature of violence in some sports and not in others that we cannot identify easily the hooligans in each of the sports.

Newspapers throughout the world devote considerable coverage to sport, especially football. Space devoted to sports often exceeds that given to political and economic issues. As Jay Coackley says *"Sport images are so pervasive today that many young people are more familiar with the tattoos and body piercing of their favourite sport celebrities that they are with the local politicians who make policies that have a significant impact on their lives."* (Sport in Society, McGraw Hill, 2002). At the same time, there are legal fights over who owns the right to profit from selling sport images, especially images that represent the identity or persona of a particular athlete. The media coverage and marketing of celebrity-athletes is another way that sports enter our lives. Clearly, the attention given to certain athletes has turned them into celebrities at least, if not cultural icons and heroes.

All bullies and thugs benefit from weak supervision of the football authorities, and the police, to say nothing of Roy Keane's behaviour or that of his manager, Sir Alex Ferguson, whose comment during the uproar in August 2002, as mentioned earlier, was: *"[Keane] has no case to answer to".*

The law has slipped in this area of football fracas. Contrast the Keane case with the way a Scottish international Duncan Ferguson was treated in 1995. He was playing for Rangers and was jailed for three months after he head-butted James McStay of Raith Rovers in a Scottish premier league match. The verdict owed much to the fact that the incident had been filmed – but so was the Keane attack on AIF Inge Haaland. Ferguson paid a heavy price, Keane got off virtually free.

In 1997, Simon Devereux of Gloucester was jailed for 9 months for breaking the jaw of Jamie Cowie, the captain of the Rosslyn Park side.

Lord Scarman in a foreword to The Violent Society, said, *"the reader should be in no doubt when he reflects on what violence is, and always has been, a feature or a threat in human society – and will remain so"* (Moonman, E. Cass 1985).

The challenge, therefore, is not the elimination of violence, but its control and restraint. The lesson for a civilized society is that unless fear of attack, of deprivation, of frustration, is eliminated within a society the risk of violent outburst by those who see themselves as victims will be greatly enhanced. The problem is more than a maintaining 'law and order': it is also one of recognising the necessary constraints on the individual. Violence inevitably is a rejection of society's norms.

In sport, there are all manners of violence, some within the game but one should not confuse the competitiveness and determination to win to be an aggressive part of the violent characteristic. Nor is violence new to sports. A brutal element is to be found in history with blood sports in ancient Greece and throughout the Roman Empire. Tournaments during medieval time were clearly a preparation for war. Each country has its own form of violence in sport.

There is also a language of violence – often used to wind up the combatant and to intimidate the opponent. This is particular true of boxing where for instance Mike Tyson goes to extreme lengths to taunt and threaten his opponent that he will "die because of his power". The very staging of the boxing match encourages this, when the referee brings the two men together and they are within inches of each other so that before the boxing starts, the men try to do what they may be unable to do physically.

Commercial and marketing of boxing demands that hostility and drama will ensure "more bums on seats" if there has been much displayed anger and hassle at the weigh-in (though it did get out of hand prior to the contest between Lennox Lewis and Mike Tyson); and even in women's boxing the two contestants in a commercial bout between the respective daughters of Joe Frazier and Mohammed Ali angrily protested that the "other boxer would be destroyed". In American football, in baseball and soccer, the coach will use the language of success for his team and denigrate and intimidate his opponents in the team talk.

The videos of sport sell. On both sides of the Atlantic there are a considerable number of videos of violent actions in each of the sports. In Britain, the video on dirty play in football has been a consistent seller.

Sadly, the enjoyment is based on glorification of the violence – always carefully edited – so one could well imagine that the violence is total and consistent throughout the game.

Pain and injury is a price players pay. In *Violence in Sports (2001)* Howard Nixon (USA) and Ivan Waddington (Britain) suggest that over 80 per cent of the men and women in top-level intercollegiate sports in the United States sustain at least one serious injury while playing their sport, and nearly 70 percent are disabled for two or more weeks. Nearly all players, both men and women, say that they play while they are hurt, and many experience chronic pain. Nixon notes that the rate of disabling injuries in the NFL is over three times greater than the rate among workers in high-risk construction jobs. The rate of disabling injuries varies from sport to sport, but they are high enough in many sports to constitute a medical problem as well as a social issue.

Waddington's research shows that the health benefits of playing sports are highest when participation involves rhythmic movements under conditions that can be controlled by the athletes themselves. The health costs are highest when participation occurs in highly competitive contact sports played under conditions that are outside the athletes' control. In other words, the violence inherent in power and performance sports takes a definite toll on the health of athletes.

Where does this leave the question of ethics in sport? This may be answered in two ways. First, that the players are subject to the same temptations as any other group in society and they will indulge in violent acts without regard to any moral consideration. This is confirmed, rather depressingly by Jennifer Beller of the University of Idaho Centre for Ethics. *"The average adult athlete has the moral reasoning of a 13-year old, a level at which impulses often impede good judgement. Sports figures who go astray, often don't consider how their actions affect other people. For years, people said sports build character. Our research, on 35,000 athletes, shows it negatively impacts character".*

The second consideration, more positive was when the British cricketers made a moral stand against the Zimbabwean government's oppressive regime. It was a rare moral action, but as Simon Barnes said the day after in the Times (29 Jan, 2003). "They did so without stridency or threats or pouting. They simply pointed out that their match against Zimbabwe, in Harare, raised a number of difficult and uncomfortable issues, and questioned the wisdom of playing the fixture". This action shows that some sportsmen do care. They can't ignore outrageous treatment of the people if the host country and the idiot-sportsmen administrators who say, *"never mind the circumstances, play on".*

Before concluding our discussion on Sport Violence, it is necessary to emphasise that more qualitative research is needed.

A constant complaint by academics in staff rooms is that there are not sufficient grants for research in each and every field but it happens to be true when confronted with conflict and violence. However, Malcolm, Jones and Waddington, in The Future of Football (Cass, 2000) go further: they complain that a particular neglected area is general sports' research, although there is a lot of interest in sport hooliganism.

Malcolm, Jones and Waddington point out that only four per cent of sports' research had focused on fans, yet they take little account of the work done by the Centre for Contemporary Studies throughout the 1980s and 1990's, to name but one body, which covered many aspects in its reports of violence in football as well as running seminars tackling the issues with the football authorities and the police. (CCS, London, Soccer Violence, 1985 – 92).

Researchers and would-be researchers have to justify their grants and fellowships, but some of their comments offer a distorted picture of what already exists. Although there is a great deal of information available – good quality at that – the dilemma is getting the various authorities sufficiently minded to read, act and implement some of the findings.

The Government has seen the political importance to their image of appearing to go in hard on hooliganism. They also need to ensure that in competing for international tournaments, the country is not handicapped or disgraced by hooligans.

There are difficulties in gathering information. Again, Malcolm, et al, correctly point this out. Easily identifiable sample groups - season ticket holders, buyers of programmes or fanzines, members of fan groups, and so on – are, almost by definition, maybe unrepresentative of the crowd as a whole. Moreover, as a great many fans aim to enter the stadium as close to kick-off as they can (survey data indicated that around 50 per cent of spectators aim to arrive in the 30 minutes prior to kick-off, but that a considerably higher proportion actually do so), interviewing is highly impractical and likely to reflect a bias towards certain groups, namely those arriving earlier.

If we fail to understand, or ignore, the social and psychological influences amongst spectators, then, we are likely to make some unforgivable errors. Take the report, in 2000, of <u>David Mellor's Task Force.</u> He declares:

a) Britain's biggest football clubs are creating an apartheid-style system of support, with local people abandoning the game to be replaced by affluent whites from the suburbs.

b) The racism that permeates football at all levels has become so bad that young Asians and blacks are turning their back on the game.

c) The report warns that clubs that fail to tackle prejudice could find themselves in financial crisis within 10 years. .

These are all relevant and debatable issues yet absolutely no research to justify these three declarations.

The heart of any Saturday afternoon game in any of the divisions is the local fan. He will grumble, walk away at the end of the game and, if the results justify it, may be angry and maybe will shout 'never again,' but such is the competitive nature and the fun of the game that– like many of us – he or she will be back come the following home fixture.

It does seem an exaggeration to suggest that Asian fans are deserting the game, as they have never been there anyway except for very small numbers. The football environment can be narrow, and therefore there is not a formal way of being made "welcome" except to attend on a regular basis and meet up with some neighbours. One Asian supporter said to me *"we don't need special welcomes for everyone – just a team that does the business on the pitch."*

The third assertion of the Task Force is the most remarkable of all: what possible evidence could there be to warn clubs that if they fail to tackle prejudices (which, of course, they should) they could find themselves in a financial crisis within 10 years. As we have seen, quite starkly, over the past five years, the financial scars of the clubs do not lie in racism, but in over-spending and high wages of players.

As a series of opinions Mellor's working party was quite lively but in terms of reality and substance it offered little to help the game and any violent behaviour of supporters. Violence may come in all shapes and sizes. Yet the original description remains. To violate another person, possession or family is a profane act and to combat such violence much care and understanding is required to support those violated and to ensure that all the agencies - the local community, the police and the local authorities - fully understand their responsibilities and act accordingly.

CHAPTER 5
INTERNATIONAL VIOLENCE
AND TERRORISM

What is new about contemporary terrorism? It is still "organised violence," but there is a greater emphasis today on an organization and a constant search, by the terrorists, for new technology to dislodge and divert the authorities; it is still both indiscriminate and arbitrary. We have come a long way since the attacks by groups threatening the State in the 18th century to the suicide (more accurately, homicide) bombers of today. The definition of terrorism, adopted by the Jonathan Institute in 1979, still applies today. (Terrorism: How the West Can Win, ed. B Netanyahu, New York, Farrar, Straus Giroux, 1986 p9.) *"Terrorism is the deliberate and systematic murder, maiming and menacing of the innocent to inspire fear for political ends"*. This definition has never been surpassed for clarity and concision.

In this chapter we shall explore terrorism, its "fixture" in history and why it may be described as a "cheap war". For many, certainly in the United States, the defining moment in recognising terrorism were the events of September 11 2001, which illustrated the accuracy of the Jonathan Institute definition. September 11 struck into the heartland and the business sector of a super-state and revealed that there is another significant type of terrorism to have emerged in recent years - the homicide bomber.

In the second section of this chapter, we shall examine the proliferation of weapons and the financing and proliferation of terrorist groups themselves. In the context of the development of new technology, we shall also specifically look at ricin, a deadly poison which threatens the welfare of the general public. Finally, we shall examine the growth of new and sophisticated weapons, and the transfer of technology, such as that provided by Russia to Iran, to help enhance its nuclear capability.

Causes of terrorism may range from those associated with the Colombian rebels, to the IRA and Hamas, all of which provide significant opportunities for shared training and weaponry purchasing even though the philosophies of the respective groups may be of the extreme right or left.

The high level of terrorist activity means that the British intelligence services should be given a higher priority in receiving government financial support than hitherto. A great deal has been achieved in searching out quality information, whether from the United States or from the French and German authorities; but it has taken western powers a long time to realise that, in the battle to overcome terrorism, no one country can go it alone.

To know the enemy, their movements, lifestyle, and origins are all part of the search in order to understand how best to overcome terrorism from whatever quarter. Here the public responsibility and need for vigilance is critical.

For a considerable time, the hazards of terrorist actions were considered to be someone else's problem. Yet, international terrorism today can transfer easily from one country to another, utilising local cells and safe houses. The 12 October 2002 bombing in Bali made a statement. Local fanatics were not merely reacting to the tourists who came to party in their towns but, more importantly, they were making a statement - with the help of Al-Qaeda - against the whole of the Western ethos while headlining Muslim fundamentalism.

Many governments have ignored the insidious international nature of the terrorist: they have chosen to regard the actions of the IRA as a "British problem," the Basque bombings as a "Spanish problem", the "Hamas problem," as peculiar to Israel. With the transfer of terrorist personnel, equipment and intelligence from one part of the world to another, there has to be a global response by governments if terrorism is to be marginalised. As we have seen with soccer violence and hooliganism, intelligence services need to cooperate to defeat the common enemy.

There is confusion, both in terms of definition and ethical issues, over what constitutes terrorism, as every state defines terrorism in its own political, domestic and foreign circumstances.

For example, Syria and the United States disagreed, in November 2001 over the status of the Lebanese group Hizbullah, with Syria arguing that it should not qualify as a terrorist organization. Thus various countries develop their own legal definition of what they consider terrorism. Professor Yonah Alexander reminds us (Combating Terrorism) that Canada's description is based on its Security Offences Act (1984) and its Security Intelligence Service Act (1984), which do not explicitly define terrorism but apply to *"threats to the security of Canada."* Such threats include *"activities within or relating to Canada directed toward, or in support of, the threat or use of acts of serious violence against person or property for the purpose of achieving a political objective within Canada or a foreign state."*

In its Penal Code (chapters I and II of Title II), France, refers to terrorist-related acts as *"acts by an individual or group that uses intimidation or terror to disrupt public order".* Although this definition does not mention political motivation, an act would not be labelled an act of terrorism unless linked to some political motive or cause.

An analysis of various governmental as well as academic views indicates that there is no consensus of what exactly constitutes terrorism. Nevertheless, there seems to be an agreement related to several components, such as the nature of the act (unlawful), perpetrators (individuals, groups, or states), objectives (fear and frustration), targets (victims), and methods (hostage taking).

Conferences on these issues, have dealt, (perhaps excessively) with the roots of terrorism. Given the killing, maiming and damage terrorism can achieve, one should not be over-concerned about where and when it started, unless we can learn from the attitudes behind the early attacks.

In its modern form, terrorism appeared with all the violence displayed during the French Revolution, with the "Reign of Terror" unleashed by Robespierre, when the guillotine was extensively used on dissidents. In the late 19th century, radical nationalist groups like the Irish, Macedonians, Serbs and Armenians used terrorist methods in their struggle for autonomy or national independence. In the Soviet Union, there was a wave of terror after the Bolshevik Revolution in 1917.

Whatever the period, democratic governments have often delayed actions against terrorists and have hesitated using the full force of the law against criminal activities such as those of the Mafia in Italy. In part, this is due to the failure of governments to understand the pernicious nature of terrorism. Many governments see terrorism as a social or political disease that will disappear if a remedy is found. The recommended remedy varies according to the political position of the government.

Moreover, governments often delay action so as not to offend allies or financial backers both within and outside their country.

We return to the quality and level of information of terrorist activity. Ironically, it appears that only when there is an outright act by terrorists do governments feel that they can delay action no longer, no longer take refuge in caution, when their own credibility becomes paramount.

TERRORISM – THE LAW

The confusion over just what constitutes terrorism stems from the fact that every sovereign state reserves for itself the political and legal authority to define terrorism in the context of its domestic and foreign affairs. Governments speak with a bewildering variety of voices on the subject of terrorism. The United States is a case in point.

In the US federal system, each state determines what constitutes an offence under its criminal or penal code. States have generally defined terrorism as a crime, thus ending the need for the use of specific statutes covering other selected criminal acts that are identified as terrorism. For instance, the Arkansas Criminal Code states that *"a person commits the offence of terroristic threatening if with the purpose of terrorizing another person, he threatens to cause death or serious physical injury or substantial property damage to another person."* In Britain and in other European countries, separate authorities deal with the various aspects of terrorism whether it is victim compensation, street terrorism, the threats to national security or ecological terrorism.

In the US legislative branch, no consensus has been reached. Indeed, over the past 30 years, the U.S. Congress has held numerous hearings, considered bills, adopted resolutions, and passed laws on terrorism. A comprehensive working definition that can address the different forms of terrorist attacks has not emerged from Congress thus far. In recent years, however, the Department of State has adopted a definition, stating that the term 'terrorism' means *"premeditated, politically motivated violence perpetrated against non-combatant targets by sub national groups or clandestine agents, usually intended to influence an audience".* (For sources on the definition of terrorism see, Yonah Alexander, ed., Terrorism: An International Resource File 1986-1990, Ann Arbor, Michigan: UMI, 1991).

Other countries, such as the United Kingdom, have adopted an evolutionary definition of terrorism. The UK defines its position in s.1 of the Terrorism Act 2000. Section 1 (1) provides that "terrorism" means the use or threat of action where the actions falls within subsection (2), i.e. violence, serious damage, endangering life etc. and (b) "the use or threat is designed to influence the government or to intimidate the public or a section of the public, and (c) the use or threat is made for the purpose of advancing a political, religious or ideological cause."

Attempts to define terrorism on the part of the United States and the United Kingdom reflect a divergence of national dispositions. Similarly, international organisations, such as the United Nations, have failed for decades to agree on a common universal definition. While both the United Nations General Assembly and the Security Council repeatedly affirm their determination to combat terrorism in all its forms *"irrespective of motive, wherever and by whomever committed,"* the world body was reluctant for political reasons to define precisely the nature of the terrorism challenge (UN Security Council Resolution 1269, 12 Oct 1999).

An active effort by the United Nations to craft a definition occurred in December 1999, when the General Assembly adopted by consensus the text of a draft "International Convention for the Suppression of the Financing of Terrorism". It states:

"Criminal acts intended or calculated to provoke a state of terror in the general public, a group of persons or particular persons for political purposes are in any circumstances unjustifiable, whatever the considerations of a political, philosophical, ideological, racial ethnic, religious or other nature that may be invoked to justify them". (UN General Assembly Resolutions 54/109, 9 Dec, 1999.)

Some additional references that may assist the reader in grappling with the "cheap war" follow below, but while it may be true that "one man's terrorist is another man's freedom fighter," there are certain commonly accepted elements in all the definitions. Various descriptions of the phenomenon include the following:

- Terrorism is the use or threatened use of force designed to bring about political change. – Brian Jenkins, Under Siege 1971-1980, Santa Monica CA. Rand 1981.

- Terrorism constitutes the illegitimate use of force to achieve a political objective when innocent people are targeted. – Walter Laqueur (The Age of Terrorism, Boston. Little, Brown, 1987.

- Terrorism does not have a clear-cut and internationally recognised definition, yet there is broad consensus on its various aspects. Violence is a sine qua non for terrorism. It is lethal. In the political sense, terrorism is an assault on civil order. Murat Karagoz Perception Sept - Nov 2002. Vol VII No.3.

Terrorism provides a "cheap war," yet some operations are massively expensive. The attack of September 11 2001 must have involved considerable planning and co-operation with at least one national state, a massive budget, and a substantial call on personnel in many parts of the world. A management structure will operate throughout but, in the main, the unit and cells are kept rigidly separate to mount operations. The terrorist, however, needs a steady and predictable cash flow to pay for weapons, food, service charges, wages, etc.

These costs are unimportant set alongside the vast millions required for a state to set in place opposition or to commit its people for an attack on another country. One significant item of expenditure for the terrorist is travel ensuring that there are safe houses and safe people to make travel "healthy".

State-sponsored terrorism is more difficult to control, because the use of state apparatus makes it that much easier for groups to conduct their operations and escape the clutches of the law. Cross-border terrorism is often supported and sponsored by the intelligence agencies of the neighbouring countries. The international community must engage on a steep learning curve and act upon information about the make-up and travel intentions of terrorist groups. Britain and the United States already share such information.

In reviewing the nature of violence we must stress that terrorism is not a synonym for violence in general. Terrorism is a special kind of violence.

In Central America, for instance, terrorism is used in conjunction with rural guerrilla warfare and with economic and political warfare in an all-out bid to topple governments. But in Western Europe, which has experienced about 40% of all international terrorist incidents annually, terrorism is usually not accompanied by a wider insurgency. Terrorism is indiscriminate as innocent people are caught up in the violence. As Raymond Aron has said: *"An action of violence is labelled "terrorist" when its psychological effects are out of proportion to its purely physical result. In this sense, the so-called indiscriminate acts of revolutionaries are terrorist, as were the Anglo-American zone bombings. The lack of discrimination helps to spread fear, for if no one in particular is a target, no one can be safe."* (On War, 1985 University Press of America.) Rules of war do not apply, and since there are no rules we feel helpless and disorientated, with no inviolable rights in the eyes of the terrorist. This confirms the very nature of terrorism: indiscriminate, unpredictable, arbitrary and ruthless.

When the February 26 1993 crude bomb exploded in the World Trade Centre in New York, killing six and injuring a thousand people, the disruption of information systems was kept highly confidential. As Alvin Toffler wrote, *"Information systems are a particular target and are vulnerable. Invariably, they are not protected"* (War and Anti-War, 1994 Time Warner). Communications Consultant, Winn Schwartau, of Inter-Pact notes: *"With over 100 million computers inextricably tying us all together through the most complex array of land and satellite based communication systems... government and commercial systems are so poorly protected today that they can be essentially considered defenceless. An electronic Pearl Harbour is waiting to happen".*

A report of the US General Accounting Office to Congress voices similar concern. Fedwire, an electronic fund transfer network that handles $253 trillion in money transfers in one year alone, suffers from security weaknesses and needs "stringent security provisions."

Booz, Allen & Hamilton, the consulting firm, conducted a study of communications in New York and found that major financial institutions were operating without any communications back-up.

DOUBLE STANDARDS

When terrorists are identified, (as we have reported in the press during the Afghanistan conflict following September 11,) there are bound to be angry reactions from the families of the British servicemen and women engaged in the war.

During November 2001, British Muslims were urged by the Taliban to rise up in a national campaign of disobedience - a call which prompted fears of civil unrest in England's Muslim communities. In Blackburn, Taliban supporters were urged to engage in and spread the "campaign of disobedience" throughout Britain, prompting fears that continued allied attacks on Afghanistan would precipitate a winter of civil unrest in northern England's Muslim heartlands. The Independent (12 Nov 2001) reported that in Blackburn a crowd of more than 200 Taliban supporters gathered to hear proponents of the militant Al-Muhajiroun. To the despair of many community leaders, violence broke out, creating turmoil and riots:

"At the time an attack on a church and a vicar near the location of recent riots, took place in Bradford. A car passenger was taken to hospital with serious injuries after a brick was hurled through the window of the car and a disabled motorist's screen was smashed with an axe by Asian youths on Harehills in Leeds".

How did opposing Muslim groups react to the 11 September attacks? The Observer noted that most Muslims kept their heads down. *"Possibly they were anxious not to inspire a backlash by the wider community as British troops were involved".* (4 May 2003.) Several Muslim leaders did nevertheless speak out against terrorism, for instance, Zaid Shakir of the Light Study Group said: *"We should chose a day to mourn. On that day every Muslim family will buy 14 flowers along with 14 cards with a message explaining to our white neighbours that we are their Muslim neighbours and we wish to extend to them a small expression of condolence. We should personally deliver them to our neighbours".* Conversely, Anjem Choudary of Al-Muhajiroun, declared: *"The People of America deserved 11 September. Osama bin Laden is a hero to the people in the UK. If support for Al-Qaeda wasn't proscribed and people were free to air their views, many more would voice their support. Here at Al-Muhajiroun we fear only God and are free to speak our view - Osama bin Laden is a hero and should be loved".*

The very different expressions of the two cases demonstrates the need to be apprised of how differently people of the same faith see their enemies and friends.

CYBER – KNOW YOUR ENEMY

Acquiring new technology to enhance their missions is a constant aim for the terrorist leadership, hence the growth of electronic and cyber terrorism.

The Internet already serves as a frame for propaganda and psychological warfare, providing a recruiting and training virtual structure, a communication channel with encrypted messages and a tool for operational planning and execution. In the future, society will face an expansion of cyber terrorism including electronic jamming.

Several devastating scenarios of cyber terrorism could well damage the public services by altering formulas for medication at pharmaceutical plants, "crashing" telephone systems, misrouting passenger trains and changing pressure in gas pipelines to cause valve dislocation.

SEPTEMBER 11 2001

Dates are vital pegs in our minds, whereby we recall the horror or happiness of a particular occasion. From personal experiences, it would appear that the former dominates. We remember what we were doing on the day of President Kennedy's assassination. The events of September 11 2001 were not only a vital wake-up call to the United States from any isolationism of the past; the day also served as a reminder to the Western Powers of their own vulnerability.

A seldom-discussed report in the Turkish journal, Perceptions (March-May 2002), argues that, in the eighteenth and nineteenth centuries and for much of the twentieth century, the essential action in the global balance of power took place in Europe. Since the end of the Cold War, the European continent is no longer the focus of shifting alignments and multilateral security. Although a balance of power may now be maintained in Europe, disorderly developments in Asia, the Middle East and elsewhere negatively affect the stability of the European sub-system. The consequence of this shift affects many areas of governmental thinking. Above all, the nature of security must change, taking into account the geographical and institutional scope of new pressures including international terrorism.

Ease of travel and trans-communication across international borders add to anxieties following September 11. Professor Kestas Ifantis confirms this (in Perceptions):

"Trans-sovereign problems – problems that move beyond sovereignty and traditional state responses – fill the contemporary international relations agenda and make a mockery of state borders and unilateral state responses. Among the new factors that transcend boundaries and threaten to erode national cohesion, the most perilous are the so-called "new risks": drug trafficking, trans-national organised crime and nuclear smuggling, refugee movements, uncontrolled and illegal immigration, environmental risks and international terrorism. These are not new sources of potential conflict. They all existed to some extent during the Cold War but were largely subsumed by the threat of military conflict between NATO and the Warsaw Pact countries.

Ironically the very same policies that created open, democratic societies also threaten the trans-sovereign states. Drug smuggling illegally uses the same international financial networks that free trade creates.

Refugee movements and illegal immigration represents a further threat to European security and stability. The figures are staggering, with more than 800,000 Bosnian refugees still in Germany and Italy whilst almost a million Albanians entered Greece and Italy.

Post September 11 international terrorism has increased. All the traffickers take advantage of the infrastructure which was waiting to be exploited."

Reinforcing this view of the changing security environment, there was a great deal to dispute in the Western media about the loyalty and double standards of British Muslims in Afghanistan and, later, Iraq. Mourad A Fleming (in The Times correspondence columns) explained that the origins of Islam provide no base for terrorism, but Herb Greer, a war correspondent, rejected this view (Feb 5, 2002): *"I was one of the first Western correspondents to report the Arab side of the Algerian War in the late Fifties. The fundamentalist tendencies which founded the Armed Islamic Group (GIA) were clearly in evidence at that time, in a split between French-Westernised Algerians and strict Islamics. The anti-Western hatred among the latter was already fully developed, dating back more than a century."* According to Mr Fleming, Western military success *"can only breed more terrorists". In fact, the breeding ground for such killers lies in the Islamic doctrine, which divides the world into the Dar-al-Islam (House of Islam) and the (Western Judaeo-Christian) Dar-al-Harb (House of War).*

The conflict between the two, according to normal – not "extremist" – Islam doctrine, is interrupted only by states of truce, and will never cease until the whole world is brought under the sway of the Dar-al-Islam.

Mr Greer concludes, *"The pretence that West-hating terrorists and extremists occupy a sort of limbo which has nothing to do with Islam is supported neither by historical fact, nor by real Islamic doctrine."*

However, an argument that British Muslims would support Saddam Hussein and role model Bin Laden brought angry reactions from the majority of Muslims in Britain.

Even so, the Al-Muhajiroun organisation - whose high-profile supporters include Sheikh Abu Hamza al-Masri - warned that Britain would *"choke on the smoke"* of terrorist reprisals if it attacked Saddam Hussein.

The tabloids reacted with screaming headlines *"Kick them out!"* (Daily Express, August 16 2002). After a number of demonstrations, Inyat Bunglawala, a spokesman for the moderate Muslim Council for Britain, called for legal action against the radicals: *"Some of their remarks are very inflammatory and do enormous damage to the Muslim community. They have no standing in the community. They have been chased out of every mosque and they are despised. I really would like to see legal action. Quite clearly their antics are creating an atmosphere of hatred against Muslims".* Many senior Muslims figures said at the time they would support moves to deport the extremists. Those British Muslims who fought for the Taliban were taking a serious risk not only for themselves, but also for their fellow countrymen who stayed here and never contemplated travelling to fight in Afghanistan against Britain.

Mohammed Abbas, a delivery driver from Manchester is one such case. He told his story to Daniel McGory in The Times (September 6 2002), who wrote: *"He admits to having fought in Afghanistan for the Taliban, but has since slipped back into Britain. He lied to Special Branch detectives who questioned him when he arrived at Heathrow over what he had been doing since he flew to Pakistan two days after the attacks on the World Trade Centre and the Pentagon. His English wife and two children were with him and, while detectives doubted his account of attending his cousin's wedding and trying to start a business in Karachi they could not prove that he had been there to fight".*

There are many who now boast they were there, but it is estimated that less than 1,000 British Muslims went to Pakistan intending to fight a "holy war". Only a handful were allowed by the Taliban to get close enough to the battle. The Taliban and their Al-Qaeda allies thought the British volunteers "too soft". Britons found it hard to acclimatise to the mountain camps, and all but a few were sent back. Those like Mr Abbas, who did see action, admit that they were petrified, says Daniel McGory. What Mr Abbas's experience suggests is that there are cells in Britain who can provide weapon training and availability for action.

There are other disturbing trends which cannot be ignored.

A year after the attacks on the United States, with subsequent memorial services in Britain, rallies were staged by Muslim groups, to celebrate the "positive outcome" of the September 11 terrorist attacks. Thus, as Britain and America joined the world in solemn memorials and silent tributes to mark the first anniversary of the attacks, many Islamic extremists attended a meeting in London to highlight the "benefits" of the atrocities. This meeting was addressed by Abu Hamza and Omar Bakri Muhammed, the leader of the Al-Muhajiroun group, whose members support homicide (suicide) bombings.

Areas of most concern for terrorist recruitment and training are Tunisia, Morocco and, most seriously, Algeria. As Thomas Fuller commented in the International Herald Tribune (7/8 Sept 2002): *"That members of the North African Diaspora are involved in terrorism in Europe is nothing new. Militant groups fighting the Algerian government were behind dozens of bombings in the 1980s and 1990s, especially in France. But the last year has revealed new faces and a less structured, looser network of groups."* Presently, European and US intelligence agencies have increased the level of co-operation and the sharing of data with their counterparts in this region, particularly, Algeria.

At the same time, on a government level, the United States has been pressuring some major players that were not inclined to commit themselves to the allies. For instance, Condoleezza Rice, then President Bush's National Security Adviser, reminded Germans on a visit to the US that *"terrorists hate Berlin, London and Paris just as much as they hate New York and Washington, because these cities are symbols of a free and open society"*. This did not prevent the German government from declaring hostile opposition to the US/British-led military action on Iraq.

"Do we really still have to prove that Saddam Hussein is a threat for international stability and peace?" Ms Rice asked. Given that Saddam Hussein had twice attacked his neighbours; had used chemical weapons against his own people; had twice been caught trying to acquire nuclear

weapons, and possesses a large range of high volume weapons, this reminder from Ms Rice seems perfectly fair.

By September 2002, there was a growing awareness of the terrorist dangers in Asia. With US technical assistance in Singapore and the Philippines, for instance, much intelligence work was operating in both countries to expose plots against US – related targets. Yet this was not sufficient to prevent the bomb outrage in Bali.

Thomas Crampton in the <u>International Herald Tribune</u> (7 Sept 2002) has a somewhat cynical view of the present hunt for terrorists: *"Asian governments have started taking an increasingly opportunistic approach to the war on terror, using the broadly defined Washington backed campaign to advance long-standing domestic agendas including fights against groups without any clear link to Al Qaeda."*

Confronting the terrorist is an essential part of protecting a nation's citizens. But security is not without its difficulties and inconvenience, whether in restrictions on movement or increasing controls at air and sea ports.

Kerim Chatty, a Swedish citizen with a Tunisian father and a Swedish mother was arrested after a pistol was found in his hand luggage at Vasteras airport near Stockholm. He was trying to board a Ryanair flight to Stansted. Chatty, who has a criminal record, had recently converted to Islam. A military intelligence source confirmed to <u>The Independent</u>, *"we know for certain that the plan was to crash the plane into a US Embassy"*. That seemed clear enough, but there were still concerns expressed by Scandinavian human rights groups about Chatty's rights.

Bringing terrorists to justice is not a straightforward issue. Following the bombing of a nightclub in Bali, the suspect thought to have parked the car that exploded outside the Sari Club was given a hero's welcome as he appeared in Court in Jakarta. Supporters chanted *"God is greatest"* whilst disrupting the proceedings.

Melanie Phillips in <u>The Daily Mail</u> (26 May 2003) warns that our ineffable judiciary is busy signalling that Britain is the land where terrorists may go free. The Court of Appeal quashed the convictions of nine Afghans who hijacked a plane from Kabul three years ago, holding its passengers hostage for three days at Stansted Airport. The court has yet to publish its reasons, but it appears the crux of the matter was that the trial judge, Sir Edwin Jowitt, misdirected the jury on the law of duress, namely that the accused or his family would have faced death or serious harm if he had returned to his own country and if he had not committed any offences no reasonable person could have acted otherwise. Sir Edwin set out a list of commonsense tests for the jury to apply before this defence of duress could be accepted, including the requirement to prove that there was an immediate threat to the hijackers' lives. In the event, the Appeal Judges said this argument was wrong.

In other countries, a combination of inadequate laws and governmental weakness similarly contribute to terrorists often being acquitted.

Another on-going argument, prior to and following the Iraqi war, is the extent to which Saddam Hussein was connected to Al-Qaeda. There is no doubt that communications and logistical support operated between the two. Iraq under Saddam Hussein occupied a unique role in laundering resources from other states, which would have been compromised if seen to be funding terrorist operations directly.

But as the stakes are raised in the war against terrorism a long-drawn out struggle seems inevitable. New strategies will be required to compete with terrorists in ensuring that they don't take the initiative. Writing in The Times Rohan Gunaratna avers that the extra security measures now introduced will not be enough to deal with the growing terrorist threats. He argues, *"Al-Qaeda is not invincible nor infallible. But it will take years of painstaking efforts to hunt down its operatives who have spread across the globe as the West fail to act. The key to defeating al-Qaeda is to kill Bin Laden and the core leadership around him, almost certainly still hiding along the Afghanistan-Pakistan border. While the penultimate and core leadership remain intact, the group will not be destroyed no matter how many of the rank and file are killed or captured"* (12 June 2002).

The game plan for confronting such terrorists is to operate in both the formal arena (with governments and institutions acting against them) and the informal arena, by alerting the public to the dangers and the risks of terrorism.

In the same edition of The Times, Christopher Andrew issued the following warning shortly before the Iraqi war: *"There is no end in sight to nuclear proliferation. Since every previous human invention has spread around the globe, it is idle to suppose that WMDs will prove the first exception to this iron law of history – especially in an era when technology crosses national boundaries with unprecedented speed. The main priority of intelligence agencies will now be to monitor and slow down the ultimately unstoppable proliferation of weapons of mass destruction".*

Another problem raised in the aftermath of September 11 was why it was so difficult for the authorities and Special Forces to confront the terrorists. Judge Jean-Louis Bruguiere - who has sentenced more Islamic terrorists than any other investigator in Europe - believes that the main reason for the poor response to rooting out terrorism in Europe is the lack of standardisation by police in dealing with terrorists. He points out that such inquiries are conducted by the police in Britain whereas in France and most Western Countries, it is the judicial authorities that have jurisdiction over the issue. The two sides find communication notoriously difficult. *"We don't have a correspondent to whom we can talk in Britain,"* says Bruguiere (The Times, 18 April 2002).

Bruguiere has argued that France is ahead of the terrorist 'game'. He warns the West that France is no longer the target but North America, as they failed to heed warnings right up to the years and months before 11 September 2001. Bruguiere does not discloses the source of his information, but it is likely to come from French intelligence agents who have proved superior to their US counterparts in the struggle against Islamic fundamentalism.

The Times argues that almost all radical French-based Islamic organisations, including mosques, are infiltrated by informers, and that for some years, all journeys to Afghanistan - however circuitous - have been monitored. The findings are passed to Bruguiere, who has built up an extensive picture of the Islamic terrorist phenomenon. *"Public opinion has relaxed, but the terrorist threat is as great as ever,"* says Bruguiere. The dangers are, at last, being recognised and there is no more powerful expression of these dangers than that of the former US Secretary of State, George P Shultz, (Washington Post, 7/8 Sept 2002).

"The world has now entered the third decade of crises and dangers to international peace and security created by Saddam Hussein. In 1980 he launched an eight-year war against Iran. Chemical weapons were used, and at least 1.5 million people were killed or severely wounded. In 1990 he invaded Kuwait in a war aimed at eradicating another state's legitimate sovereign existence. As he was forced out he deliberately created environmental degradation of gigantic proportions. He has used chemical weapons against the Kurdish people in an attack on a genocidal scale, and he has sent his forces into Kurdistan to conduct widespread slaughter." Schultz argues that the history of Iraq, the achievement of its people, the degree of past civilization of the past, and its extensive natural resources all point to the possibility of a positive transformation once Saddam's yoke is lifted. In the process, a model may emerge that other Arab societies will look to and emulate. Given events following the war, this may seem somewhat optimistic. A considerable amount of trust is necessary before such a model may be established. Nevertheless, there is no doubt that the challenge offered by Iraq, also offers an opportunity for a historic turning point that can lead us in the direction of a more peaceful future.

HOMICIDE BOMBERS

Words may confuse: in the context of modern terrorism, the phrase used by the media and politicians alike, to describe those who strap explosives to themselves and enter shopping centres and buses, are what is called, "*suicide bombers*". In fact, their actions are homicidal; they are killers who set out to kill innocent people. What the individual criminal does with his or her life is not an issue; but we make a serious error, even add colour to the deed by this misnomer. Homicide bombing is not courageous but cowardly.

The recruitment of homicide bombers takes place in the training camps in Libya, the West Bank, Iran and Iraq. In addition, one of the main purposes of the Hizbullah, Hamas and Islamic Jihad websites, is to recruit. Sheik Yusuf al-Qaradawi, one of the most influential Muslim religious leaders to have issued a number of "fatwas" supporting the bombers, now has a website which is linked to the militant wing of Hamas. The website dispenses advice to eager potential homicide bombers wanting to sign up for the war against Israel and the United States. Seeking to legitimise the homicide bomber, Sheik Yusuf al-Qaradawi's fatwah formalises the attacks in the following declaration: *"The actions committed by the young Muslims who defend the land of Islam are the greatest form of Jihad for the sake of God and they are part of the permitted terror which the Quran talked about... it's mistake is to call these actions suicide because they are brave actions for the sake of God and the ones who commit them are considered "shuhadaa" for the sake of God."*

There is no substantiating material on the nature and background of the homicide bomber. A case study in the New York Times (22 June 2002) will have to suffice in providing some insight into the mental and social processes involved.

The report tells of 20 year-old Ms Arien Ahmed, a Palestinian student in business administration. Like most recruits, Ms Ahmed did not go through months of indoctrination; she had no connection to Islamic groups like Hamas and she received little preparation other than how to press a button, but she was available. The report explains that on Wednesday 22 May, she had been pulled away from a marketing lecture at Bethlehem University, shown a backpack and how to trigger the bomb inside; was put in a beat-up car with another would-be killer and sent on, dressed to pass as an Israeli woman. She had no idea where she was; she tells of being in a daze.

She wondered if she was in Jerusalem or Tel Aviv. She was actually in the town of Rishon Letzion.

Ahmed wanted to avenge the death of her fiancé, a leader of the Bethlehem group which was part of the Tanzim, the militia connected to Al Fatah. She believed that he had been killed by Israeli forces, though Israel intelligence agents said he had accidentally blown himself up. But Ahmed was now starting to wonder, as she walked along the pedestrian mall, if she was doing the right thing, or if hell rather than heaven awaited her. *"I look at the sky,"* Ahmed recalled in a later interview speaking English as she described a kind of awakening, *"I look at the people."* She said she remembered a childhood belief, *"that nobody has the right to stop anybody's life."* Ahmed, a rare exception among suicide bombers, turned back. Her companion, Issa Badir, urged her to have second thoughts, she said. But he ultimately went ahead, killing himself and two Israelis.

The case is unusual for the lack of training and information given to 'the candidate,' nor did Ms Ahmed's group engage in significant ideological "cushioning". These pointers may reflect the limits to the number of suitable volunteers and the cost of more detailed training. Yet as the New York Times pointed out: *"The range of recruits to suicide missions continues to broaden in often bewildering ways. This week, Israeli forces arrested a 12-year old Palestinian boy its intelligence had identified as planning an attack".*

Dr Iyad Sarraj, a Palestinian psychiatrist in Gaza City, has watched the trend towards suicide bombing with growing alarm. He said that Palestinian children who had grown up with the idea of suicide attacks were equating death with power. One thing is certain: here is another element in the terrorist's armoury. Other countries would do well to notice the grave consequences of suicide missions, which cause untold destruction, as well as death and psychological damage. (See Appendix B for list of incidents in one country in year 2002.)

Much of the success of a co-ordinated terrorist group over a scattered series of incidents planning vengeance or attack derives from the financing of its various operations. Efficient funding ensures the latest logistical support and the purchase of the latest weapons. One cunning device introduced by the IRA was the revolutionary tax - a tangible way of capitalising on their reputations. The levying of a revolutionary tax (or protection money), is a major source of terrorist income throughout the world and for some businesses has become an item of everyday expense. If actually kidnapping a senior executive is too dangerous for the terrorist, the threat of kidnap has proved to be a much safer and lucrative activity.

Robberies and racketeering around towns and villages were common practice by the IRA. But the big money came from the drug trade. Given the size of the drugs market, it is not surprising that an international drugs trade emerged, dominated by international crime. It is a natural development, therefore, for international terrorists to become involved in drugs. (Centre for Contemporary Studies, London 1990).

The structure of cross-boundary groupings and the well prepared transit routes set up by terrorists, with their many safe houses and safe operational points, makes an ideal communications channel for the illegal drug trade, offering a massive pay-back for the terrorist agenda.

Many countries have a terrorist group which challenges formal law and order. At the same time, for whatever reason, many incidents of terrorism are not reported. An unusual incident occurred in Spain, at a time when ETA was afraid of provoking a military coup. A lull in ETA activities was broken by a pressing need for funds. Prevailing over fears of the army, a major kidnapping took place in early 1982. This time the target was the millionaire father of singer Julio Iglesias. ETA demanded a ransom of $1m for his safe return, but ETA's luck failed to hold and after 19 days of captivity, Senor Iglesias was rescued by a special unit of the Spanish police.

If kidnapping is to succeed then conditions need to be right. ETA and the Red Brigade were successful in their use of the kidnap weapon largely because security forces were inefficient and demoralised.

A more detailed case of terrorist funding concerns the misuse of funds diverted from appeals to alleviate hardship. This was the specific charge made not only by the Israeli government, but also by a number of International Lawyers' organisations relating to grants from the European Union to the Palestinian Authority, which 'lost' or leaked funds to militant groups. During a sweep in several towns, the Israelis captured a great deal of material supporting these allegations (The Times, 6 May 2002). A search of one department of the Palestinian Authority - the General Security Apparatus Organisation - is alleged to have shown that Mr Arafat had been using monthly grants to pay hundreds of gunmen from his Fatah organisation and the al-Aqsa Martyrs Brigade. One document included in the dossier is said to be a letter addressed to "The Fighting President Brother Amu Amar" (Mr Arafat's nom de guerre), requesting a payment of $2,500 for three named gunmen. At the foot of the letter, in what is said to be Mr Arafat's own handwriting, is an order that the men should be paid $600 a head.

The European Commissioner was unconcerned that there was anything unusual in such transfers. Gunnar Weigand, spokesman for Chris Patten, the European Commissioner for Foreign Affairs, said that the distribution of each monthly grant was closely scrutinised by officials from the International Monetary Fund (The Times, 6 May 2002). Now more than two years later, a searching enquiry is underway into all monies dispatched from the E.U.

In a UN report on Al Qaeda funding (29 Aug 2002) it was noted that a worldwide campaign to block Al-Qaeda's funds was hardly successful in the four months following 11 September 2001 when up to $112 million in assets of suspected members and supporters were frozen. But partly for legal reasons and partly because the network found new ways to evade the sanctions, the international effort to clamp down on the terrorists' cash flow came to a premature halt.

According to the UN, Al-Qaeda had moved many of its assets into precious metals and gems, and was transferring money through an informal transfer system. There were also private donations to Al-Qaeda of almost $16 million a year. According to The Sunday Times (25 Aug 2002), senior members of the Saudi Royal Family paid at least £200m to Osama Bin Laden's terror group and the Taliban in exchange for an agreement that their forces would not attack targets in Saudi Arabia.

Papers filed in a $3,000 billion lawsuit in America, on behalf of September 11 victims, allege that this deal was agreed after two secret meetings between Saudi royals, Al-Qaeda and Bin Laden. These monies enabled Al-Qaeda to fund training camps in Afghanistan later attended by the September 11 hijackers.

RICIN

The other likely escalation of terrorism stems from the use of Ricin, which is easily made and cheap. Terrorists do not necessarily need a massive bomb or a willing homicide bomber to achieve the aims of destruction and chaos. They can easily use transferable poisons like ricin. Unlike any other form of traditional warfare where a particular target is identified such as, an airfield, a factory or a city, with ricin the terrorists have little need to use extensive resources or training of personnel to be successful.

It is generally agreed that biological attacks are more destructive than chemical attacks. As Christopher Harman says: *First, they may take longer to kill, making bio-agents harder to anticipate and evade than many chemicals. Second, instead of dispersing in the air, sometimes within minutes, as with many chemicals, biological war agents may spread, linger and even propagate. Thus, under proper weather conditions, a single warhead landing in a "major city" could kill more than the Hiroshima bomb. Third, ricin, as we have previously stated is cheap to produce* (Terrorism Today. Frank Cass, 2000).

Gaining access to knowledge of many of the poisons is not a particular problem. It would be possible to locate sympathisers with some training in chemistry or biochemistry. The recipe for ricin - a castor bean based biological poison - is available on the Internet. Other legitimate chemicals are freely available. There is much interest amongst terrorists in ricin; indeed, two different American militia groups in Arkansas and Minnesota have, in recent years, been found with significant quantities.

Ricin became a serious talking point in Britain in January 2003 when anti-terrorist police arrested six men after finding traces of the poison. Later in 2003, scientists at Porton Down germ warfare laboratory were not able to prove that this was in fact ricin, (The Sunday Times, 5 Oct 2003), but it remains a deadly and likely substance to be used in a future attack.

Ricin, one of the world's deadliest toxins, is twice as deadly as cobra venom and is relatively easily made; it may be inhaled, ingested or injected. There is no known antidote.

Following the arrests in Britain, the public was shocked about these findings. A hitherto indifferent public with little knowledge of terrorist activities became intrigued and then troubled. It is always likely that one attack would shock the public and the authorities into action similar to that of the United States following the finding of anthrax subsequent to September 11.

In Britain, the public mood was set not by the government, but by The Daily Mirror and other tabloids. While, two senior British Ministers were publicly quarrelling about an Iraqi intervention - on the day of the ricin warning! - The Mirror screamed Deadly Terror Poison Found in Britain (it's here) (8 Jan 2003).

Ricin provided a dramatic warning to the British of the dangers that might be introduced not just by weapons, but also by subtle and dangerously effective poisons. Hence the raids on suspects' workshops in Wood Green, London and Manchester were treated with a sober, worried reaction on the part of the public.

Another jolt to public indifference to terrorism followed a raid on the Finsbury Park Mosque. When police broke into the Mosque, they found a number of items including a stun gun, CS gas, passports and seven asylum seekers in hiding. Another tabloid newspaper, The Sun, ran an editorial on the need to get rid of one of the Muslim leaders who operated from the mosque: *"One man shows how wishy-washy liberal Britain has become a haven for those who hate us with a vengeance... With his hook hand and snarling mouth Abu Hamza is the unacceptable face of Islam. He preaches a wicked tirade of abuse against Britain, the country in which he has lived for over two decades and whose passport he carries for convenience.*

Is there another country in the world where this crazed cleric would be tolerated?" The Sun says revoke his passport and kick him out – or build our own version of Camp X-Ray and lock him in it. Hamza's praise for Osama bin Laden, his unconcealed glee over September 11 and his belligerent demands for a holy war should qualify him for the first plane to Egypt, land of his birth" (21 Jan 2000).

While the tabloids led with a denunciation of likely terrorists or sympathisers in our midst, the quality newspapers followed with a call for government action, to isolate and remove likely terrorist sources and contacts.

The links between the terrorist groups and rogue states, and the willingness of countries like France and Germany to do nothing in confronting Iraq, made the proliferation of weapons and increased activity by terrorists all the more likely.

THE PROLIFERATION OF CAUSES AND "CONVENIENCE" ISSUES

Some definitions of terrorist acts relate to their modus operandi; others describe the characteristics of terrorism itself.

In Political Terrorism, Schmidt and Youngman described 109 different definitions of terrorism, which they obtained in a survey of leading specialist academics. (Amsterdam & Transactions Books, 1988) From these definitions, the authors isolated the following recurrent elements, in order of their statistical appearance:

Violence, force (appeared in 83.5% of the definitions); political (use of political systems) (65%); fear, emphasis on terror (51%); threats (47%); psychological effects and anticipated reactions (41.5%); discrepancy between the targets and the victims (37.5%); intentional, planned, systematic, organized action (32%); methods of combat, strategy, tactics (30.5%).

Respondents were also asked the following question: "What issues in the definition of terrorism remain unresolved?" Some of the answers follow below:

- The boundary between terrorism and other forms of violence;

- Whether government terrorism and resistance terrorism are part of the same phenomenon;

- Separating "terrorism" from simple criminal acts, from open war between "consenting" groups, and from acts that clearly arise out of mental illness;

- Whether terrorism is a sub-category of coercion/violence/power/ influence;

- Whether terrorism can be legitimate, and what gains justify its use;

- The relationship between guerrilla warfare and terrorism;

- The relationship between crime and terrorism.

Some actions by states support the spread of terrorist acts even if they express surprise when challenged. When the US declared that Russia was helping to build five more nuclear reactors in Iran, with the purpose of developing nuclear weapons there was a surprised reaction by the Russians that their motives in 'helping' Iran should be so misunderstood. President Bush accused Iran of sponsoring terrorism and listed Iran with Iraq, Syria and North Korea as members of the "axis of evil" that threatened US national security. In August 2002, he warned Moscow that its project to build a nuclear reactor at the Bushehr facility on the Gulf coast would be used by the Iranians to develop weapons of mass destruction. The Russians and Iranians both refuted the claim.

The deal enabled three more reactors at the Bushehr site and another two at a new power station at Akhvaz to be built, about 65 miles from the Iraqi border. It is not surprising that Russia was embarrassed by the revelations. It has frequently taken the advantage to sell arms and to provide technical know-how to countries, without any reference to the potential of nuclear threats to international security.

The differences in the various forms of terrorism whether it is revolutionary violence or national liberation may be seen in the following studies of countries with longstanding histories of terrorist activities.

A. COLOMBIA.

Colombia was one of the three countries that emerged from the collapse of Gran Colombia in 1830. There has been a 40-year campaign by rebels to overthrow the government, aided by funds from the drug trade. Large areas of the countryside are under guerrilla influence, but the rebel movement lacks the military strength or popular support to overthrow the Government. The Revolutionary Armed Forces of Colombia (FARC) has been operating in Southern Colombia since the 1960s, growing from an ill-assorted group of only 1,300 men, in the 1980s, to a well-financed army of 18,000 men currently organised into 66 Fronts across the country.

A safe haven was ceded to FARC by the government in 1999 as part of an effort to jumpstart peace talks. But in an atmosphere of much uncertainty and suspicion the peace process broke down after FARC kidnapped a leading senator and a member of the congressional peace commission. The safe haven has since been reoccupied by the Colombian Army.

The Colombian Government also accuses FARC of using the safe haven to train new guerrilla recruits, for the smuggling and storage of weapons and cocaine, as well as the holding of kidnap victims for ransom.

In addition to the rebels' reign of terror, FARC has acted as a base and training facility for many other terrorists, in particular the IRA. This came to a head in August 2001 and April 2002, when key IRA operators were arrested and a US congressional report was published on FARC's activities (24 April 2002). The congressional report made a number of comments on the role of Colombia as a resource for the terrorist world. The report also examined the involvement of IRA members: "Colombian authorities believe that at least five and as many as 15 IRA-linked individuals have been travelling in and out of Colombia since at least 1998. The United States does not have the luxury of turning a blind eye when American lives and national interests are put at risk by IRA activity. Colombia is a potential breeding ground for international terror equalled perhaps only by Afghanistan and the IRA findings are the strongest among these global links".

The IRA denied any association with the Colombian rebels described in the report. Nevertheless, the evidence of expertise and the style of training had all the hallmarks of IRA involvement. Further, the report confirmed that the IRA was using the Colombian jungle to try out new weapons. The report concluded that, as a result of several IRA visits, FARC attacks had become far more sophisticated and deadly, while their tactics were identical to the IRA methods. *"New techniques in urban terrorism are being employed by the FARC in car bombings".*

B. ISRAEL

The main threat to the security of Israel is that of Palestinian militant groups; but they are joined by other Arab and radical elements (primarily Iranians) who are not prepared to recognise the existence of the state of Israel.

In Combating Terrorism, (University of Michigan Press, 2002) Professor Yonah Alexander identifies three different sources of Arab-Palestinian terrorism: private individuals, organisations and militia. The first type is the most primitive and least dangerous from the standpoint of military and political ramifications, since they do not respond to any outside grouping or demands. He or she simply acts on the basis of personal hatred.

The organisational type of terrorism against Israel consists of a number of people with considerable back-up by at least one supporting organisation. Professor Alexander emphasises the significance of this threat, not only in Israel but wherever they decide to take their ideology and their weapons.

Organised terrorist actions include shooting at civilians and/or Israeli forces: planting mines and bombs; attacking vehicles in Israeli territory, and penetrating Israeli population centres with booby-trapped cars.

In recent years, organized Palestinian terrorism has been almost exclusively initiated by organisations identifying with the extremist Islamic fundamentalist movement (primarily Hamas and the Palestinian Islamic Jihad). These organisations have introduced homicide bombers on passenger-filled buses or in any other place filled with Israeli civilians.

Such attacks are deeply troubling for two reasons: it is almost impossible to deter the fanatical homicide bomber from carrying out his or her mission, and security inspection systems for pinpointing such a bomber are inadequate.

The third form of terrorism involves armed and organised militias, groups located along Israel's borders. Since no country with a strong central government willingly permits the existence, let alone the activities, of hostile armed militias within its borders, the only such threat currently is from Lebanese territory. From the 1970s through the early 1980s, these militias consisted of Palestinians equipped with heavy ordnance including artillery and Katyusha rockets. Their activities across the border led to serious military confrontations, the height of which was the Lebanon War of 1982.

The militias and other terrorist organizations have the following features in common:

1. The objectives of their actions involve a total lack of distinction between harming military/defence forces and innocent civilians.

2. Even when living and operating in a friendly country, the majority of these militias do not maintain a standard military framework of units, camps, installations, uniforms, etc. Quite the contrary, they choose to mingle with the civilian population because of the concealment and refuge this provides.

The key weakness of such terrorist units derives from their dependence on the goodwill of the host country that permits their operations.

A major difference between terrorism in Israel and in other countries is that terrorism in almost all countries is directed against the governing authority whereas, in Israel, the terrorists aim to destroy the State of Israel and all its people.

Specifically, the groupings directed against Israel include:

Force 17: This is the security apparatus entrusted with the preservation of stability and order within the Palestinian Authority (PA). The organisation is comprised of 3,500 operatives and is headed by Faisel Abu-Sharkh, permanently positioned in Gaza. They are equipped with light weapons and BRDM-2 armoured vehicles; they patrol the streets of Palestinian cities as well as the "separation line" with Israel.

Tanzim: The Tanzim is the organized cadre of the Fatah movement – the largest and leading Palestinian faction in the PA. It sees itself as the dominant political force in Palestinian society. It is funded by the PA and has been responsible for most of the violence of the intifada.

Palestinian Front for the Liberation of Palestine (PFLP): The PFLP is a radical Palestinian group aimed at eliminating the State of Israel. It has opposed all peace agreements with Israel and has much in common with the violent fundamentalist religious movements, though it is a secular organisation; a rival to the Fatah faction.

Islamic Jihad: Members of the Palestinian Islamic Jihad aim to create a fundamentalist Islamic state in Palestine after fighting a holy war against the Jews, which they view as the first step toward realising their extreme version of an Islamic society. The organisation is supported mainly by Iran, and can be seen as an Iranian proxy. Islamic Jihad opposes any kind of peace agreement that the PA has made with Israel - yet it is one of the groups which were prepared to support a ceasefire in 2003.

Hamas is a fundamentalist Moslem movement, the aim of which is the obliteration of the Jewish state. Hamas is trying to transform the Middle East conflict from that of a national struggle of Arabs against Israelis to a religious war of Muslims against Jews. The agreements between the Palestinian Authority and Israel were a catalyst for heightened Hamas activity, which brought about an escalation of hostilities against Israel – homicide bombings in particular. The spiritual leader of Hamas is Sheikh Ahmed Yasin. In addition to its presence on the streets and its terrorist activities, Hamas is a populist organisation that works to improve the educational level and social welfare of local communities. (Hamas also supported the ceasefire in 2003.)

And after Yasser Arafat? There has been little formal opposition to Yasser Arafat, partly because the management system he initiated did not provide for it. He held the purse strings for all who made his system work.

Occasionally, a Palestinian emerged to express an independent view: one example is Taw fig al-Ghussein, a 40-year-old businessman educated at Georgetown University in Washington and SOAS in London. Taw fig al-Ghussein is a likely future Palestinian leader, who has spoken out against the Palestinian Authority (The Daily Telegraph, 29 Aug 2002).

Al-Ghusseins's most scathing criticism of Arafat concerned his failure to build a functioning economy when the world's gold was being showered on the Palestinians in the hope of ensuring the success of the "peace process". Arafat, he says created "a rentier state" living off foreign aid and using the money to buy political loyalty. The "Tunisians", Arafat's lieutenants from the days of exile in Beirut and Tunis, are bleeding the ordinary people, says Al-Ghussein.

All who want to alter the system of an organisation need a power base and finance. Arafat's position was held together by the loose connections of many diverse groups, including hard-line terrorists.

C. FRANCE & ANTI-SEMITISM

In the past ten years, anti-Semitism has been much more organised than for any period since the Holocaust. Some countries have acted swiftly to deal with it. This is true of Britain and the United States. In France, with a large Jewish community (700,000), attacks have been recorded by the Weisenthal Centre and the Anti-Defamation League (ADL), drawing attention to the knifing of rabbis, the slashing of young Jews, firebombs thrown at synagogue walls, and harassment of young Jews at school. Many of the incidents against Jews are not otherwise formally registered, making the French authorities' figures on anti-Semitism an inaccurate reflection of the current scene.

The French press has hardly addressed the phenomenon and, despite a condemnation by the Prime Minster, political reaction has been ambiguous and thin on the ground. President Jacques Chirac was reported to have warned against exaggerating anti-Semitism for fear of encouraging its increase!

The Jewish community in France is beginning to feel that the government lacks the political will to take the problem seriously. Some see this arising out of a heightened perception of the Arab constituency's voting power in the elections. One of the Creteil worshippers, whose synagogue was twice attacked in a year, asked, *"Why are only synagogues targeted? How come no mosques, or churches? And still the authorities call it general violence and claim that we the Jews are over-sensitive. The policy of silence regarding Islamic Judeophobia must end!"* (World Jewish Congress Report 2002.)

Nevertheless, the French continue to vacillate. French Foreign Minister, Hubert Vedrine, claimed recently that, *"one is not shocked when young French Jews instinctively sympathise with Israel regardless of the policies, so one should not be shocked when young French citizens (of North African background) feel compassion to the Palestinians"*. What Vedrine failed to point out is that however disenchanted Jews may be with Palestinians, they do not burn down mosques or attack Muslims in the street.

There are similar incidents of anti-Semitism in Belgium but, equally, the Moslem population is a focus of robust attack by the extreme right (mostly Flemish) and Holocaust denial activists. The post-Holocaust years (1945-1980) have slipped away and whatever sympathy and concern was shown towards the Jews has largely evaporated.

The Washington Post columnist, Charles Karauthhammer sums up the rise in anti-Semitism in the following stark terms: *"What we are seeing is pent-up anti-Semitism, the release with Israel as the trigger... holocaust shame kept the demon corked for 50 years. The genie is out again."*

D. NORTHERN IRELAND

In Northern Ireland, the cheap war waged for over a quarter of a century by the Provisional IRA, INLA and the loyalist terrorist groups, the UVF and the UFF, has recently been overtaken by a series of peace initiatives. Nevertheless, the pain and killings continue and peace talks have not moved on without a number of fundamental setbacks. The reluctance to show absolute good faith in the decommissioning of weapons has been paramount in holding up the peace initiatives. Perhaps it is not surprising that decommissioning is such a critical issue. There has never been a single case of a West European terrorist group voluntarily relinquishing the bomb and the guns to become a political party.

Whatever the nature of the particular brand of terrorism in Northern Ireland, it takes place against a background of discussion and international concern. This highlights another aspect of the terrorist's modus operandi, namely to keep one hand firmly on the gun while extending the other in a handshake to meet international concern in creating a likely *"peace process"*.

In the 1990's there were many examples of such stops and starts, with many people killed or maimed in the process. In the years immediately following April 1998, there was a breakthrough agreement (overwhelmingly approved in referendums in Northern Ireland and the Republic in May of the same year), offering extensive home rule in Northern Ireland, with some Republic of Ireland participation, and all paramilitary groups disarmed.

When the deadline of 1 February 2000 came and went without the IRA or other armed groups disarming, the British Government suspended the Northern Ireland Government that had been functioning for only 10 weeks (since 2 December 1999). In May 2000, the IRA pledged to put its arms "beyond use" and permit inspections. All seemed promising, yet by 1 July 2001 the refusal of the IRA and other paramilitary groups to disarm led to the resignation of the Protestant leader, David Trimble, as First Minister. Once again the peace accord was in jeopardy. While the politicians continued to argue, there were many acts of violence of various degrees by both the IRA and Protestants.

An example of the cruelty and cynicism of the terrorist mentality in Northern Ireland is shown in the following cameo. 17-year-old Jonathan Adair, the son of Johnny "mad dog" Adair, was shot in both calves by gunmen from the loyalist Ulster Defence Association. It was a "punishment attack" committed by a group that the boy's own father controlled. Although Adair Senior denied that he had ordered the shooting, senior security sources said that it was almost inconceivable that he had not been made aware in advance of the attack which took place within 200 yards of his home (The Times, 9 Aug 2002). It was not immediately clear why Adair's son had been targeted, although punishment shootings and beatings are routinely meted out by Republican and Loyalist gangs for offences ranging from petty theft and joy-riding to looking at a paramilitary personnel the wrong way.

It should be stressed that, despite the deeply distressing level of terrorism in Northern Ireland (and on the UK Mainland) these past 30 years, there was an organised attempt by the IRA to communicate with the public, to alert and warn of an immediate 'strike'. In no way does this action alter the seriousness of IRA activities or the murders they have committed; but the special coding employed by the IRA to warn the authorities (often by calling newspaper offices) in many cases enabled buildings or estates to be cleared. Furthermore, unlike terrorist groups in Israel or Al-Qaeda's operations, generally the IRA and its associated groups planned for 'safe houses' to ensure the escape of their personnel. Homicide bombers were not deployed, suggesting a different philosophy on the part of their leadership both to violence and the indiscriminate taking of life.

As of January 5th, 2005, substantial progress has been made by the various factions to reach agreement on the removal of arms and to ensure a return of all parties to the Northern Ireland parliament. However, a small but apparently significant issue has hindered the "peace agreement", namely that the removal of the IRA weapons should be photographed and recorded. It seems, that the many days and weeks of talk had good effect in narrowing the differences but the ability to trust "the other side" had not materially altered.

A further development occurred in July, 2005 when the IRA announced that the war was over. However, there were many politicians in Ulster and in England who were extremely cautious about the IRA's willingness to end the longstanding suffering and undermining of law and order. The bill for this war has been paid and it makes most tragic reading including: 3,637 killed, 45,000 wounded, 15,300 bomb incidents, 36,000 shootings, 30,000 terrorist convictions and the burden of 300,000 troops deployed since 1969 with an overall cost, according the Daily Telegraph of £100bn (July 29, 2005)

E. SPAIN

The significant terrorist activity in Spain is a domestic one, through ETA (Euskadi ta Askatsuna), although there is also an active group GRAPO (Anti Fascist Armed Group of October 1st). The GRAPO is based on the Reconstituted Common Party of Spain. Many have died because of the activities of this group.

ETA was set up in 1959. Although ETA's members were nationalists, they differed from the traditional and conservative Basque nationalists of the Partido Nacionalista Vasco (PNV), in particular because they rejected calls for moderation and passivity: members of ETA were committed to action. In fact, they were determined to adopt violent measures several months before the death of Txabi Etxebarrieta, the first casualty of ETA, and the killing of Meliton Manzanas, the chief of the Political and Social Brigade of San Sebastian, in August 1968.

ETA has maintained itself by so impressing the local public with the theory and importance of nationalism, that funds have not been slow in following.

In reality, ETA members who pursue their campaign by killing or kidnapping form a small part of the total grouping. Between 1968 and 2000, 796 people have been murdered by ETA, and there are many hundreds of terrorist incidents every year.

The relationship between Spain and France is relevant to the understanding of the way terrorist cooperation functions. France has lent a sympathetic ear to many ETA activists, partly on account of the French support for ETA in opposing the Franco regime. Thus, France provided asylum to hundreds of members of ETA and refused Spain's request to extradite them. Slowly, French attitudes and support for ETA have changed, partly because of French concern with its own terrorists.

With the admission of Spain to the European community in 1984, further progress was made, which has been strengthened over the past few years. The French government has launched aggressive campaigns against ETA, limiting the ETA links quite substantially.

Steps have been taken by the Spanish government towards banning Batasuna, the political wing of the Basque separatist group ETA. Seizing on new international support against terrorism, the government of Prime Minister Jose Maria Aznar toughened its already hard line against Basque violence, stepping up political and police pressure on the separatist group Basque Homeland and Liberty (ETA by its Basque initials). Other tough measures now operate. Most important of these is the power granted to the Supreme Court, at the request of the government or 50 MPs, to ban any political party seen to be supporting terrorism.

Interestingly, Tim Golden of The New York Times comments: *"The government's new actions go well beyond its previous anti-terrorism stance, possibly marking an end to the policy of accommodation with more moderate Basque nationalists that Spanish leaders have generally followed since democracy was restored after the death of the dictator Franco in 1975. Since then, autonomous Spanish regions like the Basque country have amassed more powers of self-government than any similar areas in Europe, taking control of their police forces, schools and social welfare systems, with ample tax revenues ceded by the state"* (29 Aug 2002).

As a strategy to undermine separatist violence, however, the autonomy policies have largely failed. ETA has continued attacks which are blamed for more than 800 killings since 1968, when the group began its fight for a Basque state straddling Spain and France. Moderate nationalists have also continued to find a common cause with Batasuna, confounding the government's efforts to isolate those who condone terrorism.

In this instance, terrorism occupies a unique base in a region of a country, which allows it to formulate policies of its own, while not hesitating to use the stock-in-trade of the terrorist.

During rush hour in Madrid on the morning of March 11, 2004, 10 bombs exploded in three commuter train stations, killing 190 people and wounding 1,600. It was certainly the most devastating act of terrorism in Europe, except for the 1988 bombing of Pan Air Flight 103 over Lockerbie, Scotland.

There was much speculation about the operation and the involvement of likely terrorist groups. In the absence of any immediate theory, the government lost credibility and also an immediate General Election. The outgoing government - and its leader - Jose Maria Aznar - blamed the

ETA. In the weeks that followed, the investigators found evidence that Islamic elements were involved. The new Prime Minister made much of anti-American policies which had contributed to his successful election campaign.

Where did responsibility rest for this barbaric act of terrorism? Al Qaeda's network may have provided the significant inspiration as well as various levels of planning but local Muslims probably did the basic implementation. The police discovered an alliance of many groups of dissidents whilst an ETA link could not be ruled out.

F. INDONESIA

Abu Bakar Bashir has been a central player in the network of Indonesian Islamic leaders since the 1970s. Now, Mr Bashir is accused of being the spiritual leader of Jamaah Islamiyah who, according to Amy Chew, The Times correspondent, is a "shadowy South-East Asia terrorist group and the chief suspect in the Bali bombing." Mr Bashir runs the al-Mukmin Quranic Boarding School in Ngruki village in Solo, central Java, where his students are estimated to number more than 2000. It is a source of profound anxiety that his teachings concentrate on jihad. Students are taught to defend Islam against all infidels.

Bashir's attacks on the United States come thick and fast. Two days before the bombing in Bali, he travelled to Jakarta, in order to condemn the West. Yet he remains a free man in Indonesia. The authorities say that they have no evidence that he is a terrorist. Even with evidence, it is unlikely they would move in on him. A backlash from world Muslim leaders would merely add to the government's woes, which often appear at full stretch in dealing with its terrorist fringes.

Bashir's supporters say that the masses will be mobilised to wage a jihad if Mr Bashir is arrested at the request of "foreigners". In such circumstances, *"we will call upon Muslim youths to prepare to sacrifice their body and soul to defend and protect ulama (teacher)"*.

With a population of 212 million, Indonesia remains a powerful voice for Islam, having 186 million adherents, the largest number of any country.

There is much that is kept from Western eyes. The media seem reluctant to get too close to the conflict in many of the islands. Most serious has been the brutality between Muslims and Christians as thousands have been killed and many churches burnt down. On the island of Surakarta, there is a base for militant Islamic groups advocating sectarian violence across the nation. The seeds of religious strife are everywhere in Indonesia, a factor which helps explain the destruction in Bali. The common cause for many militants is an attack on Western mores and resentment at the tourist trade as reflected in the Bali bombing.

G. INDIA AND PAKISTAN

Terrorism has claimed more lives in India than anywhere else in the world. This claim is made by a specialist in Indian affairs, Ved Marwah (Combating Terrorism. Ed. Y Alexander, 2002). He points out that:

"More than one hundred thousand persons have been murdered by terrorism in various parts of the country. It continues to cause large-scale death and destruction in states like Jammu and Kashmir. Terrorism claimed its first victim in Punjab in 1978 although communal and ethic violence has been a part of the Indian scene since independence in 1947. One of the critical features of terrorism in India is that the country's neighbour, Pakistan, has been assisting every terrorist group in India."

In a large pluralist country like India, the problems of internal security management are considerable. Relatively minor incidents can escalate into major ones. The size of the country, its vast population and the gathering of large numbers of people for meetings, all add to the opportunities for the terrorist as well as inter-religious strife.

The Indian government often seems helpless to combat such widespread terrorism, a problem equally shared with Pakistan.

An increasing armoury of weapons in India has brought the wherewithal to commit violence. As Ved Marwah says, *"The United States pumped in a huge supply of small arms to the Afghan mujahedeens* (those who wage jihad – Islam's holy warriors) *through Pakistan's agencies. These arms have found their way into the hands of many terrorist groups operating in the region. The smuggling of arms into India has been facilitated by the thriving arms bazaars at Dara Adamkhel, Landikotal, and Miran Shah on the Pakistan-Afghanistan border".*

Pakistan also has made use of weaponry to boost its own particular brand of terrorism. In the Punjab, police officers were the favourite targets of Pakistan terrorists and political disputes remain unresolved to this day.

Christians have also been a target in Pakistan. Many have died as buildings and churches have been destroyed, but such outrages have elicited little reaction from the Christian church, either in Canterbury or locally in Pakistan.

A particularly disturbing incident took place on 9 August 2002, in Taxila, when three Pakistani nurses were killed and 23 other people injured as Islamic militants hurled grenades at Christian worshippers leaving the chapel of a Presbyterian missionary hospital near Islamabad. The attack in Taxila was the second on a Christian institution in days and the fourth since President Musharraf (much to the fury of Islamic extremists), joined America's anti-terrorism coalition as a result of September 11 2001. Militants also killed six Pakistanis at a Christian school in the town of Murree, 40 miles to the east.

Increasingly, Christians in Pakistan have become the target of fundamentalist rage over the US led war in Afghanistan. In the period 2001-2, more Christians have died in violent incidents than have members of any other community; they live in constant fear.

Sixteen Christians and one Muslim were killed in October 2001, in a church in the Punjab province, Bahawalpur. Five people, including the wife and daughter of an American diplomat, died in a grenade attack on a church in Islamabad in March 2002.

In Pakistan, wealthy Muslim British businessmen have been condemned for financing training centres seen as a breeding ground for terrorist groups. An investigation in 2002 found damning evidence of prominent Muslim businessmen in Great Britain using bogus charities to funnel millions of pounds to seminaries that produce as many gunmen as they do clergy. A report by the International Crisis Group (ICG), revealed that *madrassas* - hard-line Islamic schools - receive more than £800 million a year through charitable donations – almost the equivalent of Pakistan's income tax revenue. Most of the money comes from abroad, mainly from Muslim countries or from wealthy expatriates living in Britain and the US. Pakistani Government officials say that the main difficulty is to get Britain to stop the funding.

President Musharraf of Pakistan has now stressed the need to bar these schools from taking foreign donations without government approval. India totally supports its neighbours in the claim that Britain has long been a haven for terrorist fundraisers. In July 2002, a team of investigators from India, came to offer Scotland Yard evidence of 14 businessmen in Britain funnelling cash to Islamic seminaries and terrorist groups. At the same time, a senior Indian diplomat said: *"We began this campaign long before September 11 but still nothing is done. The gun is the terrorists' first weapon. The second is dirty money."* (The Times 10 Aug, 2002.)

Whatever the reasons for the degree of inertia by officials in Pakistan and India, the fact remains that Britain has a primary responsibility to act, yet virtually no action has followed the visit to Scotland Yard by the Indian investigators. It goes without saying that large sums of "dirty" money and the training of terrorists needs to be stopped. The Pakistan/Indian scene of conflict hardly needs such an inflammatory operation within its midst.

South Asia is a serious item on the terrorist agenda. An Al-Qaeda statement (issued November 2002) stated that the American people should reject any support for Israel, Russia, the Philippines and India. In a coherently argued article, Jeeran Deol said the West could not afford to ignore South Asia. *"It is yet another front in the War on Terror, even if the US's and Britain's' foreign policy does not recognise it as such"* (The Times, 27 Aug 2003).

Recent events testify to the growing strength of Al-Qaeda in the region. Its activities in India, in particular, are focused on the continuing insurgency in Kashmir. Deol writes that: *"The extent of the connections between Islamist groups in Afghanistan, Pakistan and India began to become clear in the aftermath of the hijacking of an Indian Airlines flight from Kathmandu in December 1999. The Bombay bombings (in August 2003) seem to be yet another link in this chain of terrorist attacks. The perpetrators chose a particularly sensitive juncture in communal relations, with the publication of a long-awaited archaeological report on the religious site of Ayodhya, the cause of an earlier spate of religious-inspired killings. The terrorists behind the bombing were undoubtedly seeking to incite India's 120 million Muslims, one of the largest Muslim populations in the world, against the Hindu majority. Their task is difficult in a country where Muslims are bound by other strong ties of place and ethnicity".*

The Deputy Prime Minister of India, Lal Krisna Advani, did not let the occasion pass without saying *"The attacks raise doubts about our neighbour,"* adding that *"Pakistan's aim was to destabilise the whole country because India's advances in science and technology would work against them"* (The Times, 27 Aug 2003).

The threat of nuclear conflict between India and Pakistan has encouraged Europe and America to determine a defence strategy; but the pace needs to be speeded up, otherwise terrorist groupings will take advantage of the many years of Western indifference.

H. TURKEY

Similar to the case of Colombia, Turkey has had to struggle with the exploitation of drug traffic and terrorism. It is worth noting both the strength of the terrorists' configuration and the link with the bankability of drugs. The question is often put, why terrorism and drugs?

Drugs generate a high level of income, and are easy to transport. In addition, buyers are plentiful, with the possibility of using cash in circulation. Again, in both the smuggling of narcotics and the activities of terrorism, the organisational structure is often identical.

The Kurdish Workers Party (the PKK) is at the centre of the terrorism movement, and is responsible for the murder of **(more than 30 thousand people including women and children)** thousands of innocent people over the past 30 years.

The PKK - **(Kurdish acronym for the "Kurdish Workers' Party," (changed its name to KADEK (Kurdistan Freedom and Democracy Congress) in April 2002, and then to KONGRA-GEL in October 2003, (Kurdistan Peoples Congress), alleging that PKK has fulfilled its historical mission and would now like to be accepted as a political organisation.)** - was formed in 1978 by Abdullah Ocalan.

It has long been regarded as one of the most notorious terror organisations, waging a campaign of terror against Turkey since 1984 with the support of external states and groups, the aim of which is to destabilise Turkey.

PKK was identified as one of the 30 main terrorist organisations in the world by the US Secretary of State in October 1997, and it was described in similar terms in US State Department "Patterns of Global Terrorism" reports. **(PKK/KONGRA-GEL has also been outlawed by a number of countries and the EU).**

The terrorist record of PKK is both similar and compelling. To date, PKK activities have resulted in the death of thousands of people, including the elderly, women, and children. **(21 press members, 5546 security personal, more than 10 thousand civilians)** The PKK has also murdered over one hundred **(116 teachers lost their lives and 48 teachers were wounded)** schoolteachers, who became inevitable targets of the terrorists as a consequence of the realisation that PKK's subversive views could be most easily imposed on the uneducated and ignorant (see appendix C).

Terrorists target ordinary people because they aim to coerce the local population in south eastern Turkey into supporting them. The PKK has attacked whole villages in south east Anatolia, with the object of making the region uninhabitable. The PKK have destroyed schools; set forests on fire; blown up railways and bridges; planted mines on roads; burnt down construction machinery, and demolished health centres.

In response the authorities trained villagers to defend themselves and move the more vulnerable people to locations where they would be safer.

As in other cases of terrorism, the very people on whose behalf they act, Turkish citizens of Kurdish origin, are often those who are murdered or have their homes destroyed.

Owing to its ability to strike Turkey from Syria and (after the 1994 Gulf War) from Northern Iraq, the PKK for some time proved a serious threat to law and order. The PKK has been supported and sheltered by some of

Turkey's neighbours, as well as by others outside the region. It would seem that Syria and Greece are the principle countries that have been supporting the PKK. However, with the signing of the Adana memorandum on 20 October 1998, the Syrian connection has been broken. Syrian authorities have promised not to support terrorist activities against Turkey and have taken steps in this direction. Turkey closely monitors compliance with the Adana agreement, but finds that Greece - a NATO ally - often supports certain elements of the PKK.

A 1995 report prepared by the Drug Enforcement Agency of the US Department of Justice emphasises that the PKK is engaged in drug-trafficking and money-laundering activities and is well established in the production and smuggling of almost all kinds of opium products. The revenue from these activities is used for purchasing firearms, munitions and other equipment used by the terrorists. The report cites other sources of revenue through extortion, robbery and counterfeiting.

"Political Violence and Narco-Trafficking," - a booklet published by the Paris Institute of Criminology in October 1996 - examines PKK's narcotics networks and functioning, drawing attention to the amount of narcotics captured by the European security forces, and documenting the PKK's role in drug trafficking.

The involvement of the PKK in all stages of drug trafficking has been further documented in a conference held by Dr Francois Haut, of the Paris Institute of Criminology, in Brussels on 25 April 1997. It stated that the PKK is engaged in producing, refining and marketing drugs and has contacts in numerous countries. The PKK's turnover from drug trafficking is estimated at "millions of US dollars". Dr Haut notes that the problem of narcotics trafficking has entered the Parisian suburbs thanks to the PKK, which he thinks is responsible for 10-80 % of the heroin smuggled into Paris. In 1996, a report had already been prepared by Haut, Jean Claude Salomon and Jean-Luc Vannier for the Paris Institute of Criminology, utilising reliable and impartial sources such as Interpol, the British NCIS and the national policy authorities of the EU member states. This report notes that the narcotics route that runs through Turkey to the Balkans and Western Europe, benefits the "separatist" organisations of Turkish/Kurdish origin and the PKK militants and their intermediaries.

The March 1997 issue of "The Geopolitical Drug Dispatch," a monthly report prepared by the "Observatoire Geopolitique Des Drogues," points to the role that PKK continues to use the "Balkan route," to smuggle drugs, emphasising the fact that the PKK has started using Romania and Moldova as bases. The Turkish traffickers arrested in these countries are of Kurdish origin and many criminal activities attributed to Turkish individuals or groups are in fact carried on by Kurds, usually with links to the Kurdistan Workers' Party (PKK)". At the same time the PKK often hides behind its umbrella organisations, such as the ERNK, business, youth and women's associations.

The concluding report of the thirty-third session of the Sub-Commission on Illicit Drug Traffic and Related Matters in the Near and Middle East, held under the auspices of the UN International Drug Control Programme (UNCDP) in Beirut from 29 June to 3 July 1998, noted that *"there were clear linkages between some narco-terrorist organisations, for example the Kurdistan Workers' Party (PKK), and other organized trans- national criminal groups"*. PKK personally manages the distribution of narcotic substances.

Why the Linkage between PKK and other Trans-National Groups?
These common properties may be counted as follows:

- In both organisations, as outlaws of society, secrecy is essential.

- An activity of cell operations is carried out.

- There are responsibility areas according to activity areas.

- They form pressure groups in the countries where they are present.

- It is essential that the various leaders should not be revealed to other members of the organisation.

In the 5th item of the United Nations Organization International Narcotics Control Bureau (INCIB) 1992 report, the linkage was expressed very bluntly: *Illegal narcotics production and smuggling has increased in the World, and apart from this, it is pointed out that the same organisations are involved in the production, distribution and marketing of drugs in order to finance the terror activities.*

A Further Note on the Financing of Terrorism: (Saudia Arabia)
Apart from utilising drugs as a source of income to terrorist groups, payments are laundered directly from state to terrorist. On 18 September 2003, The Times reported the United States had stepped up pressure on Saudi Arabia, to halt financial support for terrorist organisations, after fresh charges that millions of pounds had been sent to Hamas, the Palestinian militant group, via a charity.

According to a report from Riyadh in The New York Times, (17 Sept 2003) Khalid Mishaal, a senior Hamas official, visited Saudi Arabia in

October 2002 and allegedly attended a fundraising conference, where he met Crown Prince Abdullah, the de facto Saudi ruler. A summary of the meeting recorded by a Hamas official, said that Mr Mishaal and other Hamas figures thanked the Saudis for sending aid *"despite all the American pressure exerted on them,"* and praised them for *"a brave posture".* US officials believe that Hamas receives half of its annual £6 million budget from Saudi donations. A copy of a Hamas document apparently seized by Israeli forces during a raid last December in the Gaza Strip was shown to the newspaper by a former Israeli official.

This is all the more remarkable given the Saudi assurance, during the summer of 2003, of their determination to confront terrorism.

KNOW YOUR ENEMY

The intelligence services are constantly searching for the links between the various combination of cells – not just to identify a particular terrorist cell. It is likely that there are in Britain - at any one time - some 20 active cells.

Keith Doukants and Steve Boggan shocked many with their revelations of the strength and determination of the Algerian terrorists in Britain. (Evening Standard, 16 Jan 2003.) The video, "Algeria", which is partly a training document, shows among other incidents, how a young man's throat is cut. The camera lingers over the fountain of blood that spurts and bubbles from his carotid artery. The victim is a soldier in Algeria's militia; his executioner is a member of a terrorist group that distributed the video to Muslims in London as part of a drive to recruit new volunteers. Copies of the film were sold for £10 in mosques and black market bazaars.

What is the organisation of the cell? Christopher C Harmon, (Terrorism Today, Cass 2000) says a cell provides for recruits to a particular cause, a base, an "office". The recruits once trained are subsumed into the cell. The group may be inactive for a lengthy period of time depending on its role:

"Whether a group's objective is to survive as a persistent thorn in the government's paw, which may be all that the Greek group November 17 expects, or whether it is to develop into a full-blown insurgency that rivals the government in power, which has always been the intention of the New People's Army in the Philippines, eye-catching actions can only succeed when supported by a quiet, systematic, effective infrastructure. Clandestine cells make up the heart of this structure; they are its essence, whether or not the group also has overt political fronts. Cells evolved readily out of Second World War resistance movements in Soviet Russia, France and Scandinavia, and were promptly copied after 1945 by insurgents eager

to take advantage of global changes and opportunities opened up by the war. The Vietnamese, Malaysian and Philippine movements all included methods and personnel from the anti-Japanese war. To these were added entirely new movements, especially the FLN insurgency in Algeria. Whilst French forces managed to destroy the cell structure in the Algerian capital, they could not do so in the countryside, nor could they deal effectively with army units across the borders in safe havens in Tunisia and Morocco".

The strength of the cell organisation is its simplicity and its apparent loose structure so that its links with other cell partners is not explicit. *"Within each cell,"* says Harman, *"which is typically three to ten persons, a member may not even know all his or her compatriots. When cells may act in ignorance of the strategic purpose of the action, or even about the full dimensions of the operations; one knows only what one must. The result is an organisation which can act decisively and quickly. Also such an organisation cannot easily be "rolled up" by security forces who capture some personnel and use them to identify the others. Only a senior leader can give away that kind of intelligence to security forces and he or she rarely does".* Consequently, the members of the cell are unaware of the total organisation and therefore they are not able to identify the composition of the other cells. Infiltrations are likely, but they will need to be actively involved and contribute to the cell's moves for many months or years.

Nevertheless it is the task of the intelligence services to monitor all likely groupings and, as such, their role demands equal organisation and patience. Maintaining efficient scrutiny and monitoring on a particular house or houses may involve considerable resources and personnel. The strain on the intelligence services is considerable.

An additional complication for the intelligence services in Britain is the growing number of asylum seekers, who have little or no papers to establish their previous status. As Norman Lebrecht said: *"Under present rules, immigration officials cannot discriminate between a Muslim from Iraq who spent months in one of Saddam's jails and a mullah from Algeria who is silenced by the militarist regime in his own country but ferments extremism here"* (Evening Standard, 17 Jan 2003).

There are about 50,000 Iraqi refugees presently in Britain. Of particular concern are the illegal asylum seekers, many of whom have been refused entry by other EU countries, particularly France and Germany. The UK government needs to act to break the link between illegal asylum seekers and possible terrorist recruitment. The best means of dealing with international terrorism is to educate the public as to the extent and scale of terrorism. It may be too much to penetrate the terrorist mind and the particular root causes of terrorism, but the intent and resources of the terrorist are open to explanation. As the UK Home Secretary said, clearly and unambiguously, *"Although we are in a new era of terrorism, I am determined not to close down Britain".* The Prime Minster followed this up at the Lord Mayor's Banquet, when he announced that, *"The Intelligence services are defecting terrorist threats against British targets on a daily basis."* (11 November 2002). He went on to say that, *"The purpose of terrorism is of course not just to kill and maim. As the name suggests terrorism is about terror. It is to scare people, disrupt their normal lives, produce chaos and disorder distort proper and sensible decision-making... The dilemma is reconciling warning people without alarming them; taking preventative measures without destroying normal life".*

But a large section of the public doesn't want to know about such unpleasantness. It is disruptive to our social habits. "Where is the evidence?" has become the standard aimed at deflecting attention from uncomfortable issues.

In a dossier published in December 2002, Giles Whittell, describes the abuses of the Saddam Hussein regime (The Times, 5 Dec 2002). What makes the dossier all the more powerful is that it is based on documents captured from the Iraqis. *"Saddam Hussein takes pride in the velvet glove,"* reports Mr Whittell. *"This is after all a bureaucracy that has an entire agency devoted to reminding its members of each other's birthdays and wedding anniversaries. But non-members are more likely to have felt its iron fist".*

"We do not object to the decapitation of traitors," said 'Chemical Ali' Hasan al-Majid, Saddam Hussein's chief enforcer in response to a query from one of his northern commandants about killing methods. *"But it would have been preferable if you had sent them to Security for the purpose of interrogating them. Security personnel could have extracted significant information from them prior to their execution".* Behead by all means, but torture first. Such was the likely fate, both organised and savage, of Saddam's Kurdish prisoners at the time that their less fortunate brethren were being gassed before the first Gulf War. Once Kuwait was invaded, protocol suffered. One Iraqi general wrote to another that Kuwaitis were in the habit of praying in large numbers on their rooftops, only to be told: *"This can be remedied by opening fire on the roofs in question with all weapons".*

To improve the quality of British intelligence is a major priority. It starts with training personnel in such a way that they learn to project themselves into the mind of Al-Qaeda or any other terrorist leader who wishes to harm, maim or destroy British subjects and its institutions. Unfortunately, Britain is regarded as a soft touch, a safe haven for terrorists and murderers. This is the view of Mohamed Sifaouri, who wrote a four-month diary whilst posing as an Islamic militant. In a <u>Sunday Times</u> interview, he insists that London has become the European nerve-centre for hard-core Islamists: *"They can plan attacks, recruit members and spread their ideology whilst often receiving state benefits. It is every terrorist's dream"* (3 Aug 2003).

In his diary, he relates how he and his group met in cafes on the Edgware Road with leaders who were wanted for terrorist acts in other countries, but were living openly in London, often on social security and housing benefits. He also describes coming into England on the Eurostar with Al-Qaeda members travelling on fake passports. Watching the police at Waterloo reserve their questioning for those in Islamic dress, one Al-Qaeda member remarked contemptuously: *"They still haven't understood that the day the brothers come to commit an attack they won't be wearing beards or djellabas".*

Preventative action is always the preferable course. Following the outrage in Bali, the Indonesian President Sukarnoputri set up a joint Indonesian and Australian investigative team, helped by officers from seven countries, including Britain. Despite vast resources, the investigators had little to go on. The force of the bomb had destroyed a lot of evidence. Much of what was left was ruined by panicking holidaymakers, rescue workers, journalists and others who rushed to the scene. Today, we need to learn to live with an increasing number of terrorist actions. Mistakes have been made by the various security services, both in Europe and the United States, with serious consequences.

Apart from the increasing number of teams monitoring, appraising and identifying likely suspects and cells, the financial back-up is a more obvious clue as to the power and strength of terrorist organisations. For instance, the terrorist network of Osama Bin Laden struck deals in blood diamonds several months before 11 September 2001. <u>The Observer</u> newspaper recalled the extent of the stockpile (20 Oct, 2002).

The stones were illegally mined by the Revolutionary United Front rebels in Sierra Leone: *"Given that the attacks on America cost only about $500,000 it is terrifying that al-Qaeda managed to convert $20m of its cash into diamonds,"* said Alex Yearsly of <u>Global Witness</u>. *"The ease with which terrorist organisations can use diamonds as a source of funding and money laundering is frightening; they can easily transport them over borders without detection and convert them back into banknotes whenever they need the money."* According to information leaked by European and Belgian government officials, Aziz Nassour, a Lebanese diamond merchant, employed couriers to exchange $300,000 for diamonds every week between December 2000 and September 2001.

More input of terrorist planning comes from their own revelations about their previous attacks. For instance, two of Osama bin Laden's closest aides gave an interview to Nick Fielding on how they prepared for September 11. The two ringleaders, Khalid Sheikh Mohammed and Ramzi Binalshibh are among the FBI's most wanted terrorists. They have evaded capture despite the $25m bounties on their heads.

Khalid, the head of Al-Qaeda's military committee, devised the idea of targeting prominent buildings in America. Binalshibh co-ordinated the operation from his base in Hamburg, where he shared an apartment with Mohammed Atta, a leading hijacker. At least four reconnaissance units were sent to America before Atta and the would-be hijack pilots crossed the Atlantic for their training at flying schools in the summer of 2000. Atta communicated with Binalshibh in German through the Internet. He posed as a student in America contacting his girlfriend "Jenny" in Germany. They referred to the targets as university departments. The Twin Towers were the "faculty of town planning"; Atta's academic speciality, Capitol Hill, was the "faculty of law," and the Pentagon was "the faculty of fine arts". Even allowing for the terrorists' likely intention to mislead, the information gives a picture of the speed and nature of their procedures (The Sunday Times, N Fielding, 8 Sept 2002).

Perhaps an even more valuable source of information is obtained about the enemy mind with the capture of terrorist leaders in their cells, which the United States was able to achieve in Afghanistan.

In September 2002, before the UN Commissioning force landed in Iraq, the International Institute for Strategic Studies (IISS), London, published a comprehensive study of the dangers imminent in Iraq's impending nuclear capability. The ISS examined every scrap of evidence in the public domain. Paul Beaver, of Jane's Defence Weekly, described its findings as the best available documentation (10 Sept 2002). Beaver comes to the striking conclusion that: *"If Iraq had sufficient material it could probably make nuclear weapons on short order".*

Intelligence material is also supported by journalists such as Sam Kiley, of The Evening Standard, who wrote a graphic account of the city's social environment, describing the decapitation of wives and mothers by sword-wielding execution gangs in public squares. (A Social Review of Baghdad Life Today, 7 Nov 2002.) The crime of these women lay in criticising the regime. Kiley says, *"News of the executions was kept out of the Iraqi media but it spread by word of mouth amid fearful speculation about the reasons behind the killings".* According to Human Rights' groups, one of the women murdered in October 2000, was Najat Mohammed Haidar, a middle-aged obstetrician. Opposition organisations said she was killed because she complained about the black market in medicines at her hospital. Kiley's account is revealing about the horror of living in Iraq.

A state bent on destruction and violence will go to great lengths both to conceal what it wants to remain hidden and to reveal "information" which a gullible or intimidated public will be only too willing to believe.

A conspiracy of silence is also found in North Korea, where mountains are being cut into in order to house their latest nuclear machinery. Choon Sun Lee, a senior official in North Korea's military infrastructure told Peter Beaumont of The Observer, just how this was achieved (29 Dec 2002). "He described a massive tunnel extending more than a mile into the heart of the mountain. That tunnel opened into vast underground facilities housed in the chambers carved out of the rock. Included in those facilities, is a process line for turning uranium ore into yellowcake, the first step in the process towards enriching it into weapon-grade material." From there, said Choon, the ore was taken by truck and helicopter to an underground facility in a hidden valley.

Hawkish Western opinion has been bolstered by defections that reveal North Korea's plans to target US bases first in the event of a new Korean war: North Korea's goal would be the domination of the entire Korean peninsula.

In all these instances, we are reminded of the need to know the level of commitment of institutional and state terrorism. The information may not be comprehensive, nor will it answer all the questions posed by the West but, at the very least, it offers a picture of the way in which many countries are prepared to violate the human rights of their citizens.

ARE THERE REMEDIES IN DEALING WITH INTERNATIONAL TERRORISM?

There are opportunities for governments, public bodies and individuals to divert and challenge the terrorist group and the terrorist state, but vigilance and prompt action are essential. Apart from the political demands and alignments of the world's former blocks and the failure of many world institutions (such as the UN), to deal with terrorism effectively, there are still issues to be confronted. Understanding the causes of terrorism and the mind of a terrorist is crucial. For the would-be terrorist there is considerable pressure on the individual once he or she is accepted into the groups. They will already be brainwashed and they will be promised much, not only in this world but the next (the "many virgins" waiting for Muslim fundamentalists). They will have had training, often quite extensive, to hate everyone associated with the government or legal system they are opposing. They are robotic in their thinking; they are repeatedly warned about the traps of the enemy. They will acknowledge that their role is a limited one, particularly if they work in cells. The cell is supreme; it is confined, and this very confinement also provides their security.

A second major constraint for the terrorist is that in many cases they have been chosen because they want a payback for their family. The rewards for some individuals in the group are high.

Thirdly, a significant constraint is the terrorist's fear of his own unit. The IRA and, more recently, the real IRA developed the technique of fear so that the terrorist not only does not stray, or inform, but also keeps up a high level of performance and loyalty. Kneecapping and shooting off limbs are warnings, with death the ultimate penalty, both for the individual and for members of the family who get in the way. If an IRA member was known to have defected or perhaps even disappeared, the close family would be in grievous danger - the authority of the group and its dominance over the individual is thus firmly established.

Part of the response in countering terrorism is to infiltrate lines of communication and informants. Following 11 September 2001, President Bush made it clear that not enough had been done by the CIA and associated agencies to counter terrorism and he pressed for a large number of people to be recruited specifically for this purpose.

Fundamentally, combating terrorism depends on the way governments provide resources and personnel for the work demanded. The answer lies also in tackling the issues at the roots of terrorism to ensure and, as far as possible, guarantee a stable economy and sensitivity to basic human needs.

Yet for all the intended solutions, terrorism is likely to be a permanent fixture of international life. As Yonah Alexander remarks:

"Terrorism will continue epitomizing the state of anarchy in modern societies that is becoming a universal nightmare. It is safe to assume, therefore, that terrorism will continue into the twenty-first century. This prognosis is born from the reality that many of the causes that motivate terrorists, such as ideological, political and national animosities, will remain unresolved, thereby encouraging terrorists to instigate violence to achieve political, economic and social change." ("Combating Terrorism", 2002.)

Terrorism has proved to be very successful in attracting publicity and disrupting governments and business. The public finds it difficult to come to terms with the scale of impact and unless there has been a major incident involving a significant city - let alone a country - there will be a dismissive reaction rather than a determined response. So we do not think about the "unthinkable". Advances in science and technology make the equipment and know-how easily transferable between terrorist groups, so there is no immunity for the non-combatant nation. With both technological and financial pulling power, terrorist groups will attempt to improve their bargaining leverage by resorting to mass destructive violence. No serious-minded government can ignore such dangers. Alexander puts this argument even more strongly: *"In view of these considerations the arsenal of tomorrow's terrorist might include biological, chemical and nuclear instruments of massive potential. These weapons are capable of producing from several thousand to several million casualties in a single incident and of causing governmental disruption of major proportions and widespread public panic".*

What can be done? This is a question often asked at lectures, inevitably towards the end of any session as the audience, anxious or disillusioned with the way terrorism has become a growing threat to a civilised modus vivendi, seeks to establish an opportunity for peace and, specifically, some containment of the menace.

Before dealing with specific issues, let us consider a positive development and response to terrorism at a laboratory complex in New Mexico, USA, where technologies are being delivered to combat the terror threat. The Sandia complex was established especially to provide knowledge and competence to deal with terrorist attacks armed with weapons of mass destruction.

A U.S. Department of Energy (DOE) research and development laboratory that also works for the Department of Defence (DoD) and other federal agencies, Sandia has ties with other federal groups, universities, and private industry, to provide scientific and engineering solutions to meet important national needs. Sandia's primary mission for more than 50 years has been to ensure the safety, security and reliability of the US nuclear stockpile. In the 1970's, Sandia's involvement in counter-terrorism and anti-terrorism programmes took off as part of the work to develop technology which would protect nuclear weapons and nuclear energy facilities against terrorists. Much of this technology proved valuable for securing other important facilities and is now helping to fight terrorism throughout the world. Further technological advances will undoubtedly follow at Sandia in response to the growth in terrorism.

Current advances include designing 'smart buildings,' with sensors that detect the faintest presence of chemical, biological or radioactive agents in the air. These sensors are linked to computers that can seal off the buildings air-intake system and alert specially trained decontamination teams. Sandia are perfecting a new type of glass that turns to powder during explosions, rather than lethal, high-velocity shards. "We can engineer buildings to withstand terrorist attacks like we engineer them now to withstand fire or earthquakes," says Sandia's chief executive.

Sandia's mission is to meet national needs in four key areas:

- Nuclear Weapons – ensuring the stockpile is safe, secure, reliable, and can support the United States' deterrence policy;

- Non-proliferation and materials control – reducing the proliferation of weapons of mass destruction, the threat of nuclear accidents, and the potential for damage to the environment;

- Energy and critical infrastructure – enhancing the surety of energy and other critical infrastructures;

- Emerging threats – addressing new threats to national security.

7,000 permanent employees have responsibility for the task in hand. All the anti and counter-terrorism work is laid down in a five-part proposal devised by the Advanced Concept Group. The aim, according to its Director, Gerry Yonas, is to restore the sense of safety and security enjoyed prior to September 11: to turn terrorism into a psychosocial problem similar to fire (The Telegraph Magazine, 5 April 2003).

The nearest equivalent to Sandia in Britain is the MOD's Defence Science and Technology Laboratory. Increasingly close relations exist between these two bodies.

On the global level, terrorism may have to be met by a nation's full force. This came to a head with Iraq and provoked virtually a world debate, as the US stance was to search out the links between Al-Qaeda and the leadership of Iraq. The "modern war," which the US and Britain were attempting, required UN endorsement to ensure a fully co-ordinated response; in the event this was not forthcoming. A combination of anti-war protesters found their voices, ignoring the dreadful record of Saddam Hussein, some even going to Baghdad, to act as human shields. Predictably one British MP and one former MP succeeded in getting themselves press coverage as they went to interview Saddam and his supporters. At the same time, opinions were changing towards a reasonable use of force to overcome the terrorist menace exposed by The Observer editorial on 19 January 2003, a paper normally of the left on these issues and sister to the (anti-war) The Guardian: The Observer made its position clear: *"The debate in Britain and Europe continues to focus largely on what America is doing and why.*

Too often, it is overlooked that it is Iraq, which remains, at the eleventh hour, in defiance of the will of its region and the wider world".

Some will still argue that because the world contains other unpleasant dictators, why get rid of this one? The recent past contains several examples of military intervention against sovereign states where the outcome, if not ideal, has certainly been much better in humanitarian terms than what went before: Vietnam's removal of Pol Pot from Cambodia; Nato's Kosovo campaign, resulting in the subsequent indictment of Slobodan Milosevic, and the removal of the Taliban from Afghanistan, are surely steps in the right direction.

Mary-Ann Sieghart, added an interesting aside in <u>The Times</u>: *"I would be instinctively opposed to war without UN sanction, but I can see why it was worth threatening it. France and Russia are both tempted to curry favour with Saddam – and win lucrative oil contracts – by vetoing a Security Council resolution. However, once they know that Saddam will be removed whether they like it or not, they realise that a veto will be completely counterproductive. It will leave them with no influence (or oil contracts) in a post Saddam Iraq"* (29 Jan 2003).

In other words, France and Russia, engaged in trading even in the early stages of the Iraqi War. The only way to deal with this kind of chicanery is to challenge it - hard. To achieve the result that you want – either no war or war with UN backing – you have to threaten something worse. That is why, contrary to all appearances, Bush and Blair have done the right thing.

Some commentators argued that to go to war with Iraq would divert attention and resources away from the main terrorist threat, Al-Qaeda.

Others argued that the Israel/Palestinian conflict was a factor in the Iraqi war. This is a dubious proposition. Israel only seeks a secure peace, and clearly it would be to her advantage to have a more reliable, trusting, democratic ethos in the Arab states around her. This view is supported by Dr Adel Safty in <u>Perceptives</u> (June/August 2002). He urges the Arab regimes and Muslim countries to mount a credible and sustainable response to their critics:

"The most effective and truly lasting response can only come from a renewed and sustained serious commitment to the process of democratisation that has already started in many countries in the Middle East and the Arab world.

In many (Muslim and Arab) countries the powers of the judicial and legislative branches are constrained, and opposition parties have only limited access to the media. New political parties must receive governmental permission to become legal. The executive office continues to be largely uncontested".

Safty is right, since this would enable the Israelis to take a new gamble in the peace process, secure in the knowledge that the "other side" also has democratic processes and a free media, so that the debate which takes place about government actions in Israel would also take place in the Arab world - a debate which might well loosen voices against the fundamentalists and the terrorists.

Further, Safty argues: *"There is no doubt whatsoever that the failure of various governments in the Middle East and the Arab World to broaden the basis of their popular support to provide more avenues for power-sharing, and address chronic issues of corruption, and socio economic inequities, can only add to people's distrust of, and disillusionment with, their governments. It also plays into the hands of groups advocating a fundamentalist and restrictive interpretation of Islam and seeking to establish a more restrictive political order."*

CHAPTER 6
TELLING THE PUBLIC

Despite many difficulties confronting the Western powers following 11 September 2001, a number of critical issues need to be acted upon. Never again should the West be so paralysed. The public services in the United States acted admirably in the emergency but, from the military point of view, there was no immediate counter-offensive to pursue and attack Al-Qaeda. Although the military eventually moved into Afghanistan, it was not a broad-based campaign to knock our terrorist targets and key operatives.

Along with an improvement of our intelligence services, the corresponding PR machine needs overhauling. More needs to be done to give a consistent message to the public in Britain on terrorist activity and dangers. The PR success of the Falklands war was the daily press commentary surrounding events and progress, and the sure touch of the presenter. What we have witnessed in Britain is a number of senior Ministers of State giving their own version, or interpretations, of the terrorist threat rather than a coordinated approach. Something similar happened in the United States but, fortunately, President Bush cut a swathe through red tape and bureaucracy. There can be no double meanings or ambiguous messages while a country is at war.

Despite the resources put into fighting the Iraqi war and confronting the danger of a terrorist attack in Britain, we remain vulnerable, according to a Foreign Affairs Select Committee report, which found that: *"Al-Qaeda remains the world's best funded terrorist group despite the war and the seizure of £74 million in assets. As a movement Al-Qaeda has more actual trained militants with expertise that can be used in terrorist operations than any previous international terrorist movement that we have known.*

At least 17,000 Al-Qaeda foot soldiers are at large around the world" (1 Aug 2003). The report as a whole confirms the enormity of the danger to the Western World and the need for Britain to stay alert.

The dangers of confronting terrorism need to be explained more closely. In the United States, for instance, in late 2002, there was wide public discussion on smallpox jabs. In Britain, well into 2003, there were some government announcements but, when challenged about the dangers of smallpox, the appropriate minister said *"no comment"*. Whilst we hesitated on the more appropriate action, a million Americans were given smallpox vaccinations. At the initial stage, 500,000 military personnel and 510,000 civilian medical workers also received the jab.

The second step involved up to ten million frontline workers such as the police, the emergency services and other healthcare staff who would be the first to respond to a bio-terror attack. The smallpox vaccine was then made available to any member of the public who wanted one.

Much of our expertise in dealing with emergencies and major incidents needs upgrading. A priority would be to get the public to be given regular, reliable information to enable them to understand the extent of a likely terrorist threat.

The media has generally been helpful. The Times, along with other newspapers, printed a "Most Wanted Terrorist" list (6 Sept 2002) explaining their records and why they are such dangerous criminals. It is conceivable that such a dramatic presentation may have had a deterrent effect on many young Muslims in Britain who might have been tempted to join up on the side of Iraq.

On another level of exposure, it is worth noting that it was admitted in a Cabinet Office document that, since the end of the Cold War, government offices have not been geared up for a major attack on the population. It also suggested there are problems over funding: *"The current position is that while many government offices possess a cadre of staff with experience in helping respond to emergencies, they are prevented by resource constraints from developing a full planning and crisis management capability"*.

The government should demand more support and backup from local councils, health services, fire and police. Matters have improved since 11 September 2001, but then we were living in "cloud cuckoo-land" – major terrorism could not possibly happen here!

It is to the credit of the Essex County Council, that they began to inform people of terrorist activities through a series of advertisements and leaflets. *"The idea is not to scare people, but it is important to inform them of sensible steps which everyone can take,"* said a spokesman. In short, the media also has a part to play in explaining the dangers and issues of terrorism without being contrived or overstated.

By November 2002, some positive steps were being taken. Government Officials told <u>The Observer</u>: *"Emergency security measures including a rapid reaction forces of Army reservists and a squadron of fighter jets on constant stand by, have been set up to cope with a terrorist strike in Britain"* (10 Nov 2002).

Special "quick response" fighter jets are now based at the RAF bases at Marham in Norfolk, St Mawgan in Cornwall and the Royal Naval Air Station at Yeovilton in Somerset, to provide extra protection from any hijacked planes. The pilots have had psychological training to prepare them to shoot down a civilian plane being used as a terrorist weapon.

There were further signs that the government were now taking the terrorist threat more seriously. Britain's Defence Minister agreed to a missile shield. At the Foreign Policy Centre, London, he admitted that the country could be targeted by rogue states, which were now trying to arm themselves with long-range ballistic missiles and weapons of mass destruction. If deterrents failed, Britain would need a back-up system to pre-empt such an attack. The government was seriously considering joining the Americans in deploying a missile defence barrier against rogue states (13 Nov 2002).

"The reality is that once a ballistic missile has been launched against us, deterrence has failed and the only recourse left to us is to try and shoot it down. Thus, a further capability to this current range of responses, is by acquiring missile defences for the UK and for Europe as a whole, in the way the US has already decided".

The big cities are particularly vulnerable. London was slow to take up the New York initiative in spending, but in the end, allocated a mere £1m on a couple of mobile emergency trailers filled with containment vessels that can isolate, analyse and transport samples of suspected germs or chemicals. The vehicles also carry antidotes and medicines. They would be the capital's front-line tanks after a bacterial invasion. After some delay, the decontamination units have been acquired for London.

Whatever the outcome of events in the next two to three years, all households should be encouraged to understand how to survive a major terrorist attack.

Such a measure by the government to encourage local authorities, would mean a wide range of considerations, including householders advised to have a reserve supply of food and water, and be shown how to access evacuation plans, if the danger of radiation or gas poisoning proved too great.

The health sector would have a critical role in any terrorist attack. In 2003, a study by the National Audit Office (NAO) reported that nearly a quarter of hospitals across Britain were unprepared for a chemical, biological or radioactive terrorist attack. More than a year after September 11, a third of hospitals had failed to test their plans for a major disaster and many trusts admitted that they have not trained staff properly in decontamination techniques.

In London, where the threat of attack is deemed greatest, the ambulance service told the Audit office that it did not have the resources to deal with mass casualties (anything over 500 people).

The National Audit Office report warned:

"Acute trusts have identified some major gaps in preparedness, specifically in relation to chemical, biological, radiological and nuclear threats. Reasons included lack of equipment, training and expertise". The chief executives of hospital, ambulance and primary care trusts should be urged to continue to act with speed to improve their planning and readiness.

A great deal of information now exists as a result of the many bomb attacks around the world on proper evacuation processes. Experience elsewhere argues for evacuation plans to be put into government leaflets, to avoid people leaving the area immediately without waiting to hear of the nature of the attack. *"This could prove disastrous in the event of certain kinds of chemical attack or a second explosion".*

A booklet by the Home Office has appeared late in the day (February 2003). It gives warnings along the lines we have urged on coping with chemical, biological, radiological and nuclear attack. The 38-page booklet makes a valid point, namely, that in the event of an attack the public may not automatically realise they are involved in a serious emergency. *"It is likely that a terrorist attack would involve a specific target such as a VIP, critical or iconic location, or high-profile event."* The document also noted that the public may not display any symptoms for hours or even days following a sudden biological, radioactive or chemical attack.

Thus the plans of all the emergency services need to be merged and tested again and again. There is no room for error in this type of crisis.

More security is needed when travelling on holidays abroad. Brian Newsome, a lecturer in security at the University of Reading, claims that not enough is being done by the travel industry to warn us (The Times, 18 Jan 2003). Newsome believes that an attack on a large group of British tourists is Al-Qaeda's main aim now that they have scored major hits against Americans (on 11 September 2001), Australians (in the Bali bomb) and Israelis (in the Mombassa hotel blast). In his opinion, package tours are too exposed. He proposes that we fundamentally change the way we take holidays if we are to stay safe. For example, taking package holidays to destinations in Africa and South East Asia is a bad idea, he says, as they oblige one to travel on western-style tour buses emblazoned with the holiday company's name, and to stay in big resort hotels that are often, in terms of the dress, demeanour and wealth of the guests, a world away from the lives of the local people outside the gates.

Whilst this advice may be regarded as unrealistic in the travel industry and may not be altogether convenient for many travellers, his words appear to be more intelligent than the blanket information offered by the Foreign Office, where information is often presented without taking into consideration specific local conditions.

Finally, to improve our understanding of the terrorist mind it would be of considerable value if research into the various terrorists' activities and objectives could be made more readily available in simple pamphlet form.

In Britain, we could also benefit from the example of institutions and research bodies such as the International Law Institute, Potomac Institute and the International Centre for Terrorism Studies in Washington. In visiting these institutions in Washington, one is struck by their ability to bring together teams of people from all disciplines to consider the wide variety of issues thrown up by terrorism. Invariably, their reports land on the desks of congressional leaders and of the President's advisers. The bodies mentioned educate policy makers and the public in general on the nature and intensity of the terrorist threat in the twenty-first century. The purpose of the International Centre for Terrorism Studies (ICTS), is four-fold:

First, to monitor current and future threats of terrorism; second, to develop response strategies on governmental and non-governmental levels; third, to effect continual communication with policy-makers, academic institutions, business, media and civic organizations; and fourth, to sponsor research programs on critical issues, particularly those relating to technological policies and sharing the findings nationally and internationally.

At the very least such bodies help to prepare policy makers not to be caught out by growing terrorist sophistication, for example in the dramatic incident, in December 2002, when a Northern Korean ship attempted to smuggle scud missiles through the Arabian Sea. The view of the International Centre for Terrorism Studies, is that a maritime disaster is not a matter of if but when.

Recent events have provided us with a bleak outlook. In October 2002, the French oil tanker, MV Limburg, was targeted by an Al-Qaeda fishing craft laden with explosives, as the tanker was headed into Yemeni waters. The terrorists killed one crew member, caused a fire, and released 50,000 barrels of crude oil along the coastline.

An earlier attack on 12 October 2000 saw the bombing of the USS Cole in the port of Aden. Suicide operators crashed their boat, equipped with specially designed charges, into the hull, killing 17 and wounding 30 American sailors, and causing $100 million in damage to the vessel.

These are serious issues, because the sea offers opportunities for terrorists to transfer equipment without crossing boundaries and achieve considerable damage to supplies and loss of life. Maritime industries remain extremely vulnerable to attack.

Another particular area of growing concern relates to the offshore oil platforms. Offshore targets are susceptible to attack from the surface, underwater and air. A well-placed explosive or a guided missile could seriously damage or destroy an offshore facility. The relative ease with which such an operation could be carried out makes offshore facilities inviting targets. A determined and dedicated terrorist element, directed by or linked to Al-Qaeda is a very strong possibility, in which a facility could be captured and the crew held hostage. Terrorists could threaten to blow up the rig, causing a major oil spill unless demands were met. Thus far, American oil executives have been reluctant to confront the problem, fearing that discussion might invite criticism from their shareholders!

Another worrisome area is the vulnerability of nuclear maritime targets. Their historic record provides some clues about future threats. It is unlikely that terrorists would attack a well-protected target, such as a nuclear submarine. But they will, no doubt have opportunities for related options, directing their attention to the essential components for nuclear weapons – most notably plutonium and enriched uranium, both of which have application in non-military commercial nuclear reactors.

One example of a vulnerable commercial target is the trans-oceanic energy shipping industry between Europe and Asia. In mid-June 2002, two British transport ships carrying nuclear materials - the Pacific Pintail and the Pacific Teal - arrived in the port of Takahama, Japan. The two ships were loaded with rejected mixed plutonium and uranium oxides, or MOX, and between them carried fuel for 17 nuclear bombs.

These ships then set sail for Britain on 4 July 2002 under the direction of British Nuclear Fuels. Even though the Japanese Coast Guard was monitoring these ships, there was widespread international criticism as the boats were regarded as 'floating bombs', inviting ignition and detonation.

What makes this event potentially catastrophic is not only that it illustrates maritime vulnerability to acts of extremism and terrorism, but also reveals an additional hazard: an international event with 2.7 million people on hand in Japan and nearby South Korea, to celebrate the World Soccer Tournament, creating the perfect "target audience" for terrorist groups.

SECURITY IN THE UK

Much greater checks need to be made on immigrants. Questions surrounding asylum seekers need to be met head-on and not fudged. Sensitive though the subject may be, it must be explored.

Norman Lebrecht of the <u>Evening Standard</u> made a telling contribution to this debate, arguing that it cannot be right for those who profess allegiance to another country with different values to be admitted to the UK: *"Those who are now gaining entry include Muslim fundamentalists who proclaim their desire to convert this country to sharia law, put its women under chadors, ban music and restore capital punishment for the crime of adultery. These fanatics congregate around rabble-rousing mullahs, who adulate Osama Bin Laden and preach death to America and its allies"* (17 Jan 2003). It is a dilemma which the Home Secretary has itemised very carefully, pointing out the dangers if the level and numbers of illegal immigrants continue to rise.

There is a world of difference between the asylum seekers who came here to the UK over the centuries and what is happening now. As Lebrecht says, *"The problem is not the degree of danger from which asylum seekers have fled, but the degree of threat they might pose to this country. Previous waves of immigrants came to Britain because they admired our way of life... Many Algerians, on the other hand, are here because they embrace a militant doctrine. They spew hatred on those who give them shelter and despise British Muslims who have merged Westernism with their religious traditions. Such fanatics, along with others from Saudi Arabia Egypt and Yemen should never have been allowed in."*

There is a further worry. <u>The Muslim News</u> has reported on crimes against British Muslims, including attacks on women, arson and bomb threats. The Islamic community exists in a "climate of fear" since the advent of 11 September 2001. More than 100 confirmed incidents were reported by the <u>Muslim News</u>, as "a very small sample" of anti-Islam attacks over a period of 15 days. In one of the worst incidents, a woman was beaten on the head with a metal baseball bat by two white men while on her way home from work in Swindon, Wiltshire. In Glasgow, a female student was viciously assaulted orally and physically, while travelling on a bus.

CONCLUSION

The sheer vulnerability of modern society; the ease of transferring sophisticated weaponry around the world; the ambivilent responses of many governments to attacks of terrorism, and the complex structure of terrorist cells have all contributed to the success of world terrorism. Notwithstanding the fact that many serious attempts have been anticipated and prevented, we continue to face considerable danger at every level of civilisation as we know it.

We have identified the extraordinary complexity of the nature of terrorism and the determination of the individual terrorist to succeed in his/her mission. Homicide bombers have brought death and destruction to Israel, and have been a dangerous influence on terrorists operating in Russia, Indonesia and India.

Despite all apparent advantages which the terrorists possess, there are considerable opportunities for counter-terrorism measures to match terrorist action. As Professor Yonah Alexander says, *"States possess enormous legal, economic, police and military resources that terrorists cannot match".* (Combating Terrorism, Michigan, 2002.) Perhaps the reason we find ourselves in a quandary in assessing how best to deal with terrorism is that governments have not fully utilised their powers - with the possible exception of the United States and Britain, although even here, the response has been spasmodic and understated.

If a fully committed counter-terrorist strategy could be implemented within the next two to three years, starting with the United States, Russia and Britain, then many of the essential steps towards dealing with terrorism could be implemented whilst continuing to be alert to the long-term hazards. In the short-term, these measures must include stricter admissions at airports as well as sea movements and the setting up of national anti-terrorist groups fully committed to the sharing of information. In the long-term, we must continue to look ahead to likely new tactics by the various terrorist groups of the future. The terrorist war cannot be won by confronting each incident as a one-off. Instead, we need to examine and monitor the pattern of likely interventions over a number of years and prepare a response for (say) ten years ahead.

Along with the various ways of helping to confront terrorism, it would be prudent to help those countries unable to fund a campaign against terrorism by the establishment, through the US and Britain, of an International Fund (a kind of modern *Marshall Plan) to help meet all contingencies.*

CHAPTER 7
WHAT CAN BE DONE?

WITHIN THE COMMUNITY

Racism provokes angry reactions by those discriminated against and this must be dealt with forcefully. There are many in Britain – including distinguished churchmen and politicians – who speak out against racism, but they need to be more rigorous both in their denunciations and their actions. Understating the problems arising from racism and the need for urgent action will otherwise be exploited by extremists with their own agenda. The United Nations declarations on human, political and religious rights appear in appendix D.

In Britain, efforts to deal with these issues are being made. The steps taken by the Office of the Deputy Prime Minister to foster and support racial equality and diversity show what may be achieved using the law to scuttle racism. Race and employment directives, when fully implemented, will go some way towards tackling discrimination: *"We need to have a clear, shared understanding of basic minimum standards. Unfair discrimination – whether at the point of recruitment, in conditions of employment or through harassment – is wrong. It can have a devastating impact on the lives of individuals. It can impose huge costs on business and the economy more generally every year. These costs may not always be highly visible – but discrimination inevitably undermines companies' efficiency, productivity and ability to compete. In that situation everyone loses."*

VIOLENCE IN SOCIETY AND RELATED OFFENCES

A wide range of employment and race directives, ranging from disability care and respect for religious beliefs and observance, has been distributed to many businesses, a large of number of which have since been implemented.

In an attempt to deal with violence in the city, there has been a unique initiative to bring together Protection Panels, to assess and manage the risks of dangerous offenders. In London, the Metropolitan Police Force has set up a specialist unit to help the panel ensure good practice and consistency. This initiative also highlights the close links between the police force and the Probation Service.

MAPPP (the Multi Agency Public Protection Panel) is a borough-based unit dealing with information of a highly confidential nature. The coordination officer told me that the panel meets monthly and that he is *"responsible for preparing the list of cases for review at each panel meeting. A typical Harrow MAPPP may review between 30 and 40 cases each month, though a proportion of those cases under review are brought for the purpose of sharing information only. These may include cases that are still under investigation or going through the judicial process. Looking at those cases serves as an early warning"*.

Some novel techniques are employed by the unit. In the Victim Liaison Service - a specialist branch of the Probation Service - work is carried out with victims whose attackers have been sentenced for more than 12 months. The Service consults with the victim over the conditions they would like to see imposed on the offender upon release from prison, such as keeping to specific locations, avoiding the victim's place of work or home, etc. Communication is perhaps the single most important aspect of the work of MAPPP, which not only provides a full range of public protection measures but, when possible, seeks to reduce re-offending.

Modern technology is also useful in searching out the potential offender. All cities and towns now make use of CCTV technology. In large cities, CCTV cameras are even more comprehensive. In Manchester, for instance, potential criminals can be monitored by up to 1000 swivelling cameras operated from a sophisticated control room. The system is so powerful that it can zoom in to identify faces from 600 yards or provide pictures of criminal behaviour from five miles away, providing valuable courtroom evidence. Operators in the central control room monitor up to 180 high-resolution digital images displayed on broadcast-quality back-lit projection screens spread across a 58-foot wall. Possible offenders can be tracked across the city with extraordinary clarity on 400 cameras based on main thoroughfares and side streets, in stores, bars and car parks. The aim is to have 1000 cameras running 24 hours a day.

The digital platform can store images for 92 days or 30 years in the case of sensitive material. All are instantly retrievable. Of course, like all tracking devices, these are costly. The IBM system costs £3.2m, but it has been credited with thwarting a murder and a kidnapping, and has resulted in 150 arrests.

Violence in schools has also grown over the past decade. Stronger measures to support teachers are being introduced and the public reaction has been generally positive. Many parents however, are opposed to a tougher regime.

In August 2002, the National Association of School Masters and Women Teachers (NASUWT) told Head Teachers that they should take a "zero-tolerance" approach to pupils who use foul language in the classrooms. It is the first time that the recommendation has been contained in the Union's advice to members (The Times, 17 Aug 2003). The NASUWT, which is the second largest teachers' union, with about 200,000 members, said that Heads would have to make their own judgement about what constituted offensive verbal abuse.

Chris Keates, the Union's Deputy General Secretary, said that Heads should take into account what the pupil said with how he or she said it. *"The pupil could say 'Go away Miss,' which would be fine, but if they said, 'you go away,' and combined it with threatening body language, then it would take on a different meaning."* The most common insult is 'fuck off!' followed by name-calling and insults directed at the teacher, which is unacceptable.

New approaches to alerting children to the dangers of the gun culture are being introduced in a series of anti-gun and gang culture lectures. These lessons have been launched as part of the crackdown on gun culture following the deaths of two teenage girls in a shoot-out in Birmingham. (The Observer, 12 Jan 2003.) The danger of being drawn into the gun-and-gang culture is illustrated in the fascination of the young with glamorous images on the cinema and television scenes.

In addition to problems of behaviour in schools, increasing evidence is available from psychologists about the way video "nasties" may harm children, particularly as many parents seem unaware that their children have access to such videos. Much of this argument is pertinent to the James Bulger case, where the Judge suggested a link between watching the film "Child's Play 3" and the killers' behaviour. Now, psychologists say that the availability of such video films should not be allowed to continue and that restrictions are necessary on the type of videos hired for viewing at home. (The Times, 1 April 1994.) Psychologists argue that children must be protected from damaging material as much as from other forms of child abuse.

Elizabeth Newson, Professor of Developmental Psychology at Nottingham University maintains that studies at the time of Bulger's killing show that in many video films, the viewer identifies himself with the perpetrator of violence, rather than the victim. She argues that psychologists failed to predict the amount of damaging video material that would be on the commercial market or the ease with which children could acquire it. *"Many of us hold liberal ideas of freedom of expression dear, but now begin to feel that we were naïve in our failure to predict the extent of damaging material and its all-too-free availability to children "* (The Times, 1 April 1994).

Germany has taken a tough line to curb TV violence. In May 2002, the Chancellor summoned TV chiefs to work out how to reduce the level of violence on television. This media summit held on the eve of a funeral service for the 16 teachers and students murdered in Erfurt, was aimed at calming an increasingly nervous German public rather than solving the riddle of whether violent images create violent people. The Erfurt killer, 19 year old Robert Steinhauser, had a television in his room and told school friends that his favourite film was "The Terminator", starring Arnold Schwarzenegger.

SHOOTINGS

Britain has not entirely escaped the shootings and the horrors of school serial killers, which has been such a serious crime in the United States. The American Beltway Sniper provoked much cause for psychological and social analysis in 2002. The leading American profiler, Robert Ressler, who has produced profiles on serial killers for over 20 years reported that, *"the killer is doing things that he's thought out very carefully. It's not precipitous in any way. I think a person like this is very much into his own ego. They are dysfunctional to start with. They're introverted. They're loners for the most part"*. Ressler's methods were first brought to public attention by the author, Thomas Harris, who used Ressler's research as a basis for his thriller, "The Silence of the Lambs". While police call on citizens to report strange behaviour, Ressler does not think the sniper's actions would be known even to close friends and family. *"For someone to know that this person is doing this sort of thing is unlikely at this time,"* he said. James Alan Fox, a Professor of Criminal Justice from North-Eastern University in Boston, USA, said: *"We know that respect is an important issue with this man. He talked to the police with a very respectable tone – 'Dear Policeman'. Maybe he doesn't get a lot of respect at work or at home and he's trying to grab respect with a gun. He is someone perhaps in his twenties, thirties. Maybe he wanted a career in the military, but never actually made it. And this is his chance, this is his battle, this is his attempt to be in charge"* (The Times, 17 Oct 2002). The sniper enjoyed interacting with the police and sending messages, such as the "Death" tarot card left at one murder scene.

Increasingly, we are learning more about the motives, the lifestyle, and the pressures on the killer, the sniper, or even the youngster at school who wants to shoot it out with his fellow pupils. Even the gene factor is not overlooked. A newly discovered gene may explain why some boys who are maltreated grow up to become violent, antisocial yobs while others do not. Research at King's College, London, has found that among men who were abused as children, those who became violent, criminal or antisocial adults were likely to have a particular gene variant on their X chromosome (The Times, 2 Aug 2002).

This discovery may well lead to 'good behaviour' pills analogous to cholesterol-lowering drugs used to prevent heart disease. A long shot, the cynic would say, but it shows the lengths to which we need to go, as incidents of violence become increasingly frequent.

HOSPITALS

Initiatives against criminal acts in the public sector, such as hospitals, are being undertaken with renewed vigour.

When Karl Hein took over as Head of Security at the Royal and Broadgreen Hospitals, Liverpool, he sent a public message to those who terrorise patients and staff: *"We will not tolerate criminals in our hospitals"*. Hein operates a zero tolerance approach towards thieves, abusive patients and aggressive visitors. Other hospitals have followed Merseyside's lead. More initiatives should be taken in more hospitals, and this means giving security a much higher profile and status than hitherto. From personal experience in the health services over 20 years, I have to admit that security was hardly a prime issue for Management, becoming paramount only during a crisis.

The Liverpool Royal and Broadgreen are not alone now in operating schemes to protect vulnerable staff working on their own at night. Steps have also been taken to safeguard social workers making home visits. Hospital staff are trained to know where all exits are, and can request personal panic alarms. Staff who go alone to see patients are expected to check in and out with Security when making home visits. The backgrounds of patients are also screened to assess the risk they may pose to a hospital employee. In addition, care is taken to ensure that those people who work night shifts are offered security escorts to the bus stop or their cars in a bid to make staff safer after dark.

RACISM: EUROPE

There is a racist element that taunts, injures and preaches violence in order to rid the UK of blacks, immigrants and Jews. Countering racism on a European level however, the European Monitoring Centre (EUMC), has yet to make a true impact on the insidious nature of racism. A positive programme by the European Monitoring Centre is now underway with the Community Action Programme, providing around one million Euros to support activities across Europe to combat discrimination on grounds of race or ethnic origin, religion or belief, disability, age, or sexual orientation. The first phase of its main capacity-strengthening component is now completed. In October 2002, a conference in Brussels brought together partners from 71 funded projects. At the Opening Session Bob Purkiss, EUMC Chairman, spoke about the need for the different target groups of discrimination to overcome division and join forces in their common struggle for racial equality.

In Phase 1 of the project, participants agreed to develop partnerships and have provided a strategy for joint activities to strengthen the transfer and application of good practices in tackling discrimination. This programme has considerable merit and vigour and will run through until 2006.

The dilemma for the European Monitoring Centre is that they are often forced to make political generalisations about racism which may affect their independence and credibility. Their strength is in reporting what is happening in Europe. They work in the area of good practice, finding out and reporting on what they discover, but their critics say they need to take this a stage further and report on how to do it. To improve the methods, they have already called together a group of international researchers, to identify problems of data collection and to look for "pathways towards increased data and comparability." Personal initiatives on a national level are to be welcomed. The Everyman project in London, for instance, is a voluntary charitable organisation and works at the "sharp" end, offering a range of services for men who want to stop behaving violently. It runs a number of counselling programmes and works with all types of male violence.

MOVES IN THE RIGHT DIRECTION

Out of a morass of racial incident, in Northern Ireland, for instance, some positive action has emerged, as groups of women have sought to make peace across an often violent religious divide.

In Bradford, a group of white and Asian women drew together in the summer of 2002, to challenge the violence on their streets, setting up a self-help project called "Safe Areas for Everyone" (SAFE). Frankie McGowan reported on this remarkable answer to violence in The Times (9 July 2002): *"SAFE is the brainchild of a middle-aged housewife, Elizabeth Hellmich, a professional foster mother. She raised two daughters of her own, is an active member of Neighbourhood Watch and works for Stage 84, a children's theatre group.*

A year ago she realised that the future was in danger. For three dreadful days she and her neighbours, white and Asian, watched helplessly as the worst racial violence in Britain for 20 years erupted around them. Businesses were set on fire, Asian and white youths threw bricks and planks of wood at each other, and 300 police officers were injured".

After the riots, women across the divide started to talk to each other. The project helps women to combat the background of fear through lectures and training. The Bradford Regeneration Fund gave them £11,500 to start and, apart from attracting the inevitable element of condescension - *'Mum's army on the look-out for troublemakers'* - these women are succeeding in recognising trouble and reporting back to their group. There are many practical things that they teach: *"If someone is vandalising a car, check what they are wearing. Forget the colour of their jumper; they whip that off when they are around the corner. We tell members to clock their trainers".* It is hoped that this project, will extend into other areas because it works so simply and effectively.

Some national initiatives now exist with the prime purpose of confronting racism, for example, in the football arena, with 'Community Days' involving the clubs, which have opened up their stadiums for a variety of events. But the major role of 'Football Unites, Racism Divides' (FURD) is a willingness to regularly review the extent to which their various initiatives have been implemented.

One should not deny the passion to be found in sport generally, but in football in particular. Arthur Koestler, the Anglo-Hungarian philosopher and writer, once said that there are two kinds of patriotism: ordinary patriotism and football patriotism. Incidentally, although he wrote in English, he always remained a Hungarian 'supporter'.

Football and sport may divide people, but it can also bring people together, acting as a cathartic force. At the Winter Olympics in 1972, the Czech ice hockey team succeeded in beating the Soviet Union. The excitement and enjoyment of that victorious moment will not be lost on anyone who witnessed the defeat of the Czech team in 1968 - a defeat which seemed to compound the tragedy of Russian tanks entering Prague.

ON THE MEDIA

The media has an important role to play, not only in the way it reports racism and related incidents, but also in the presentation of those reports. The CRE (Commission for Racial Equality) has been active over the years in providing seminars and reports, which offer guidelines as well as details of national awards on scrutiny and monitoring for shoddy and unfair reporting, Prejudice in the media is insidious and widespread. Anyone who complains about reporting standards is referred to the Press Complaints Commission - a totally inadequate body that has terms of reference which appear to have been prepared in-house by the newspaper owners themselves.

Along with the control of news by the media, there is a trend in some police forces to stop releasing details of crimes because - according to one West Country police force - such details scare the public (The Times, 22 Nov 2002). Could there be anything more preposterous than for a police force to censor what one should know about the security of our local community?

'Avon and Somerset', which encompasses Bristol, Bath and Taunton, now concentrates on publicising appeals for witnesses and the outcome only of successful court cases. For decades, a mid-Somerset chain of weekly newspapers has published a Crime File, giving details of minor incidents such as car thefts and break-ins of apparent interest to its readership. It would be enlightening to know why this has now stopped.

On the other hand, Scotland's second largest force, 'Lothian and Borders', halved its crime figures simply by recording and publicising incidents, including serious assaults, robbery and arson.

Confronting Violence

With a dramatic increase in the numbers of young offenders, it is imperative that measures are taken to bring this under control. The use of electronic tagging has produced some positive results. Recent changes in the law on sentencing will mean that several hundred Offenders a year will be given twelve months of intensive supervision, consisting of up to 30 hours of classes and activities a week, instead of a much lesser requirement of Community Service. With electronic tags, offenders cannot go out at night without alerting security guards and risking being sent to prison.

Electronic tagging flopped when it was first tried in the UK in 1969, but with increasing technological sophistication, tagging has become more reliable and the devices have now been successfully used to monitor more than 35,000 adult offenders released early from jail.

IMMIGRATION ISSUES

On the higher scale of international terrorism, drastic measures are needed to confront the terrorist cells and to minimise the danger they pose. The dilemma for security officials is the scale of the menace and the number of potential suspects. In the case of the Algerian militants, they concentrated first on Algeria, then France and now, with the reputation of the UK for being soft on immigrants, we find ourselves in the front line. One should stress that it is not only those terrorists who have been trained as part of a group who constitute a threat to our society. An additional hazard are the hundreds of trained 'freelancers' who do not necessarily share a common goal with a particular terrorist group, but are available for assignments.

The dilemma for the Government and the security authorities remains: how do the police warn the public against the danger of Islamic terrorism without causing panic?

An open policy of communication, with clear messages on the broad strategies of police and security forces would be a start.

The Home Office Report on Strategic National Guidelines, published in February 2003, dealt with action in the event of an attack by chemical, biological, radiological and nuclear substances and, as such, is of immense value to the health, police and fire services. The report is not alarmist; the language is direct, the content helpful and most informative. Following September 11, British people were surprised that families in the US began to store goods in case of future terrorist activity - this is a positive way of meeting a problem, forewarned and forearmed.

Following the Crumsall arrests and the murder of one of his officers, Chief Superintendent Todd (of the Manchester police force) said: *"the message to the public is don't think 'this can't happen in any town', because it can"*. That is surely the essential message in relation to violence in today's society.

It is hard for British people to accept the Government's appeal to be vigilant; to look at neighbours and new work colleagues. The UK has a good record of welcoming those escaping from persecution and arrest.

Indeed, the UK has always consisted of different ethnic groups, quite apart from post-war immigration. Britain's history of migrant settlement dates back many centuries. During the 16th and 17th centuries, French Huguenot Protestants fled religious persecution and poverty, to settle mainly in the East End of London. By the 18th century, the slave trade resulted in almost 20,000 black people being brought into the UK. From India and China, settlers came to Britain in the 18th and 19th centuries, respectively. Most importantly, Britain's wide empire provided the basis for the 1945 post-war migration.

After the Second World War, labour shortages caused the government to encourage migration from the former colonies - and then they came from Pakistan and India in the 1960s, from Uganda and Asia in 1968, Nigeria and Ghana in the 1980s.

Immigrants came because they wanted to live here, either because of available jobs, or to join fortuning relatives or simply to make a 'new start'. The public today is worried: it wants to know why people come to Britain, when a number of immigrants have expressed contempt and hatred for our society and a dislike of everything Britain represents. As Monica Porter wrote in The Times, *"Why should we welcome as our neighbours, for example, those who consider it is a moral imperative for a father to kill his daughter for refusing to enter into an arranged marriage? Yet political correctness has made such cowards of us that we overlook murder, even, for fear of upsetting ethnic sensibilities, so subverting the ideas that underpin our democracy. It was very different for us Hungarian refugees - 20,000 in all - who fled after Soviet tanks crushed the uprising in 1956. My family didn't just flee from terror and repression; we fled to something – the freedoms and civil rights offered by the democratic West. In our case, the United States"* (The Times, 12 Feb 2003).

THE ENVIRONMENT

Let us return to the question 'why violence?' The art world offers one answer, inevitably controversial. (www.artrenewal.org) in the United States maintains that the Art Renewal Group environmentalists across the country are increasingly coming to believe that Modernism, in all its forms, has led to a relentless lack of respect for nature and the real world. Paintings and sculpture that show the beauty of nature and humanity have been denigrated and ridiculed, in favour of abstract expressionism. No wonder that the city and countryside are all too often littered with garbage or drenched with acid rain and that our environment is every day looking more like a Jackson Pollock painting.

The leading force behind the Art Renewal Group is Dann Hoekstra, an artist who uses the argument that a society, which ignores its environment, will lose its culture. In their disillusionment with cities and violence, his supporters go further. But society is changing: *"By far the most significant cultural development of the 21ˢᵗ century, is this passionate shift towards nature,"* says Hoekstra. *"It is like a tidal wave, apparent in secular, political and religious realms alike"*. Hopefully, this movement might add weight to a general concern with minimising conflict and understanding the dynamics of non-violent lifestyles.

A group with similar aspirations is the <u>Non-Violence Foundation</u> in Britain, which encourages openness in understanding the danger of violence. Their project *"Telling it like it is,"* aims for a better understanding of the risks and dangers to which young people are exposed. Initial research explored the perception and experience of violence and violent crime, and examined its influence on young lives. This data was collected in the London borough of Tower Hamlets, the site of the Non-Violence Project's year-long pilot programme. The various findings included references to bullying: nearly two thirds of young people surveyed perceived bullying to be a serious or very serious cause for concern; one in two are worried, or very worried, about being bullied themselves.

On abuse, two thirds of young people surveyed perceived racial abuse to be a serious, or very serious, problem in their area. The research found that as many as half of all young people in Tower Hamlets live in constant fear of racial attack.

When interviewed, young people, particularly young males, spoke of a world in which violence and the threat of violence was a constant and routine feature of their day-to-day lives. Individual disputes often escalated and led to group conflict. Mobile phone technology has aggravated this tendency, dramatically increasing the speed at which such disputes can escalate. At least one quarter of fights among the young people of Tower Hamlets are gang-related.

Police harassment is perceived to be a problem by as many as half the young people surveyed. The manner in which 'stop and search' exercises are conducted by the police was the main cause of concern.

The research indicated that both the threat of violence and the actuality figure prominently in young peoples lives. Survey findings indicated high levels of concern among all young people, and while the anxieties of young women were far higher than those of young men (itself a serious cause for concern), young men's fears and worries also ran high.

In focus groups, young men described a world characterised by a 'geography of fear', marked by places and spaces they considered dangerous to visit. Danger here was registered in terms of a real threat of violence towards them, possibly involving the use of weapons.

The findings of the research pose a number of serious questions about the way in which the media and government legislation present and represent young people, raising serious questions about the adequacy of existing structures of support. The findings also reveal a complex and contradictory set of dispositions. On the one hand, young people could easily become involved in a range of harmful activities from joyriding to street robbery to gang fights. On the other, all those interviewed had internalised many social aspirations considered healthy and positive. They respected their families and their religion, and all wished to obtain good jobs and do well in their exams.

RELIGION AND RACISM

Discrimination is not confined to personal actions; it is also an institutional problem. Laws are not enough to remove this kind of unequal behaviour and unfair treatment. Such derogatory behaviour results in the unequal treatment of persons in the legal, public and private spheres on the grounds of sex, national or ethnic origin, colour, sexual orientation, age, religious affiliation, or suchlike. What is required is not only a policy that will help to change the social climate, but also anti-racist education. The principle aim of contemporary society should be to root discrimination out and it will make a significant difference at all levels, including the way nations exist and co-exist with one another.

It will not solve the terrorist threat indeed, it will not reach the terrorist in the medium term. Neither will it be comprehensible to the suicide/ homicide bomber. But an anti-racist strategy needs to be in place to explain and persuade at many different levels. It is difficult to ignore irrelevancies, such as whether the Archbishop of Canterbury should be spending a single moment of his day challenging the Walt Disney Corporation for having marketing tie-ins with their films. This seems absurd when the Archbishop might have challenged the violent content of films in general.

The Rev. Dr Dennis Duncan takes a more fundamental approach in encouraging Christians to be sensitive to the social changes all around us and, importantly, how to cope with such changes. In his splendid book, Rainbow Through the Rain, the Rev. Duncan writes: *"The confessional and the counselling room are places where domestic violence is revealed or acknowledged in the most unexpected of people. There are writers who would campaign strongly against all forms of violence, but do it in the most aggressive language possible. While physical violence would be claimed to be abhorrent to them, verbal violence carries no such stigma"*. The Rev. Duncan continues: *"All responsible members of society would say they were against violence, but in our proper condemnation of violence it is essential that we are aware how near the surface violent feelings can be in all of us. People of gentle natures can, in certain traffic situations, demonstrate active forms of road rage. There are those - are we among them? – who would be deeply offended if they were accused of racial prejudice or intolerance but whose reactions change perceptibly if those who are putting them - or us – under pressure, physical or otherwise, belong to another culture, nation or race"*.

Another route towards understanding and mutual respect is to be found in a number of institutes like the Centre for Jewish-Christian Relations in Cambridge. One of their major tasks is to produce material for teachers wishing to convey to their pupils the values underpinning good citizenship. It contains a range of innovative and stimulating classroom activities aimed at pupils aged between 11-16. A particular focus of the activities is on interfaith dialogue.

The inspiration for the Centre's work comes from three remarkable people of the last century. Hugo Gryn was born in 1930 in Czechoslovakia. He and his family were transported to Auschwitz. Together with his father, he was separated from the rest of the family and survived for a year in slave labour camps. Throughout his life, he remained aware of the evils that arise from hatred. In the 1960s, as a young rabbi, he befriended Martin Luther King and in this, Hugo Gryn saw beyond the divisions between different communities. He inspired many thousands of Jews and non-Jews.

Sister Edith Stein was born in 1891, the youngest of eleven children in a devout Jewish family. Edith became a brilliant student of philosophy and a remarkably successful woman in a male-dominated world. She then converted to Catholicism, but she continued to value her Jewish identity and attend the synagogue with her mother. After the German invasion of neutral Holland, the Nazis arrested all Catholics who had Jewish origins. Edith Stein refused to deny her Jewish heritage, and she and her sister both died in the gas chambers of Auschwitz.

Elie Wiesel is another inspiring individual. He was born in 1928 in the close-knit Jewish community of Sighet, now part of Romania. The first years of the Second World War left his village relatively untouched. In 1944, however, Elie's childhood ended abruptly as the Nazis took over Sighet and deported all the Jewish people living there to concentration camps in Poland. Later he vowed never to speak about his experiences in the concentration camps. Eventually, he was persuaded to break his ten-year silence by the distinguished French Catholic writer, Francois Mauriac.

Elie Wiesel published his memoir of the genocide, 'Night', in 1958. He has supported the struggles of many people, including the victims of apartheid in South Africa. In 1986, Elie Wiesel won the Nobel Peace Prize.

These three different people, in different ways, all inspired those who came to them, whether for advice or support for action.

The next decade will demand strong trusty leaders, determined in their dealing with international terrorists. They must ensure that there are comprehensive measures in place to challenge the dangers from outside the country as well as the violence and crime on our streets and in our communities.

This is where the integrity of the likes of Gryn, Wiesel and Stein becomes relevant. Of course, we are dealing with a totally different set of issues, but the courage to deal with the perpetrators of violence is critical. Too often the message from the national leadership has been ambiguous. Following the terrorist attack on September 11, various warnings were given by governments, but their advice appeared suspect when different government departments in Britain offered different views on the central issue. Nevertheless, the determination by the Prime Minister to support action into Iraq was correct. This did not prevent the media and some politicians from launching a campaign on the issue as to whether WMDs would be found and who took the decisions in preparing memos on the dangers posed by Saddam Hussein - a campaign out of all proportion to its significance.

As Lord Scarman pointed out, however, the essential issue of violence - at whatever level - is that it is, and always has been, a feature or a threat in society. (Foreword to The Violent Society, Eric Moonman, Cass, 1985.)

The challenge, to civilisation is not the elimination of violence, but its control and restraint. And the lesson for a civilised society is that, unless fear of attack, deprivation and frustration are eliminated within a society, the risk of violent outbursts by those who see themselves as victims, will be greatly enhanced. The problem is more than maintaining "law and order"; it is also one of achieving a just society.

DESTABILISING A NATION

For a country to act against violence in the international arena, with the full force of law to explain all the implications involved to the public, requires a closer working relationship with other nations in sharing source material. The issues are stark. If there is danger that might destabilise a country, it is necessary to explain how and why this needs to be dealt with – and the preferred options. It takes courage for a public leadership to speak out on issues that the public neither sees nor experiences for itself. In this respect, the terrorist has a considerable advantage. The IRA bombings in the mid-1990s were real enough because there were many people killed or maimed in Britain as well as in Northern Ireland. It is a terrifying prospect, if the only way the public can relate to such destructive and brutal acts is through personal experience, rather than an impartial understanding of the sheer cost - at every level - to community and country.

Fortunately for Britain, the risks and hazards of terrorism, and the threat to the State itself, has been emphasised by the Prime Minister (and to some extent by the Leader of the Opposition). However, support from other public figures has been slow in coming and vague in delivery. The new Archbishop of Canterbury, Dr. Rowan Williams, did himself and his church a disservice when he declared that: *"The attacks on the United States on September 11 should not be seen as an act of war...it is an act of terror, of violence...but war does not come in to it"* (The Times, 26 Aug 2002).

The Archbishop was perhaps striving for some form of distinction - somewhat naively, given the risks involved in appeasement. His subsequent comments were certainly more confusing: *"The role of religious leaders in such circumstances (Sept 11) was to be a focus for self-criticism, to persuade a community where it had gone wrong, where it had failed and what mistakes it had made."* In the ever more likely event of a terrorist attack utilising massive weapons of war, including the biological and nuclear, there is little time to engage in such cerebral indulgence.

Making peace with terrorists is at best a dubious business. The IRA made a public apology on 17 July, 2002, the 30th anniversary of the IRA operation in Belfast. *"While it was not our intention to injure or kill non-combatants, the reality is that on this and on a number of other occasions, that was the consequence of our actions. It is, therefore, appropriate on the anniversary of this tragic event, that we address all of the deaths and injuries of non-combatants caused by us. We offer our sincere apologies and condolences to their families."* (The Guardian, 17 July 2002.) There was no immediate acceptance from the Loyalists, but they did say that *"the statement came a little too late, given that it came eight years after [its] ceasefire".* As Rosie Cowen pointed out, this statement *"only expresses repentance regarding victims the Provisional deemed 'non-combatants'."* (The Guardian, 17 July 2002.)

Hatred and violence is expressed not only by terrorists, but also by those who support their causes or philosophies. This was apparent in Durban, in South Africa, at the UN World Conference Against Racism in September 2001. The World Conference was an unlikely venue for a massive demonstration against Jews. Although the purpose of the conference was to examine areas of ageism, sexism and other forms of discrimination, the meetings were dominated by a highly professional group who insisted that the Middle East was the core of all debates. In consequence, the conference consisted of a week of considerable fear and anxiety for the Jewish participants, who had to contend with considerable prejudice. The conference leadership appeared unable to control or cope with events in the main plenary and workshops.

Jews were abused on the streets of Durban; T-shirts were worn sporting logos: "Zionism-Nazism: two faces with the same coin". The mood of violence was everywhere.

The build-up to the conference began three years previously when many lay leaders and professionals were invited to London, to attend preliminary briefings in preparation for an event on discrimination before the gathering in Durban scheduled for September 2001. Because of the distant venue, relatively few people present would be able to attend the conference itself. Nevertheless, we all worked hard in sifting out the various reports on prejudice and likely hostility. Major items included: discrimination and how it affects the role of women; ageism; the lessons of the Holocaust; and problems of multi-faith communities. We worked easily and with trust, because so much needed to be done in explaining and informing one another of the dangers of prejudice.

What happened in Durban was not about these issues, nor did anyone bother to adhere to the agenda. Some delegates tried to instil a positive note, including former Irish President, Mary Robinson. As Conference President, she appealed for tolerance and compassion. Time Magazine reported that, *"The behaviour of some of the non-Governmental organisation forums was contemptible."* The Protocols of the Elders of Zion were on sale; flyers asking: *'WHAT IF HITLER HAD WON?'* were freely on display. Many Jewish delegates said that, after a full week of such treatment, they could stomach no more and left.

"This is the first time I've ever felt ant-Semitism this personally, at such a level of intensity," said David Matas, Senior Counsel for B'nai B'rith, Canada. *"It's a kind of collective guilt,"* said Matas, a refugee lawyer, *"but instead of saying that the Jews killed Christ, they're using the modern-day language of human rights to accuse us of some of the worst sins known to humanity".* Could there be a greater irony than the fact that a Conference, convened to combat the scourge of racism, should produce the most racist declaration from a major international organisation since the Second World War? For the future, it is incumbent on all involved in the preparation of

such meetings to define precise objectives and to insist that controls for adhering to the agenda are in place.

Among its many responsibilities, the United Nations and its agencies are concerned with protecting human rights. It is therefore, of paramount importance that its own declaration of human rights is fully understood, safeguarded and adhered to, so as to avoid a repetition of the mob rule witnessed at the Durban UN Conference on Racism (See Appendix D).

VIOLENCE: FROM WITHOUT

Terrorism

London's reputation as a haven for Islamic extremists has been a source of embarrassment to successive British governments as Western countries, as well as Russia and the Arab states, have accused Britain of turning a blind eye to terrorism.

At one time, in September 2001, at least six suspected international terrorists were being held in Brixton jail awaiting extradition for acts of terrorism around the globe.

They included:

- Khalid al Fawwaz, wanted by the US for the bombing of its embassies in Africa. A Saudi dissident, who has been in London since 1994, he is an alleged leader of Osama bin Laden's London group.

- Sheikh Abu Hamza, head of supporters of Shariah, based at Finsbury Park Mosque.

- Sheikh Omar Bakri Mohammed, leader of a religious group calling itself Al-Muhajiroun, which produces inflammatory leaflets and posters attacking Jews. Born in Syria, he has lived in Britain since 1986, when he was deported from Saudi Arabia.

In addition, as a confused public learnt on 19 February 2003 - fourteen Taliban militiamen were seeking asylum in the UK and three had already been granted it.

Witold Gutt, a former prisoner of Dachau, said: *"The 1951 Geneva Convention that allows protection of such people (asylum seekers) needs to be rapidly modified in order to distinguish between victims and persecutors who are escaping from well deserved retribution. I wonder if the same law would have led to asylum for Nazi murderers such as Eichmann?"* (The Times, 19 Feb 2003).

Ricin hit the headlines on 7 January 2003, when six terrorist suspects were questioned after traces of one of the world's deadliest poisons were discovered in Wood Green, London. The inevitability of biological weapons being used as one of the tools of terror was described in a disturbing, but necessary reminder as long ago as 1989. *"The outlook for biological weapons is grimly interesting. Weaponeers have only just begun to explore the potential of the bio-technological revolution. It is sobering to realise that far more development lies ahead than behind".* (Commander Steven Rose, "The Coming Explosion of Silent Weapons," Naval War College Review, Summer 1989.)

If it was a sober warning in 1989, it is now very real and actual, given the use of ricin and other poisons by terrorists in the past two years. Biotechnology has undoubtedly added a new dimension to the nature of weaponry and to the way violence can be perpetrated.

There are some who disagree with this view. Professor Matthew Maeselson of Harvard University, argues that no matter how available new weapons maybe, there is always an element of restraint which prevents the wider use of such weapons. He cites a similar history of restraint for chemical weapons. *"Although massively used in World War I and stockpiled in great quantity during World War II and the Cold War, chemical weapons – despite hundreds of wars, insurgencies, and terrorist confrontations since their last large-scale employment 80 years ago – have seldom been used since. Their use in Ethiopia, China, Yemen, and Vietnam (if one includes harassing agents), and against Iranian soldiers and Kurdish towns are among the very few exceptions. Indications that trichotecene mycotoxins had been used in Laos and Cambodia in the 1970s and 1980s proved to be illusionary."*

He goes further, citing the case of Richard Nixon who, soon becoming President, ordered a full review of US biological weapons. Shortly afterwards, President Nixon announced that the United States might consider a moratorium.

The Soviet Union did not respond in kind and, aware that the United States had previously invested heavily in biological warfare, continued its production of biological weapons on a large scale.

In support of his argument of restraint, Professor Maeselson cites the facility built in the early 1980s, for the production of anthrax bombs at Stepnogorsk, now Kazakhstan. Recently dismantled under the US Cooperative Threat Reduction Programme, in collaboration with Kazakhstan, it was equipped with ten 20,000-litre fomenters; apparatus for the large-scale drying and milling of the agent to a fine powder; machines for filling it into bombs, and underground facilities for storage of the filled munitions. According to its Cold War Director, Stepnogorsk conducted numerous development and test runs, but never produced a stockpile of anthrax weapons. Nevertheless, there is no doubt that its purpose was to provide a capability to commence production on short notice if ordered to do so.

But it is naïve to imagine that terrorist groups with no formal world body or government to relate to, or be held account by, work to a restraint clause. Their actions are arbitrary, with no warnings, and the trend of their armoury is always in the direction of new technology, not because one weapon has failed, but because they want ever more sophistication in weapons of increasing effectiveness and deadliness.

The real dilemma for the Security Services and the Government is highlighted by the admission of Taliban asylum seekers, groups which are damaging the image of genuine asylum seekers. In a published interview one Taliban asylum seeker, Wali Kahn Ahmadzai said: *"I live here, but I still think America and Britain are enemies of the Afghan people and Muslim people"* (The Times, 18 Feb 2003). He said this while at his new home, a first-floor flat, in West Hampstead, North London.

The problems posed by Taliban asylum-seekers are unlikely to go away. Ahmadzai and others like him will remain here. Under the 1951 Geneva Refugees Convention, asylum seekers cannot be returned to a country where they have *a "well-founded fear of persecution or death"*.

With all the uncertainty in our present society, it is easy to make generalisations and fall into the trap of the prejudiced or the discriminating. Ziauddin Sardan, a Muslim writer, said: *"Don't look at your Muslim neighbours with suspicion. We too, find the twisted, evil minds of a suicide bomber impenetrable. He is a special breed and he stands outside normality, beyond reason."* (Evening Standard, 13 Sept 2001.) Other Muslim writers have expressed similar views, even if many of the religious leaders have remained silent in the face of the Muslim fanatics.

More voices need to be raised on all sides of the community: Muslim, Catholic, Protestant, Jews and Hindus. Surely, a united response is the only answer to the frenzied and unstable world of today. Leaders of all peoples need to be reminded that we care and understand that there can be no winners in a world armed to the teeth, with terrorists ready to exploit any chink in the armour, any moment of weakness.

LEARNING TO LIVE

Preparing the public for an understanding of a likely terrorist attack using chemical or biological weapons, will require a commitment by the

Government and Opposition Parties to treat the issue without seeking political advantage. There will always be opportunities for politicians to want to "contract" out of an agreement, to support a narrow or sectional interest, but this must be resisted. The new type of warfare is unlikely to produce the national patriotism seen in the two World Wars of 1914-1918 and 1939-1945. That passionate feeling for England would appear to be relegated to England's football matches!

Learning to live in a violent society means essentially being a more involved and active citizen. It means a great deal of persuading and, in some cases, pushing the elected representatives - whether in Parliament, the European Parliament or in the local Council - to listen and to be alerted to the dangers. The average politician is hardly likely to be any more enlightened on issues of security than any other member of society. Violence and, worse, terrorism, are nasty, cruel and hardly ensure rational, defined arguments. One MP said to me, *"there's no votes in it"*. I reminded him that, *"When your constituent is considering the security of his children and their future, together with all he has created and worked for, then any security challenges which could destroy all that will quickly transfer his concern into votes"*.

Learning to live in a violent society inevitably means some discomfort and watchfulness, and it would be helpful if the Government provided the same information to all citizens, so that there was a realistic assessment of the risks from wherever they are most likely to come.

There will of course be inconvenience associated with travel or when attending major large-scale gatherings. In the United States, tight new controls have been introduced at airports and seaports. The millions of foreign tourists, business travellers and students etc, who arrive each year will be finger-printed, photographed and checked against a terrorist watch-list before entering the country. The new rules will affect all visitors who are required to have a visa - at least 23 million people or sixty percent of those who travel to the United States each year. This will not only increase delays in obtaining visas, but also raises concerns about how personal information could be used. Nevertheless, immigration lawyers have praised federal officials for a programme that does not single out any ethnic groups. (San Francisco Chronicle, 20 May 2003.)

But the measures we have been forced to take to deter and deflect terrorists is a small price for reducing the potential dangers accompanying their incursion into a country.

Straightforward messages are essential. Neither the American nor the British governments have seriously educated their public about the many practical steps to take in the event of an attack. With the exception of the

Home Office guidebooks (referred to earlier), these booklets are for public officials and those manning control points in the event of an emergency, but these do not reach the public.

In the United States, one such manual has emerged, The Survivors Guide: What to do in a Biological, Chemical or Nuclear Emergency, by Angelo Acquista (Hodder & Stoughton, 2003). Dr Acquista confirms the view that an alert public can successfully confront the terrorist danger. He wrote the guidebook because the common denominator among people who are afraid is ignorance. The guide, he says, is one way to educate them and thus take away the terrorists' weapon of fear. *"Nobody is going to train the public,"* he says, *"But if people are better prepared they won't be afraid, and they will be able to save their own lives and the lives of others".*

Following Tim Reid's interview with Dr Acquista, he reported that: *"There is a total lack of knowledge about what would happen in biological, chemical and nuclear emergencies. Despite the fact that we call biological agents weapons of mass destruction, people should know that there are treatments and therapies for most of them and once the initial cluster of victims is finished, the damage is usually very limited"* (The Times, 11 July 2002).

Dr Acquista's guidebook is timely if only to offset the way government information is distributed, often in a spasmodic and unconnected fashion. The result, says Dr Acquista, is to scare everybody witless in the United States.

A key element of the 285 page survival kit, says Tim Reid, is a series of information boxes on each possible weapon, poison and nerve agent, detailing the name of the disease, the organism responsible, how it is contracted, the time from exposure to illness, major symptoms and, crucially, how to treat it, and what vaccines or antibiotics should be taken.

In addition to the survival kit, it is essential that the media - particularly the BBC - should move away from its combative role with the Government and concentrate on producing programmes with more substance. For instance, Knights Under the Prophet's Banner (2001), a book by Ayman Zawahiri, Bin Laden's chief Lieutenant, presents a list of terrorist principles, which should have been brought to the attention of the wider public. Zawahiri also mentions *"the need to concentrate on the method of martyrdom operations as the most successful way of inflicting damage against the opponent and the least costly to the mujahideen in terms of casualties".* A recruitment video accompanying the book, highlights the usefulness to the terrorist cause of martyrdom operations. The concept of martyrdom is something the British public needs to understand and grapple with: life to the Muslim fanatic is neither precious nor personal, but to be used for the destruction of the Western powers.

Learning to live in the violent society means that we need reassurance from our political leadership. Taking space in newspapers and posters may be a drop in the collective mind of public awareness, but both these communication vehicles should be used to transmit ideas, new initiatives and products. The advertisement, "we commit ourselves," was free of excessive claims, and displayed unity of purpose in face of a specific danger. This could prove as valuable as the following:

"We commit ourselves to prevent terrorists, or those that harbour them, from acquiring or developing nuclear, chemical, radiological and biological weapons; missiles and related materials, equipment and technology". This advertisement placed in <u>USA Today, 2 June, 2003</u>, signed by 8 world leaders: Berlusconi, Blair, Bush, Chirac, Chretien, Koizumi, Putin, Schroder. Eight world leaders announced their commitment to cooperative action against global threat. One year ago they agreed to a $20 billion Global Partnership aimed at stopping terrorists from obtaining nuclear, biological and chemical weapons and materials. Our leaders must put their words into action at future G8 meetings.

Along with a national call alerting the public to likely terrorist danger, an agreement by the major powers to commit themselves and their resources under the following headings would also seem appropriate:

1) To reach an international agreement regarding an exhaustive definition of terrorism and to endorse a means of classifying countries according to the features and the level of their sponsorship of terrorism.

2) To define a clear "price scale" to be paid by countries engaged in terrorism.

3) To adjust the "price scale" to the various types of state sponsorship of terrorism, aiming to change their balance of interests.

4) To impose a secondary boycott on States and companies that continue to maintain economic and other ties, whether open or covert, with States on which a boycott has been imposed because of their involvement in terrorism.

These conditions would set the minimum level of an agreement to combat terrorism. Should the United Nations hesitate or delay supporting measures to combat terrorism there are still significant methods which the United Kingdom could introduce to counter terrorism. These could even begin at the point of entry into Britain. New technology is now available on a considerable scale, so that biometric tests could be conducted before the admission of likely terrorists.

A pilot scheme in which fingerprints, iris or facial recognition data is contained in a microchip on visas for visitors from Sri Lanka, is to be extended to countries from which there are large numbers of immigration offenders. The UK Passport Service's business plan for 2003-8 showed that officials were hoping to begin to implement the "smart" passports by 2005/7.

A chip implanted in the card would carry facial recognition data. Within a year of the new high-tech passports, the agency hopes to introduce a "passport card" - similar to a credit card - to be used with the paper document.

The card would be valid for travel within the EU and "certain other countries".

Whilst concentrating on immigrant offenders, the intention is to use the new technology to include some countries such as Jamaica and Zimbabwe where there is widespread abuse of the immigration and asylum laws.

Is Violence Natural?

The fierce debate over nature and environment is bound to be re-opened again following a new study, which reveals that teenage boys have a natural tendency towards violent and aggressive behaviour. The Edinburgh Study of Youth Transitions and Crime tracked more than 4,300 children over five years (The Observer, 11 Aug 2003), in a study which revealed that teenage boys have a natural tendency towards violent and aggressive behaviour which they argue, is part of being a male.

We have looked rather more widely at the circumstances of violence and its many constituent parts. The various patterns of violence explored in this book are different for different people living in different countries. Children are at risk from those who have access to them, the home and school featuring prominently as locations of child abuse. Those who have experienced discrimination because they are disabled or disfigured, or members of religious, racial or ethnic minorities, also report high levels of violence.

Then there is the question of domestic violence. Even low-level violence can have a profound effect on all the individuals in a family. Low-level violence may consist of name-calling, petty theft and minor injuries against a person because of what she or he is, or worse still, because the abuser feels that the victim's vulnerability can be exploited. The public are often disenchanted with the law, which they perceive as taking "sides" with the criminal rather than the victim, and this has been the source of many angry articles in the press and a number of programmes on TV and radio. Whether this disenchantment with the law is wholly correct or not, confidence needs to be restored in the community along with all the other measures mentioned, by for example, increasing the level of policing. The law - and the way - the law interprets and understands the plight of the victim is an essential starting point. To be the victim of violence is a frightening experience, and the legal system possesses the power to provide protection to those who are living alone, disabled or vulnerable.

In the United States, the legal system has moved on in conceiving ways of strengthening and supporting the victim through a system of restorative and balanced justice. As in Britain, restorative justice now offers hope for the victims of crime in a system that too often (it seemed) had failed them. Restorative justice works on the basis that the Offender has a responsibility first to the victim and then to the community. It concentrates on the scene of the crime - how much has changed by the offender's action and how it can be restored and at what cost and in what ways of satisfaction for the victim.

In dealing with the wider issue of terrorism, we have stressed that the public has a role to play, no matter how frightening the scale of the enemy's operations. Many terrorist acts are well planned and highly organised, with specific objectives to cause panic or to target a large number of airports, postcard sites or commercial buildings. Our response demands equally well-defined anti-terrorist programmes from our governments. The comment sometimes heard after a terrorist act, *"those killed happened to be in the wrong place at the wrong time,"* is totally unacceptable. Of course, no authority can forestall every single terrorist action; but we can certainly insist that, by sharing a dialogue with our elected representatives, we identify the levels of danger and what capability we have to withstand likely attacks.

When confronted with a likely major change in their lifestyle the public will search, I suspect, for spiritual support or uplift. Too often this is not forthcoming. Dr Denis Duncan explained that people are here to make their choices. Is it not conceivable that troubled people want even a little more support in periods of loneliness or stress? Dr. Jonathan Sacks' 'credo' article puts it like this: *"We are a mix of good and evil. We have compassionate instincts, but also cruel ones. We have a sense of justice, but human beings are also capable of oppression and injustice on a massive scale. God took a momentous risk. He created the one being capable of destroying what he has made. That implies something so strange, it sounds like a paradox. More than we have faith in God, God has faith in us"* (The Times, 23 Sept 2002).

Everyone wants an end to violence. Violence engenders extreme discomfort in both the individual and the community. The law does not appear to be sufficiently comprehensive or sufficiently determined to protect the public, with a judiciary seemingly tilted in favour of the criminal and not the victim. At least that how it appears to many people.

Internationally, we are aghast at the way terrorism travels across state boundaries to recruit and set up cells with people born in our own country. It is worrying that people who live and work in Britain today are prepared to take part in a terrorist cell for the purpose of killing and maiming fellow Brits.

The public, in anger and frustration, wants to draw a line through many of these areas of violence. In this book, we have examined areas of violence in which domestic, national and international incidents occur. Hopefully, we have identified a counter-reaction at every possible level. The individual may well feel helpless; he or she will not be able to confront the dangers alone. Here one will need to form coalitions with other likeminded people; to play an active role professionally, at work, and to ensure that our public representatives, whether MPs or Councillors, are fully aware of our deep concerns and willing to truly act as each individual's spokesperson.

CHECKLIST

1. <u>Learning to live in a violent society</u> depends on the motivation, willingness and determination of a nation's citizens to be kept informed of political and social developments in their city/town/country. Also to see to it that their elected officials and representatives are regularly made aware of their concerns, and if necessary, their determination to act, and to press their views.

This can also act as a trigger for people in Third World Countries to find their voices where there are limited educational and social opportunities.

2. <u>Learning to live in a violent society</u> means tackling discrimination wherever it exists. Violence often begins through discrimination. There are a number of ways to tackle anti-black, ethnic and anti-Semitic manifestations. At the national and international level there are some critical United Nations declarations of Human Rights and Covenants. They establish the rights and opportunities for groups and institutions, with a range of ideas backing up the many practices. They should be more widely known and introduced, for instance, at Sixth Form level, and not regarded as texts exclusive to politicians and lawyers.

There is also considerable scope for confronting discrimination within Europe, albeit through the European Union.

For the first time in Europe, common minimal standards for legal protection against discrimination have come into force in the EU Member States. Since 19 July 2003, the Racial Equality Directive has provided in general for the equal treatment of people, irrespective of their ethnic, cultural or religious background. It prohibits discrimination in areas such as employment, training, social assistance and health care and provides for equal access to services.

The first Directive:

- Defines direct and indirect discrimination and gives victims of discrimination a right of redress through a judicial or administrative procedure, associated with appropriate sanctions for those who discriminate.

- Shifts the burden of proof (in civil cases) once a prima facie case of discrimination has been made out by a complainant and accepted by the court or other instance.

- Requires the Member States to provide information on their territory about the measures they adopt to fight discrimination and to set up bodies for the promotion of equal treatment which will provide independent assistance to the victims of discrimination.

A further Directive includes procedures to:

- Prohibit discrimination on grounds of religion and belief, disability, age and sexual orientation in the labour market.

- Requires employers to make reasonable adjustments to cater for the needs of a person with a disability who is qualified to do the job in question. Such adjustments may, for example, need to be made in workplaces, working patterns or the distribution of tasks among employees.

Of all the EU's domestic campaigns, this is perhaps the most resourced in the search for greater public understanding. It is running a five-year information campaign in all Member States and this is crucial. The campaign will stress the positive benefits of promoting diversity and combating discrimination for all members in society and business.

In short, it is a positive expression of support to defeat discrimination in Europe.

3. Learning to live in a violent society demands considering ways of altering society as we know it. Ruth Morris (Stories of Transformative Justice, Scholars' Press, 2000), says that there are pathways to confront the negative elements in our society by using, consumer power and the creation of new techniques of information to enlarge and widen public awareness. These pathways, together with changes in our political system to enhance democracy, will further pinpoint ways in which the individual can change their life and environment for the collective good and social responsibility for all.

4. How to survive in a terrorist world Some guidelines in a crisis: The Cabinet Office's, "Dealing with Disaster" (3rd edn. 2003), is a useful guide on civil contingency planning arrangements in the event of terrorist

attack. Sections deal with the management of key operational control in a major incident, the response command, the care and treatment of people and the role to be played by central and local government as well as the voluntary sector. However, I am inclined to recommend an American paperback, "The Survival Guide - What to do in a Biological, Chemical or Nuclear Emergency," by Angela Acquista. As the Medical Director of the New York City Mayor's Office of Emergency Management, the writer instils throughout the book, clarity and deep understanding of what will be done rather than what might be done. It is not surprising that it figured, for some time, in the best selling US booklist (Random House, 2003). (Appendix E.)

As to what constitutes a "major incident" in Britain it is often unclear. The following definition is set out in the Association of Chief Police Officers Emergency Procedures Manual and in the Fire Service Major Incident Emergency Procedures Manual:

"A major incident is any emergency that requires the implementation of special arrangements by one or more of the emergency services, the NHS or the local authority for: the initial treatment, rescue and transport of a large number of casualties; the involvement either directly or indirectly of large numbers of people; the handling of large numbers of enquiries likely to be generated both from the public and the news media, usually to the police; the need for the large scale combined resources of two or more of the emergency services; the mobilisation and organisation of the emergency services and supporting organisations, e.g. local authority, to cater for the threat of death, serious injury or homelessness to a large number of people".

The broad definition above is also applicable to the NHS, as the wording indicates. For specific NHS purposes, a major incident may be defined as: *"Any occurrence which presents a serious threat to the health of the community, disruption to the service, or causes (or is likely to cause) such numbers or types of casualties as to require special arrangements to be implemented by hospitals, ambulance services or health authorities".*

A list of websites dealing with a major incident is to be found in Appendix F.

LONDON 7/7 AND 21/7, 2005

The death toll of the London July 7, 2005 bombings grew to 52 with some 700 people injured or needing medical attention. We came to terms with the fact that the terrorist had extended their range of activity to yet another city after New York, Madrid and Moscow.

The transport and communications network, in many parts of the capital, came to a standstill as subway trains and a bus were targeted by the terrorist. However within a few days and whatever any previous uncertainly amongst the security and police services prior to the bombings, rapid strides were now made in moving things along and attempting to return to business as usual.

But no one living in the greater London area and beyond could pretend that we were living in other than a cautious, uncertain environment. Of course some parts of the media overstated the public's reaction like The Independent with a bold headline on their front page, 'city of fear'. The London public was not fearful but rightly cautious and angry. Yet this became soon translated into a positive reaction as the police called for assistance and got it – some 800 witness statements were offered to them as well as 3,500 calls on likely identities of the bombers.

Many questions were asked of the authorities? Were we in a proper state of readiness to meet the terrorist attack? Probably not. The manual of counter operations used by the police was virtually that used to cope with IRA. Yet this was a different enemy and at a different time. With the IRA there were frequent contacts between them and the authorities; there were 'familiarities' and a willingness by the IRA, despite their serious differences and readily available arms, to alert those living or working in their potential targets. Nor did they resort to use of suicide bombers. Sophie Goodchild in the Independent on Sunday has since pointed out (June 17/05) that the Association of Chief Police Officers has circulated a manual to all forces urging them to "revise procedures on evacuating civilians and dealing with suspects planning an attack".

Other questions? International connections?

It is as thought that three of the July 7 bombers had visited Pakistan, two of them at the same time and may also have been to Afghanistan. Some of the suspects have links to East Africa.

With modern technology, as we have described, I consider it likely that whilst the team and the supporting cells were home-grown British it is certain the overall executives decision to act at this particular time came from outside. With regard to the second incident, it is more than likely that again it was home grown but with an executive decision based in the UK. It was altogether less professional and consequently a botched assignment.

Al-Qaeda connection? Senior police sources have stressed that they are dealing with al-Qaeda inspired groupings.

What kind of explosives were used?

Security specialists believe that the 7/7 blasts were caused by the kind of home-made chemical based explosive similar to material found in a bomb factory in Leeds where three of the suspects lived and in a car in Luton. They were likely to be nail and shrapnel bombs. They are designed to "tear into flesh". The devices, made from bottles packed with explosive and nails were found in a Nissan Micra rental car used by Shahzad Tanweer, one of the bombers. These nail bombs are easy and cheap to produce. Possibly acetone, peroxide is packed into milk bottles then wrapped in cling film with nails placed on its outer rim.

Fortunately within days of 7/7 new procedures were quickly learnt and introduced by the authorities.

The use of CCTV in identifying and pursuing likely suspects is a sensible investment. To those planning security procedures in all other cities it would be prudent to recognise this as an aid to all extra policing policies. For instance, the four men involved in the London bombings were seen on CCTV at Luton station prior to their arrival in London. They were identified together on a Thameslink train to Kings Cross. This information resulted in a considerable response from the public.

A backlash against Muslim communities seems inevitable. Wisely, some of the Muslim leaders have anticipated such a reaction and have made it clear that terrorism has no part within the Koran.

Yet multiculturalism in Britain has taken a serious battering. This is similar to the view in Holland where the country's General Intelligence and Security Service (AIVD) spokesman Vincent van Steen said that "Dutch police and security services do not just assume the country will be hit by a terrorist attack, they know one will come. The attacks in London have only made that sense of imminent threat sharper." Van Steen said, "in the Netherlands we have some 10 to 20 radical Islamic groups of a violent nature, consisting of a few hundreds members, we think, who are potentially violent."

The sense of tensions at the AIVD is palpable. Its 1,000 or so civilian staff have worked gruelling hours since the Madrid bombings last year.

The sense of urgency is very strong and it became stronger after the London attacks. Initially, the politicians and the public in Holland did not want to hear this message as it clashes with the compromise with Holland's 900,000 Muslims.

Just as we mentioned the linkage between football hooligans and other groups in creating disorder and violence, it was perhaps no surprise that an alliance arose to extract "revenge" on Muslims (Guardian July 15).

The police monitored their activities as the original plan was to cause widespread fear and injury with attacks on mosques and high-profile "anti-Muslim" events in the capital.

The Guardian reported that "football hooligans communicating over the internet have spoken of the need to put aside partisan support for teams and unite against Muslims. Hooligans from West Ham, Millwall, Crystal Palace and Arsenal are among those seeking to establish a common cause.

But there have been positive signs from the Muslims themselves. By July 19, they had set up their own website to denounce their fellow religionists who caused the havoc in Britain.

Following the success of the "We're Not Afraid" (a website campaign), a London businessman has created "Not In The Name Of Peace", a website for followers of Islam and others to send pictures and messages opposing terrorism.

Muslim convert Muhammed Payne told the Evening Standard, "I just wanted to say something positive about Islam and put forward the point that the religion is about promoting peace.

"I didn't want to be too political, just get the message across. The site has only been running for a few days and we have had many messages."

To get things running, IT consultant, Mr. Payne, 29, put a picture of his nine-month-old son Zakariyya on the site wearing a Crystal Palace football shirt, next to the message: "I want to grow up, not blow up."

As we have explained elsewhere, the tightening up of controls regarding the movement in and out of the country is another crucial part of the package in dealing with future terrorist threats.

The Prime Minister's statement to tighten up the way suspected terrorists are dealt with is crucial (August 2005) It is welcomed by newspapers as diverse as The Daily Telegraph, The Times and The Sun despite some Muslim critics, as a necessary initiative to make sense of our security arrangements rather than a major new initiative.

The proposals include new ground to be used to deport non-British citizens, reform the Human Rights Act if courts block removals; appeals after deportation; to ban extremist Muslim clerics, (likely candidates would be Bakri Mohammed Syrian-born preacher who arrived in Britain after being deported from Saudi Arabia in 1986 and also Abu Qatada, under house arrest in West London Jordanian-born and described by a high court judge as 'a truly dangerous individual') and also a maximum time limit for extradition of terrorist suspects.

It is odd that coming late in the day that these measures should surprise anyone. In contrast, France has deported 10 radical imams in the past two years, with another one recently deported to Algeria and 10 more are under police surveillance. Interestingly enough in France no mosque is off limits to the police.

In Germany a number of hate preachers have been deported.

As so we try and come to terms with the terrorists. If you lived in Israel or Sharm el Sheikh where violent episodes occur fairly frequently you are likely to absorb the pressure. The work of the suicide bomber is indiscriminate and criminal. But 'taking the pressure' can mean keeping your spirits up and continue your lifestyle in whatever way you feel comfortable.

My encouragement for learning to live in a violent society goes further back than the current wave of bombing and terrorism. I have been there before as my parents and my family in the Liverpool blitz in 1940 saw our home totally demolished around us.

APPENDICES

APPENDIX A
EUROPE & ANTI RACISM

1. UK ORGANISATIONS

The Runnymede Trust - A UK-based independent think tank on ethnicity and cultural diversity.

Institute of Race Relations – A London-based group that conducts research and produces educational resources addressing the struggle for racial justice in Britain and around the globe.

The Commission for Racial Equality – A publicly funded, non-governmental body set up under the UK Race Relations Act 1976 that works in both the public and private sectors to tackle racial discrimination and promote racial equality.

UK Home Office – Racial equality site with links to relevant legislation and other information.

2. EUROPEAN INSTITUTION SITES

European Commission Against Racism and Intolerance – Mechanism established by the Council of Europe in 1993 to combat racism, xenophobia, anti-Semitism and intolerance at the level of greater Europe and in the perspective of the protection of human rights.

European Monitoring Centre on Racism and Xenophobia (EUMC) – Established in 1997 by the European Union as an independent body to review the extent and development of racist, xenophobic, and anti-Semitic phenomena in the EU and promote "best practice" among the Member States.

The EU and the Fight Against Discrimination – European Parliament site with information on EU legislation (including links to specific acts) and efforts to tackle discrimination.

European Court of Human Rights – Information on European human rights law and cases.

OSCE High Commissioner on National Minorities – The office works to seek the early resolution of ethnic tensions that might endanger peace, stability or friendly relations between OSCE participating States.

Equal Opportunities – Links to proposed and existing EU policy and legislation on equal opportunities within the Union.

A Compendium of Pilot Projects Aimed at Combating Racism, Xenophobia, and anti-Semitism and Integrating Ethnic Minorities.

Eurobarometer – Commission statistics on a variety of European issues, including attitudes to people of a difference nationality, race, or religion.

3. EUROPEAN NONGOVERNMENTAL ORGANISATIONS

ENAR – A network of European NGOs, originating from the 1997 European Year Against Racism, working to combat racism in all the EU member states.

United for Intercultural Action – A voluntary co-operation of more than 500 organisations from 49 European countries working together to fight nationalism, racism, and fascism and support migrants and refugees.

Minorities of Europe – Works toward the advancement of education, empowerment, and civic participation, in particular of young people from minority groups, and promotes positive intercultural relations throughout Europe.

Migration Policy Group – An independent organisation committed to improving policy development on migration and related issues of diversity and anti-discrimination.

Voices Without Frontiers Network – Combats discrimination by providing access to and the use of radio by way of the creation of transnational networks between broadcasters, anti-discrimination organisations, migrant and refugee groups as well as between broadcasters and other members of civil society for exchange of programmes, plans of action and information.

ICARE – The Internet Center Anti Racism Europe is a co-operative effort designed to promote antiracist information on the Internet.

B) COMMUNITY ACTION – PROGRAMME TO COMBAT DISCRIMINATION 2001-2006

Community Action Programme to combat discrimination until 2006

The programme, designed to promote measures to prevent and combat discrimination based on racial or ethnic origin, religion or belief, disability, age or sexual orientation, has three main objectives:

a) to improve the understanding of issues related to discrimination through improved knowledge of this phenomenon and through evaluation of the effectiveness of policies and practice;

b) to develop the capacity to prevent and address discrimination effectively, in particular by strengthening organisations' means of action and through support for the exchange of information and good practice and networking at European level, while taking into account the specific characteristics of the different forms of discrimination;

c) to promote and disseminate the values and practices underlying the fight against discrimination, including through the use of awareness-raising campaigns.

In order to achieve these objectives, the Decision lays down a strategy based on three strands:

- strengthening analysis of the nature and consequences of discrimination in the Community;

- supporting organisations taking part in combating and preventing discrimination, enabling them to compare and contrast their approaches with experience in other regions of the Community;

- raising the awareness of the main decision-makers of the possibilities of increasing the effectiveness of anti-discriminatory measures and practices.

C) DISCRIMINATION ON THE GROUNDS OF RACE AND ETHNIC ORIGIN

The European institutions, in particular, the European Parliament have repeatedly recognised the persistence of racist and xenophobic attitudes and have highlighted the importance of combating racism and xenophobia.

Efforts to develop an overall European Union strategy against racism and xenophobia were initiated by the European Parliament, which instructed a committee of inquiry to draft a report, the so-called "Evrigenis report", which recommended a series of measures to combat racism, xenophobia, anti-Semitism and intolerance at Member State level, which could be supported by further measures and action at Community level.

EUROPEAN UNION

Proposal for a directive implementing the principle of equal treatment between persons irrespective of racial and ethnic origin – COM(1999) 566

Declaration against racism and xenophobia
Official Journal, No. C158, 25/06/1986 p. 0001-0003
http://europa.eu.int/eur-lex/en/lif/dat/1986/en_486Y0625_01.html

European Monitoring Centre on Racism and Xenophobia (EUMC)
http://www.eumc.at/
DE, EN, FR
Link to the Annual Reports

EUROPEAN PARLIAMENT

Resolution on racism, xenophobia and anti-Semitism and on further steps to combat racial discrimination.

CNS/1999/0253 Equal treatment between persons: fight against racial and ethnic discrimination for employment and social sector.

EUROPEAN COMMISSION

European Commission anti-racism website
http://europa.eu.int/comm/dg05/fundamri/eu_racism/index_en.htm
EN

APPENDIX B
HOMICIDE BOMBERS

A RECORD OF THE KILLINGS AND PEOPLE MAIMED IN ONE YEAR IN ONE COUNTRY.

Jan 25, 2002 – 25 people were wounded when a Palestinian homicide bomber detonated explosives outside a café on a pedestrian mall near Tel Aviv's old central bus station at 11:15 AM on Friday.

Jan 27, 2002 – Pinhas Tokatli, 81, of Jerusalem were killed and over 150 people were wounded, four seriously, in a homicide bombing on Jaffa Road, in the centre of Jerusalem, shortly before 12:30. The female terrorist, identified as a Fatah member, was armed with more that 10 kilos of explosives.

Feb 16, 2002 – Two teenagers were killed and about 30 people were wounded, six seriously, when a homicide bomber blew himself up on Saturday night at a pizzeria in the shopping mall in Karnei Shomron in Samaria. A third person subsequently dies of his injuries. The popular Front for the Liberation of Palestine claimed responsibility for the attack.

Feb 18, 2002 – Policeman Ahmed Mazarib, 32, of the Bedouin village Beit Zarzir in the Galilee, was killed by a homicide bomber whom he had stopped for questioning on the Ma'ale Adumim Jerusalem road. The terrorist succeeded in detonating the bomb in his car. The Fatah Al-Aqsa Martyrs Brigades claimed responsibility for the attack.

Feb 27, 2002 – A Palestinian homicide bomber blew herself up at the Maccabim road block on the Jerusalem Modi'in highway Wednesday night, injuring three policemen. *Mar 2, 2002* – Ten people were killed and over 50 were injured, 4 critically, in a homicide bombing at 19:15 on Saturday evening near a yeshiva in the ultra-Orthodox Beit Yisrael neighbourhood in the centre of Jerusalem where people had gathered for a bar-mitzva celebration. The terrorist detonated the bomb next to a group of women waiting with their baby carriages for their husbands to leave the nearby synagogue. The Fatah Al-Aqsa Martyrs Brigade took responsibility for the attack.

Mar 5, 2002 – Maharatu Tagana, 85, of upper Nazareth was killed and a large number of people injured, most lightly, when a homicide bomber exploded in an Egged No. 823 bus as it entered the Afula central bus station. The Islamic Jihad claimed responsibility for the attack.

Mar 7, 2002 – A homicide bomber blew himself up in the lobby of a hotel in the commercial centre on the outskirts of Ariel in Samaria. 15 people were injured, one seriously. The PFLP claimed responsibility for the attack.

Mar 9, 2002 – 11 people were killed and 54 injured, 10 of them seriously, when a homicide bomber exploded at 22:30 PM Saturday night in the crowded Moment café at the corner of Aza and Ben-Maimon streets in the Rehavia neighbourhood in the centre of Jerusalem. Hamas claimed responsibility for the attack.

Mar 17, 2002 – A homicide bomber exploded himself near an Egged bus no 22 at the French Hill junction in northern Jerusalem. 25 people were lightly injured.

Mar 20, 2002 – Seven people, four of them soldiers were killed and about 30 wounded, several seriously, in a homicide bombing of an Egged bus no 823 travelling from Tel Aviv to Nazereth at the Musmus junction on Highway 65 (Wadi Ara) near Afula. The Islamic Jihad claimed responsibility for the attack.

Mar 21, 2002 – Three people were killed and 86 injured, 3 of them seriously, in a homicide bombing on King George Street in the centre of Jerusalem. The terrorist detonated the bomb, packed with metal spikes and nails, in the centre of a crowd of shoppers. The Fatah al-Aqsa Brigades claimed responsibility for the attack.

Mar 27, 2002 – 29 people were killed and 140 injured – 20 seriously – in a homicide bombing in the Park Hotel in the coastal city of Netanya, in the midst of the Passover holiday seder with 250 guests. Hamas claimed responsibility for the attack. The terrorist was a member of Hamas from Tulkarem, on the list of wanted terrorists Israel had requested be arrested.

Mar 29, 2002 – Two people were killed and 28 injured, two seriously when a female homicide bomber blew herself up in the Kiryat Yovel supermarket in Jerusalem. The Fatah Al-Aqsa Martyrs Brigades claimed responsibility for the attack.

Mar 30, 2002 – One person was killed and about 30 people were injured in a homicide bombing in a café on the corner of Allenby and Bialik streets in Tel-Aviv. The Fatah Al-Aqsa Martyrs Brigades claimed responsibility for the attack.

Mar 31, 2002 – 15 people were killed and over 40 injured in a homicide bombing in Haifa, in the Matza restaurant of the gas station near the Grand Canyon shopping mall. Hamas claimed responsibility for the attack

Mar 31, 2002 – An MDA paramedic was very seriously injured along with three other people at 17:00 Sunday afternoon in a homicide bombing at the emergency medical centre in Efrat, in the Gush Etzion block south of Jerusalem.

Apr 1, 2002 – A police officer was killed in Jerusalem when a Palestinian homicide bomber heading toward the city centre blew himself up in his car after being stopped at a roadblock. The Fatah al-Aqsa Martyrs Brigades claimed responsibility for the attack.

Apr 10, 2002 – Eight people were killed and 22 injured in a homicide bombing on Egged bus No 960 en route from Haifa to Jerusalem, which exploded near Kibbutz Yagur, east of Haifa, Hamas claimed responsibility for the attack.

Apr 12, 2002 – Six people were killed and 104 wounded when a woman homicide bomber detonated a powerful charge at a bus stop on Jaffa road at the entrance to Jerusalem's Mahane Yehuda open-air market. The Al-Aqsa Martyrs' Brigades claimed responsibility for the attack

May 7, 2002 – 16 people were killed and 55 wounded in a crowded game club in Rishon Lezion, southeast of Tel-Aviv, when a homicide bomber detonated a powerful charge in the third floor club, causing part of the building to collapse. Hamas claimed responsibility for the attack.

May 19, 2002 – Three people were killed and 59 injured – 10 seriously – when a homicide bomber, disguised as a soldier, blew himself up in the market in Netanya. Both Hamas and the PFLP took responsibility for the attack.

May 20, 2002 – A homicide bomber apparently bound for Afula killed himself after border policemen approached him for questioning at a bus stop. There were no other injuries.

May 22, 2002 – Two people were killed and about 40 wounded when a homicide bomber detonated himself in the Rothschild Street downtown pedestrian mall of Rishon Lezion.

May 23, 2002 – A bomb planted by terrorists exploded underneath a fuel truck at the Pi Glilot fuel depot north of Tel Aviv. The truck burst into flames, but the blaze was quickly contained.

May 24, 2002 – A security guard opened fire on a terrorist attempting to ram a car bomb into the Studio 49 Disco in Tel Aviv. The terrorist was killed and five Israelis slightly injured when the bomb exploded prematurely.

May 27, 2002 – A grandmother and her infant granddaughter were killed and 37 people were injured, some seriously, when a homicide bomber detonated himself near an ice cream parlour outside a shopping mall in Petah Tikva. The Fatah Al-Aqsa Martyr's Brigades claimed responsibility for the attack.

June 11, 2002 – A 14-year-old girl was killed and 15 others were wounded when a Palestinian homicide bomber set off a relatively smallpipe bomb at an shwarma restaurant in Herzlia

June 18, 2002 – 19 people were killed and 74 injured – six seriously – in a homicide bombing at the Patt junction in Egged bus no. 32A travelling from Gilo to the centre of Jerusalem. The bus, which was completely destroyed, was carrying many students on their way to school. Hamas claimed responsibility for the attack.

June 19, 2002 – Seven people were killed and 50 injured – three of them in critical condition – when a homicide bomber blew himself up at a crowded bus stop and hitchhiking post at the French Hill intersection in Northern Jerusalem shortly after 7.00 pm as people were returning home from work. The Fatah Al-Aqsa Martyr's Brigades claimed responsibility for the attack.

July 16, 2002 – Nine people were killed and 20 injured in a terrorist attack on a San bus no. 189 travelling from Bnei Brak to Emmanuel in Samaria. An explosive charge was detonated next to the bullet-resistant bus. The terrorist waiting in ambush, reportedly wearing IDF uniforms, and opened fire on the bus. While four-terror organizations clamed responsibility for the attack, it was apparently carried out by the same Hamas cell, which carried out the attack in Emmanuel on December 12, 2001.

July 17, 2002 – Five people were killed – two Israeli and three foreign workers – and about 40 were injured, four seriously, in a double homicide bombing on Neve Shaanan Street near the old central bus station in Tel Aviv. The Islamic Jihad claimed responsibility for the attack.

July 30, 2002 – Five people suffered light to moderate injuries in a homicide bombing at a felafel stand on *Havevi'im* Street in the centre of Jerusalem. The bomber, who was killed, apparently exploded prematurely.

July 31, 2002 – Nine people were killed and 85 wounded, 14 of them seriously, when a bomb exploded in the Frank Sinatra student centre cafeteria on the Hebrew University's Mt

Scopus campus. The explosive device was planted inside the cafeteria, which was gutted by the explosion. Hamas claimed responsibility for the attack.

Aug 4, 2002 – Nine people were killed and some 50 wounded in a homicide bombing of Egged bus No 361 travelling from Haifa to Safed at the Meron junction in northern Israel. Hamas claimed responsibility for the attack.

Aug 5, 2002 – A bomb exploded in a car at the Umm al-Fahm junction in northern Israel killing the terrorist and wounding the drive, an Arab Israeli resident of Nazareth.

Sept 18, 2002 – Police Sgt. Moshe Hekiyah, 21, of Elyachin was killed and three people were wounded in a homicide bombing at a bus stop at the Umm al Fahm junction. The terrorist, who was apparently planning to detonate the bomb after boarding a bus, set the charge off early when approached by the police for questioning. The Islamic Jihad claimed responsibility for the attack.

Sept 19, 2002 – Six people were killed and about 70 wounded when a terrorist detonated a bomb in Dan bus No 4 on Allenby Street opposite the Great Synagoguoe in Tel-Aviv. Hamas claimed responsibility for the attack.

October 10, 2002 – Sa-ada Aharon, 71, of Ramat Gan was killed and about 30 people were wounded when a suicide bomber blew himself up while trying to board Dan bus No 87 across from Bar-lian University of the Geha highway (Route 4). Hamas claimed responsibility for the attack.

Oct 21, 2002 – 14 people were killed and some 50 wounded when a car bomb containing about 100 kilograms of explosives was detonated next to a No. 841 Egged bus from Kiryat to Tel-Aviv, while travelling along Wadi Ara on Route No 65 toward Hadera. The bus had pulled over at a bus stop when the homicide bomber, from Jenin, driving a jeep approached from behind and exploded. The Islamic Jihad claimed responsibility for the attack.

Oct 27, 2002 – Two IDF officer and a non commissioned officer were killed and about 20 people were wounded in a homicide bombing at the Sonol gas station at the entrance to Ariel in Samaria. The victims were killed while trying to prevent the terrorist from detonating the bomb. The terrorist was identified as a member of Hamas.

Nov 4, 2002 – Two people – a security guard and a teenage boy, both recent immigrants from Argentina – were killed and about 70 were wounded in a homicide bombing at a shopping mall in Kfar Sava. The Islamic Jihan claimed responsibility for the attack.

Nov 21, 2002 – Eleven people were killed and some 50 wounded by a homicide bomber on a No. 20 Egged bus on Mexico Street in the Kiryat Menahem neighbourhood of Jerusalem. The bus was filled with passengers, including school children travelling toward the centre of the city during rush hour. Hamas claimed responsibility for the attack.

Jan 5, 2003 – Twenty-two people were killed and about 120 wounded in a double homicide bombing near the old Central Bus Station in Tel-Aviv. The Fatah Al-Aqsa Martyrs Brigadaes as well as the Islamic Jihad and Hamas claimed responsibility for the attack.

APPENDIX C
TURKEY

PUBLIC SERVANTS KILLED BY THE PKK TERRORIST ORGANIZATION IN TURKEY

(1.01.1984 – 13.11.1998)

	DEAD	INJURED
PUBLIC PROSECUTOR	2	-
JUDGE	1	-
GOVERNOR OF DISTRICT	1	2
TEACHER	111	32
IMAM	32	7
MUFTI	1	1
LECTURER	1	-
ENGINEER	9	2
NURSE	1	2
MAYOR	7	3
GUARDIAN	4	-
MUHTAR (Locally elected headman)	105	11
DOCTOR	6	-
GOV. OFFICER-LABOURER	59	43
TOTAL	340	103

CIVILIAN CASUALTIES RESULTING
FROM PKK TERRORISM IN TURKEY

(15.08.1984 – 13.11.1998)

CIVILIANS		
	DEAD	INJURED
MEN	3.579	4.028
WOMEN	528	787
CHILDREN	523	634
TOTAL	4.630	5.449

APPENDIX D

*Relating to Discrimination, Human and
Political and Religious Rights*

United Nations documents:

➤ **Universal Declaration of Human Rights**
*Adopted and proclaimed by General Assembly resolution 217 A (111) of
10 December 1948*

Article 2.

Everyone is entitled to all the rights and freedoms set forth in this
Declaration, without distinction of any kind, such as race, colour, sex,
language, religion, political or other opinion, national or social origin,
property, birth or other status. Furthermore, no distinction shall be
made on the basis of the political, jurisdictional or international status
of the country or territory to which a person belongs, whether it be
independent, trust, non-self-governing or under any other limitation
of sovereignty.

Article 18.

Everyone has the right to freedom of thought, conscience and religion;
this right includes freedom to change his religion or belief, and
freedom, either alone or in community with others and in public or
private, to manifest his religion or belief in teaching, practice, worship
and observance.

Available online at: http://www.un.org/Overview/rights. html

> **International Covenant on Civil and Political Rights**
*Adopted and opened for signature, ratification and accession by General
Assembly resolution 2200A (XXI) of 16 December 1966
entry into force 23 March 1976, in accordance with Article 49*

PART II

Article 2

1. Each State Party to the present Covenant undertakes to respect
and to ensure to all individuals within its territory and subject to its
jurisdiction the rights recognized in the present Covenant, without
distinction of any kind, such as race, colour, sex, language, religion,
political or other opinion, national or social origin, property, birth or
other status.

Article 4

1. In time of public emergency which threatens the life of the nation
and the existence of which is officially proclaimed, the Parties to
the present Covenant may take measures derogating from their
obligations under the present Covenant to the extent strictly required
by the exigencies of the situation, provided that such measures are not
inconsistent with their other obligations under international law and
do not involve discrimination solely on the ground of race, colour, sex,
language, religion or social origin.

Article 18

1. Everyone shall have the right to freedom of thought, conscience
and religion. This right shall include freedom to have or to adopt a
religion or belief of his choice, and freedom, either individually or
in community with others and in public or private, to manifest his
religion or belief in worship, observance, practice and teaching.

2. No one shall be subject to coercion, which would impair his freedom
to have or to adopt a religion or belief of his choice.

3. Freedom to manifest one's religion or beliefs may be subject only
to such limitations as are prescribed by law and are necessary to
protect public safety, order, health, or morals or the fundamental
rights and freedoms of others. 4. The States Parties to be present
Covenant undertake to have respect for the liberty of parents and,
when applicable, legal guardians to ensure the religious and moral
education of their children in conformity with their own convictions.

-Article 27
> In those States in which ethnic, religious or linguistic minorities exist, persons belonging to such minorities shall not be denied the right, in community with the other members of their group, to enjoy their own culture, to profess and practise their own religion, or to use their own language.

Full text available online at: http://www.unhchr.ch, click on "Treaties"

➤ Declaration on the Elimination of All Forms of Intolerance and of Discrimination Based on Religion or Belief
Proclaimed by General Assembly resolution 36/55 of 25 Nov. 1981

The General Assembly,

Considering that one of the basic principles of the Charter of the United Nations is that of the dignity and equality inherent in all human beings, and that all Member States have pledged themselves to take joint and separate action in co-operation with the Organization to promote and encourage universal respect for and observance of human rights and fundamental freedoms for all, without distinction as to race, sex, language or religion,

Considering that the Universal Declaration of Human Rights and the International Covenants on Human Rights proclaim the principles of non-discrimination and equality before the law and the right to freedom of thought, conscience, religion and belief,

Considering that the disregard and infringement of human rights and fundamental freedoms, in particular of the right to freedom of thought, conscience, religion or whatever belief, have brought, directly or indirectly, wars and great suffering to mankind, especially where they serve as a means of foreign interference in the internal affairs of other States and amount to kindling hatred between peoples and nations,

Considering that religion or belief, for anyone who professes either, is one of the fundamental elements in his conception of life and that freedom of religion or belief should be fully respected and guaranteed,

Considering that it is essential to promote understanding, tolerance and respect in matters relating to freedom of religion and belief and to ensure that the use of religion or belief for ends inconsistent with the Charter of the United Nations, other relevant instruments of the United Nations and the purposes and principles of the present Declaration is inadmissible,

Convinced that freedom of religion and belief should also contribute to the attainment of the goals of world peace, social justice and friendship among peoples and to the elimination of ideologies or practices of colonialism and racial discrimination,

Noting with satisfaction the adoption of several, and the coming into force of some, conventions, under the aegis of the United Nations and of the specialized agencies, for the elimination of various forms of discrimination,

Concerned by manifestations of intolerance and by the existence of discrimination in matters of religion or belief still in evidence in some areas of the world,

Resolved to adopt all necessary measures for the speedy elimination of such intolerance in all its forms and manifestations and to prevent and combat discrimination on the ground of religion or belief,

Proclaims this Declaration on the Elimination of All Forms of Intolerance and of Discrimination Based on Religion or Belief:

➤ Declaration on the Rights of Persons Belonging to National or Ethnic, Religious and Linguistic Minorities

Adopted by General Assembly resolution 47/135 of 18 December 1992
Article 1

1. States shall protect the existence and the national or ethnic, cultural, religious and linguistic identity of minorities within their respective territories and shall encourage conditions for the promotion of that identity.

2. States shall adopt appropriate legislative and other measures to achieve those ends.

Article 2

1. Persons belonging to national or ethnic, religious and linguistic minorities (hereinafter referred to as persons belonging to minorities) have the right to enjoy their own culture, to profess and practise their own religion, and to use their own language, in private and in public, freely and without interference or any form of discrimination.

2. Persons belonging to minorities have the right to participate effectively in cultural, religious, social, economic and public life.

3. Persons belonging to minorities have the right to participate effectively in decisions on the national and, where appropriate, regional level concerning the minority to which they belong or the regions in which they live, in a manner not incompatible with national legislation.

4. Persons belonging to minorities have the right to establish and maintain their own associations.

5. Persons belonging to minorities have the right to establish and maintain, without any discrimination, free and peaceful contacts with

other members of their group and with persons belonging to other minorities, as well as contacts across frontiers with citizens of other States to whom they are related by national or ethnic, religious or linguistic ties.

Full text available:
http://www.unhchr.ch/html/menu3/b/d_minori.htm

APPENDIX E
"THE SURVIVAL GUIDE"

(ANGELO ACQUISTA, MD)

What to do in a biological, chemical or nuclear emergency)

A list of the biological weapons include:
1. Anthrax
2. Botulism
3. Brucellosis
4. Glanders
5. Melioidosis
6. Plague
7. Plant and Animal Diseases
8. Psittacosis
9. Q Fever
10. Ricin
11. Smallpox
12. Staphylococcal Enterotoxin B
13. T2 Mycotoxin (Yellow Rain)
14. Tularemia
15. Viral Hemorrhagic Fevers
    -Ebola Hemorrhagic Fever
    -Hantavirus Infection
    -Lassa Fever
    -Marburg Hemorrhagic Fever
    -New World Hemorrhagic Fever
    -Rift Valley Fever
    -Yellow Fever
16. Unidentified Biological Agent

Chemical Weapons
17. Agent 15
18. Blister Agents: Lewisite
19. Blister Agents: Mustard Gas
20. Blister Agents: Phosgene Oxime
21. Chemical Asphyxiants
    -Arsine
    -Cyanide (Hydrogen Cyanide/Cyanogen Chloride)

Special mention includes:
Timeline of illness, symptoms, testing and diagnosis, treatment, vaccines and environmental decontamination and clean-up.

APPENDIX F
USEFUL WEBSITES
(IN THE EVENT OF A MAJOR INCIDENT)

A

Air Accident Investigation Branch
www.aaib.dft.gov.uk/accidrep/accidrep.htm

Ambulance Service Association
www.ambex.co.uk

Animal Management in Disasters
www.animaldisasters.com

Audit Commission Community Safety
www.audit-commission.gov.uk/comsafe

Awareness and Preparedness for Emergencies on a Local Level (APELL)
www.uneptie.org/pe/apell/disasters/lists/technological.html

B

British Association for Counselling and Psychotherapy
www.bac.co.uk/skipintro.htm

British Civil Defence
www.britishcivildefence.org

British Red Cross
www.redcross.org.uk

British Transport Police
www.btp.police.uk

C

Central Office of Information
www.coi.gov.uk

Chief and Assistant Chief Fire Officers Association
www.cacfoa.org.uk/main.htm

Civil Contingencies Secretariat
www.ukresilience.gov.uk

Community Documentation Centre on Industrial Risk www.mahbsrv2.
jrc.it/edeir/index.html

Crisis Research Centre, Leiden University
www.cot.nl

Crowdsafe
www.crowdsafe.com

D

Department for Environment, Food & Rural Affairs
www.defra.gov.uk

Department of Health
www.doh.gov.uk

Department for Transport
www.dft.gov.uk

Disaster Database (BASICS)
www.basedn.freeserve.co.uk

Disaster & Emergency Management on the Internet
www.keele.ac.uk/depts/por/disaster.htm

Disaster Help (FEMA)
www.disasterhelp.gov

Disaster Information
www.disasters.au.com

Disaster Insurance Information
www.disasterinformation.org/stats.htm

Disaster Survival Support
www.Egroups.com/group/DisasterSurivialSupport

Drinking Water Inspectorate
www.dwi.detr.gov.uk/h2oinfo.htm

E
Emergency Information Infrastructure Partnership
www.emforum.org/home.htm

EMGold (Disaster Preparedness & Emergency Response Association/USA)
www.disasters.org/emgold

Emergency Planning College
www.epcollege.gov.uk

Emergency Planning Society
www.emergplansoc.org.uk

Emergency Preparedness Information Exchange
www.hoshi.cic.sfu.ca/epix/index.html

Environment Agency
www.environment-agency.gov.uk

European Commission, Civil Protection
www.europa.eu.int/comm/environment/civil/index.htm

F
Federal Emergency Management Agency (USA)
www.fema.gov

Federal Nationale de Protection Civile (France)
www.protection-civile.org

Flood Hazard Research Centre
www.fhre.mdx.ac.uk

Floodline (Environment Agency)
www.environment-agency.gov.uk/flood/index.html

G
Government News Network
www.govnet.com

H
Hazardnet
www.hoshi.cic.sfu.ca/~hazard

Health and Safety Commission (Consultative Documents) www.open.
gov.uk/hse/signpost.htm

Health and Safety Executive
www.open.gov.uk/hse/hschome.htm

Home Office (Terrorism)
www.homeoffice.gov.uk/atoz/terrorists.htm

HSE Chemical & Hazardous Installations Division
www.hse.gov.uk/chid/index.htm

I

Institute of Civil Defence and Disaster Studies
www.icdds.org

International Disaster Information Centre
www.disaster.net

International Police Association
www.ipa-iac.org

Internet Journal of Rescue and Disaster Medicine
www.ispub.com/journals/ijrdm.htm

L

Local Authorities Research & Intelligence Association
www.laria.gov.uk

London Emergency Services Liaison Panel
www.leslp.gov.uk

M

Major Accident Hazards Bureau (European Commission)
www.mahbsrv.jre.it

Major Airline Disasters
www.dnsauers.d-n-a.net/dnetGOjg/Disasters.htm

Maritime and Coastguard Agency
www.mcagency.org.uk

Meteorological Office
www.meto.gov.uk

N

National Homeland Security Knowledgebase
www.twotigersonline.com/resources.html

NATO
www.nato.int

Natural Hazards Centre
www.colorado.edu/hazards/

Northern Ireland, Central Emergency Planning Unit
www.ofmdfmni.gov.uk/cepu/

Nuclear Safety Inspectorate
www.hse.gov.uk/nsd/nsdhome.htm

P

Police
www.police.uk

S

Survive: The Business Continuity Group
www.survive.com

T

Task Force on Potentially Hazardous Near Earth Objects
www.nearearthobjects.co.uk

Technical Rescue
www.pushdtp.com/trm/

U

UK Parliament, Assemblies & HMSO
www.ukstate.com

W

World Institute for Disaster Risk Management
www.drmononline.net

BIBLIOGRAPHY

HOMICIDE/SUICIDE

Appleby, L. Shaw, J. Amos, T. et al The Progress Report of the National Confidential Inquiry into Suicide and Homicide by People with Mental Illness. (1997) London, Department of Health.

Feldman, P. The Psychology of Crime. (1993) Cambridge University Press,

EMPLOYMENT

Hoel, H. & Cooper, C. Destructive Conflict and Bullying at Work. (2000) Manchester, UMIST.

Chappell, D. & Di Martino, V. Violence at Work. (1998) International Crime Victim Survey. Geneva, International Labour Office.

Beat Bullying at Work: A Guide for Trade Union Representatives and Personnel Managers. (1997) London, TUC.

RACISM

Understanding and Responding to Hate Crime (2001) A Joint Project Funded by the Home Office Targeted Policing Initiative - Racist Violence Fact Sheet.

Sibbitt, R. The Perpetrators of Racial Harassment and Racial Violence. (1997) London, Home Office.

Clancy, A. Hough, M. Aust, R. & Kershaw, C. Crime, Policing and Justice: the Experiences of Ethnic Minorities. (2001) Findings from the 2000

British Crime Survey, HORS 223. London, Home Office
www.homeoffice.gov.uk/rds.pdfs/hors223.pdf

DOMESTIC VIOLENCE

Richardson, J. Coid, J. Petruckevitch, A. Chung, W. Mooney, S. & Feder, G. Identifying Domestic Violence: Cross-sectional Study in Primary Care. (2002) BMJ 2 Feb, 2002.

YOUTH AT RISK

Ashford, M. & Chard, A. Defending Young People (2000) 2nd Edition. Legal Action Group.

Irving, A. Spergel. The Youth Gang Problem. (1995) Oxford University Press.

Beinart, S. Anderson, B. Lee, S. & Utting, D. Youth at Risk? A National Survey of Risk Factors, Protective Factors and Problem Behaviour Among Young People in England, Scotland and Wales. (2002) London, Communities that Care.

Creighton, S. Ghate, D. Hazel, N. & Charkin, E. A National Study of Parents, Children and Discipline. (2002) VRP Summary Finding. www.rhul.ac.uk/sociopolitical-science/vrp/Findings/Findings.htm

East, K. & Campbell, S. Aspects of Crime: Young Offenders. (1999) London, Home Office.

SPORT

Dunning, E. Murphy, P. & Williams, J. The Roots of Football Hooliganism: A Historical and Sociological Study. (1988) London, Routledge.

Eliminating Racism from Football. (1998) London, Football Task Force.

Garland, J. & Rowe, M. Racism at Work - A Study of Professional Football. (1996) International Journal of Risk, Security and Crime Prevention, Ch. 1,3.

Maguire, J. Global Sport: Identities, Societies, Civilizations. (1999) Oxford, Polity Press.

Szymanski, S & Kuyers, T. Winners and Losers: The Business Strategy of Football. (1999) London, Viking.

VIOLENCE

D'Cruze, S. (ed.) Everyday Violence in Britain, 1850-1950: Gender and Class. (2000) London, Longman.

Hammerton, A.J. Companionship and Cruelty. (1992) London, Routledge.

DRUGS/ALCOHOL

Loucks, N. Research into Drugs and Alcohol, Violence and Bullying, Suicides and Self-injury and Backgrounds of Abuse. Occasional Papers Report Number 1/98. Edinburgh, Scottish Prison Service.

INTERNATIONAL TERRORISM

Alexander, Y. & Brenner, E.H. (eds.) Legal Aspects of Terrorism in the United States. Vols. 1-4 (2000) Dobbs Ferry, New York, Oceana.

Alexander, Y. & Hoenig, M. (eds.) Super Terrorism: Biological, Chemical, Nuclear. (2001) Ardsley, New York, Transnational.

Clutterbuck, R. Terrorism and Guerrilla Warfare: Forecasts and Remedies. (1990) London & New York, Routledge.

Feitlowitz, M. A Lexicon of Terror: Argentina and the Legacies of Torture. (1998) New York, Oxford University Press.

Gay, K. Silent Death: The Threat of Chemical and Biological Terrorism. (2001) Brookfield, Connecticut, Twenty-First Century Books.

Laqueur, W. A History of Terrorism. (2001) New Brunswick, New Jersey, Transaction.

Laquer, W. The Age of Terrorism. (2000) New Brunswick, New Jersey, Transaction.

Laquer, W. The New Terrorism: Fanaticism and the Arms of Mass Destruction (1999) New York, Oxford University Press.

Mishal, S. & Sela, A. The Palestinian Hamas: Vision, Violence and Coexistence. (2000) New York, Columbia University Press.

O' Ballance, E. Sudan: Civil War and Terrorism, 1956-99. (2000) New York, St Martin's.

Rapoport, D.C. Inside Terrorist Organizations. (2001) 2nd Edition. London, Frank Cass.

Simon, J.D. The Terrorist Trap: America's Experience with Terrorism. (2001) 2nd Edition. Bloomington, Indiana University Press.

Stern, J. The Ultimate Terrorists. (2001) Cambridge, Harvard University Press.

Tucker, J.B. (ed.) Toxic Terror: Assessing Terrorist Use of Chemical and Biological Weapons. (2000) Cambridge, MIT Press.

Wallis, R. Lockerbie: The Story and the Lessons. (2001) Westport, Con, Praeger.

Carpenter, S. Behavioural Science Gears Up to Combat Terrorism. (2001) Monitor on Psychology, 32 (10).

Crenshaw, M. The Attack on America/Know the Enemy Mind. (2001) Newsday, 15 September, B05.

Countering the Changing Threat of International Terrorism. (2000) Washington DC, National Commission on Terrorism.

Seger, K. The Anti-Terrorism Handbook. (1990) Novato, CA. Presidio Press.

Vedantam, S. Peer Pressure Spurs Terrorists, Psychologists Say: Attackers Unlike Usual Suicide Bombers. The Washington Post, 16 October 2001 A16.

Weinberg, L. & Eubank, W. Cultural Differences in the Behaviour of Terrorists, Terrorism and Political Violence. (1994) Sprint.

Dixon, D. Mortar Bombs Attack Blamed on Dissident Republicans. The Scotsman, 5 May, 1998.

Marshall, E. Bracing for a Biological Nightmare. Science 22 October 1997, p.745 (275-5301).

Dobson, C. & Payne, R. The Terrorists: Their Weapons, Leaders and Tactics. (1979) New York, Facts on File.

Emerson, S. & Duffy, B. The Fall of Pan Am 103: Inside the Lockerbie Investigation. (1990) New York, Putnam's.

Emerson, S. & Del Sesto, C. Terrorist: The Inside Story of the Highest-Ranking Iraqi Terrorist Ever to Defect to the West. (1991) New York, Villard Books.

IRA Handbook for Volunteers of the Irish Republican Army: Notes on Guerrilla Warfare. Eire, The Irish Republican Army, General Headquarters, 1956.

Kupperman, R. & Kamen, J. Final Warning: Averting Disaster in the New Age of Terrorism. (1989) New York, Doubleday.

Miller, J. Dissecting a Terror Plot from Boston to Amma. New York Times, 5 January, 2001.

Risen, J. Foiled Terror Plot on Tourists Linked to Bin Laden Aide. New York Times, 29 February, 2000.

Barak, G. Violence and Non-Violence. (2003) Sage Publications.

Sgarzi, J.M. & McDevitt, J. Victimology. (2003) Prentice Hall.

Munn, M. Restorative Justice: An Alternative to Vengeance. American Journal of Criminal Law, 20, 299-302. 1993

Ainsworth, P. Psychology and Crime. (2000) Longman.

Gilligan, J. Preventing Violence. (2001) Thames and Hudson.

Hopkins, J. Cultivating Compassion. (2001) Broadway Books.

McElrea, F.W.M. The New Zealand Youth Court (a model for use with adults). (2000)

Galloway, I.B. & Hudson, J. (eds.) Restorative Justice: International Perspectives. Kugler. (2000)

ENDNOTES

[1] The Times, 09-01-02 (7a)

[2] Predominantly Muslim-Bangladeshi and Pakistani. For further notes see: http://www.irr.org.uk/2001/august/ak000001.html

[3] The Times 30-04-01 (7a continued)

[4] The Islington gazette 25-05-00 (7k)

[5] Metro, page 1, 07-04-00 (7L)

[6] MacIntyre Undercover, 1999 (BBC)

[7] (Ibid)

[8] Sourced from (The Evening Standard) 26-11-98, page 68 (7c)

[9] Ibid

[10] Cited from an article by Stewart Tendler, The Times 2000 (7d)

[11] Adapted from NCIS 'Incidents of Football Related Disorder' Dossier, Season 1998-1999 (7e)

[12] Adapted from NCIS 'Incidents of Football Related Disorder' Dossier, Season 1998-1999 (7e)

[13] (7g)

[14] The Evening Standard, 04-02-02 (7f)

[15] The Observer 19-05-02 (7i)

[16] The Evening Standard 01-02-02 (7h)

[17] Evening Standard 16-05-02 (7j)

[18] The Evening Standard 11-06-02 (9)

[19] (10)

[20] Evening Standard, page 90, 15-02-02 (11)

[21] (13)

[22] (14a)

[23] Times magazine 09-03-02 (2)

24 (3)
25 (5)
26 (5a)
27 (5a)
28 Metro 05-06-06 (7)
29 (10a)
30 15-07-01 (11a)
31 (12)
32 PCCND
33 (2)
34 (3)
35 (4)
36 (5)
37 (6a)
38 (7a)
39 (8)
40 (9)
41 (10a)
42 (11)
43 (12a)
44 (12b)
45 (13)
46 (14)
47 (14b)
48 (4b)
49 (6)

ACKNOWLEDGEMENTS

The author would like to thank and acknowledge the *Evening Standard* and McTrusty for the publication of his cartoon and to Angelo Acquista for his survival guide and his publishers, Hodder and Stoughton.

INDEX

ABOUT THE AUTHOR

Professor Eric Moonman, OBE, is a leading European commentator and advisor on television of the many facets of violence and, in particular, counter terrorism. He has had extensive experience in the commercial and public sector.

Professor Moonman is a member of the International Research Council of the Inter-University Centre for Legal Studies, Washington DC; visiting Professor, City University, London and a former senior research fellow, UMIST. He has developed programmes for the International Red Cross in Africa. In the 1990s he initiated the original research into soccer violence. Recipient, Commission for Racial Equality Award for outstanding communication programmes.

A Labour MP (10 years) and Parliamentary Private Secretary.

Author of many books including his highly successful The Violent Society and The Alternative Government.

www.ingramcontent.com/pod-product-compliance
Lightning Source LLC
Chambersburg PA
CBHW061400280526
45784CB00001B/321